Art, Activism, and Sexual Violence

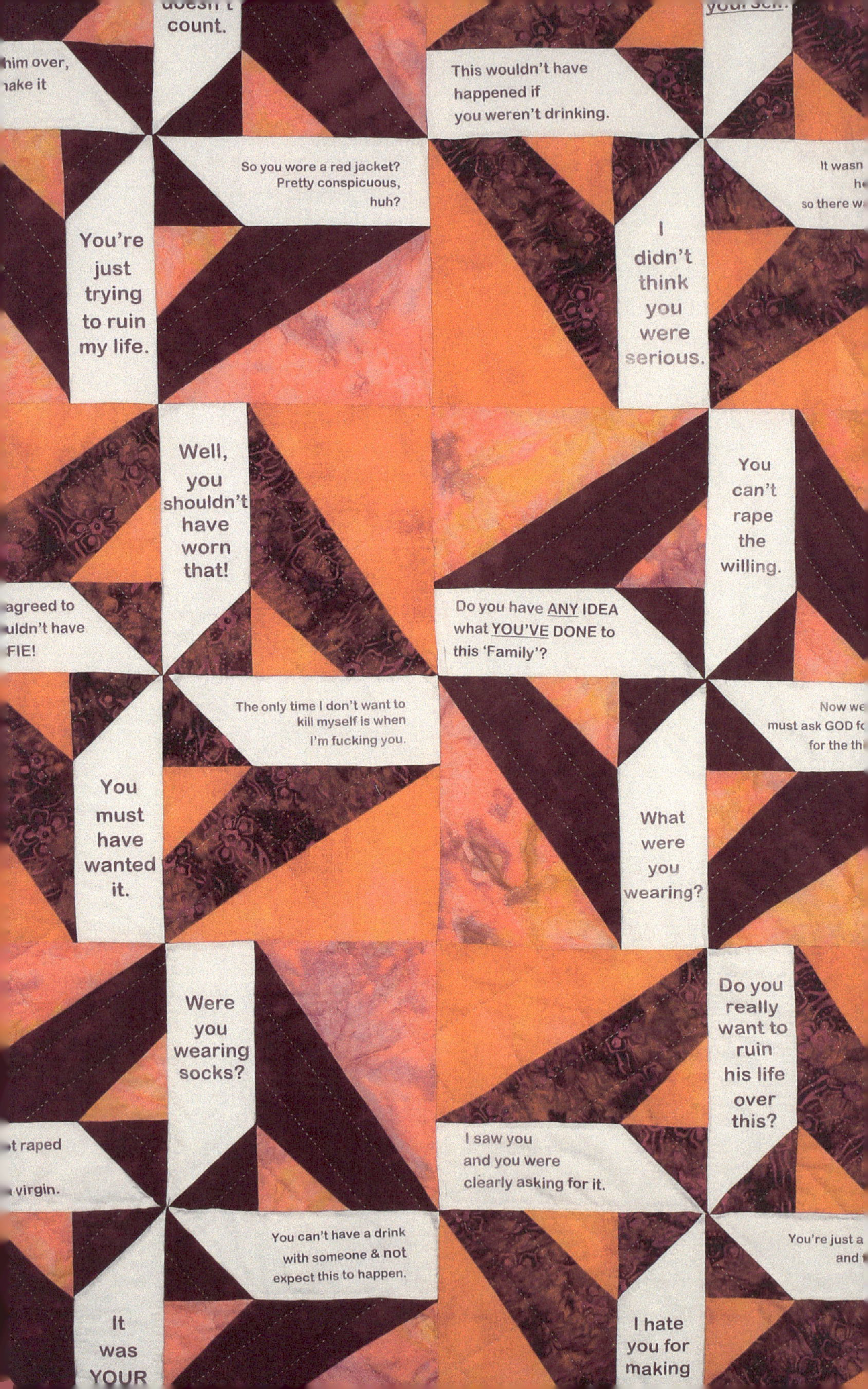
count.
This wouldn't have happened if you weren't drinking.
So you wore a red jacket? Pretty conspicuous, huh?
You're just trying to ruin my life.
I didn't think you were serious.
Well, you shouldn't have worn that!
You can't rape the willing.
Do you have ANY IDEA what YOU'VE DONE to this 'Family'?
The only time I don't want to kill myself is when I'm fucking you.
You must have wanted it.
What were you wearing?
Were you wearing socks?
Do you really want to ruin his life over this?
I saw you and you were clearly asking for it.
You can't have a drink with someone & not expect this to happen.
It was YOUR
I hate you for making

Edited by Sally L. Kitch
and Dawn R. Gilpin

Art, Activism, and Sexual Violence

University of Washington Press Seattle

Art, Activism, and Sexual Violence was made possible in part by a grant from the Humanities Institute at Arizona State University.

Additional support was provided by the Samuel and Althea Stroum Endowed Book Fund.

Design by Mindy Basinger Hill

Composed in Garamond Premier Pro and Helvetica

UNIVERSITY OF WASHINGTON PRESS uwapress.uw.edu

LIBRARY OF CONGRESS CATALOGING-IN-PUBLICATION DATA

Names: Kitch, Sally, editor. | Gilpin, Dawn R., editor.

Title: Art, activism, and sexual violence / edited by Sally L. Kitch and Dawn R. Gilpin.

Description: Seattle : University of Washington Press, [2024] | Includes bibliographical references and index.

Identifiers: LCCN 2023043122 | ISBN 9780295752099 (hardcover ; alk. paper) | ISBN 9780295752105 (paperback ; alk. paper) | ISBN 9780295752112 (ebook)

Subjects: LCSH: Sexual abuse victims in art. | Abused women in art. | Sex crimes in art. | Sexual abuse victims. | Women—Violence against.

Classification: LCC NX650.S53 A78 2024 | DDC 700.1/03—dc23/eng/20231103

LC record available at https://lccn.loc.gov/2023043122

♾ This paper meets the requirements of ANSI/NISO Z39.48-1992 (Permanence of Paper).

Contents

Foreword
CounterActing Sexual Violence through the Arts

Nik Zaleski and Elizabeth Johnson Levine

President Barack Obama declared in 2014 that preventing sexual violence on college campuses was an urgent matter. In response, Arizona State University (ASU) president Michael Crow assembled a task force that was charged with strategizing mechanisms for preventing sexual violence on the ASU campus. At that meeting, ASU Art Museum director Gordon Knox proclaimed, "Cultural problems demand cultural solutions." His observation was the seed of a three-year initiative, titled CounterAct. The initiative, begun in 2016, centered the arts as a primary prevention mechanism against sexual violence. In the following two years, CounterAct catalyzed 880 creative acts as responses to the 880 acts of sexual violence that occur in the United States every day (Rape, Abuse and Incest National Network [RAINN], www.rainn.org/statistics). We were the co–creative directors of CounterAct—Nik Zaleski, a civic practice playwright and director, and Elizabeth Johnson Levine, a socially engaged dance artist. It was from this initiative that the inspiration for the volume *Art, Activism, and Sexual Violence* emerged.

Before codirecting CounterAct, both of us had worked at the intersection of social change and the arts for the entirety of our careers. Based on that professional and personal experience, we agreed with Knox that sexual violence is a cultural problem and that cultural problems require cultural solutions. We understood rape as an issue that was too often tackled through unimaginative means. We recognized that online PowerPoints, peer-led workshops, and resource pamphlets are not enough to disrupt the dominant cultural scripts that allow sexual violence to thrive. We also understood that sexual violence was often approached on individual rather than communal levels: targeting bad actors or survivors rather than the campus community as a whole. We also knew that anti-violence initiatives on college campuses require buy-in from all stakeholders, from business schools to women's and gender studies departments. Such initiatives need compelling narratives that capture hearts and minds campus-wide and lead all stakeholders to imagine different possibilities. Because of our more than thirty years of combined experience utilizing the arts to disrupt and redirect rape cultures, we were thrilled to receive a call from Steven Tepper, dean of the Herberger Institute for Design and the Arts, about codirecting the CounterAct initiative in 2016.

History of the Initiative

Following the initial task force meeting, Tepper took charge of deploying cultural solutions to the problem of sexual violence on campus. He ignited the effort by reaching out with a call to action to all the other deans, to Educational Outreach and Student Services, and to Sun Devil Athletics. He asked units to contribute financially to the endeavor and to nominate one to two faculty or staff members to serve on an advisory council for what at the time was called an arts-based initiative for sexual violence prevention.

In November 2016, we came to campus and facilitated a half-day gathering that grounded the group of nominated faculty and staff and launched the University Advisory Council (UAC). Activities on that day explored arts-based strategies and possibilities for sexual violence prevention efforts through the arts. The UAC then became instrumental in developing the structure of the initiative. The group also kept the visiting artists accountable to diverse ASU constituents. In order to include student voices, we hired two student ambassadors (an undergraduate and a graduate student) for the planning process and also a student coordinator for the initiative.

As socially engaged artists, we know the importance of building relationships, listening and reflecting, and being responsive. We did our best to avoid the stereotype of visiting artists who "parachute" into a community and impose artistic visions without consultation. Over the course of a year, the UAC, the student ambassadors, and the co–creative directors worked to design the structure of the initiative, which unfolded into three main areas of activity: college transition (for first-year students), arts and academic integration, and signature events. It was important to find ways to introduce discussion of the arts and sexual violence into classrooms across the university, in a variety of ways, by educators working in any discipline. Signature events would be the high-visibility tentpole moments that would serve both to raise awareness of the initiative and to disseminate the actions being carried out all over campus.

As we searched for a name, CounterAct was suggested, along with the challenge to invite and produce 880 creative acts within a single year to counter the 880 acts of sexual violence that occur daily in the United States. Not only did the initiative succeed in reaching that goal, but it surpassed it—resulting in 908 CounterActions.

College Transition Creative CounterActions

Since more than 50 percent of college sexual assaults occur in the early months of each academic year, the first creative output of the initiative was a performance for the Sun Devil freshman orientation developed by and for ASU students, under our direction (Zaleski) and choreography (Levine). The thirty-five-minute play, *With Each Other*, was viewed by over 2,700 students. Fifty-one students participated in the planning and rehearsal process, and 105 students participated in post-performance workshops.

Arts and Academic Integration Creative CounterActions

UAC members worked to ensure that CounterAct was not simply a symbolic gesture or an arts "Band-Aid." They sought sustainable change and therefore advocated that arts and sexual violence prevention be integrated into the academic enterprise by infusing arts-based sexual violence prevention strategies into existing academic structures.

The team started with an audit to identify existing opportunities for arts integration while building a structure to motivate and inspire new initiatives. ASU was already hosting an annual symposium on sexual violence in higher education, under the auspices of Kim Frick and Michelle Grab, who directed ASU's Sexual Violence Prevention Program and were UAC members. Designed for faculty and staff from across the region, the symposium promoted sexual violence prevention through professional development, conversation, and community building. In 2017, we were invited to attend the symposium and to share an excerpt from *With Each Other*. The collaboration inspired a fully arts-integrated symposium the following year, in April (sexual assault awareness month), which was attended by 180 ASU students, staff, and faculty. That "convening" launched the CounterAct seed grant program and an all-campus call to action, inviting the production of 880 creative acts between April 2018 and April 2019.

Seed grants of between $200 and $1,200 were consequently awarded to students, staff, and faculty. The seventeen seed grant projects resulting from that call ranged from consent-based body painting to *Long before #MeToo: An Art-Based Exhibit Revealing a Difficult Story* and an Alexa Smart Skill App, CounterAct Sexual Violence. Each project had to be trauma responsive, arts-integrated, and consistent with the current efforts at ASU to devise creative CounterActions that addressed sexual violence and promoted healthy sexuality.

For example, with seed grant funding, faculty member Pamela Stewart designed a new "Women in US History" class that demonstrated that the current conversation about sexual violence and related behaviors has been a consistent theme throughout history. The semester culminated in an art exhibit and an event where the class's thirty-one students displayed visual art that synthesized their research and led community dialogue. Evidence of the project's impact includes this statement by Stewart:

> [A male student who worked on this project stopped] by my office yesterday, after submitting his final reflection on the project. He was deeply involved in this project, even as he was a student who often forgets submission deadlines and such. He did a visually engaging and historically interesting project that layered quotes from Anita Hill's testimony about Clarence Thomas's actions from the 1980s (students could not assess events after the 1980s as part of the project), over a 1980s photograph of the two. He told me that the course as a whole, and especially the project, made him realize that he himself has been guilty of bad behavior and he just had never really thought about it before. The project—evidently including some of the evidence he read—allowed him to reflect and aim to do better. He noted that he also now understood "how" to do better. As amazing as the projects were overall and as positive as the comments were, I think this speaks volumes.

Re-riting Masculinity was a three-part project led by ASU alumnus and graduate student Jamal Brooks-Hawkins and graduate student Phil Weaver-Stoesz. It invited men to reimagine individual and collective masculine experiences, thereby increasing awareness about toxic masculinity and its connection to sexual violence. The project's two leaders developed conversation circles focused on changing how men understand and enact their gender and the role men can play in ending sexual violence. The culminating multidisciplinary performance portrayed narratives to examine current and lived experiences of masculinity. Brooks-Hawkins explained: "The ability to speak with several men about their masculinity journey and how those journeys either contribute to or resist rape culture was extremely eye-opening. A group of men convened to discuss their masculinity and talked about many experiences which [constituted] pillars of their masculine identities. . . . Their experiences were very different, yet messages of health, personal value, and cohesion were all included."

During the course of our work on CounterAct, several campus partners voluntarily disclosed their own experiences of survival. They mentioned that so often the narrative of trauma is focused on the trauma and the act of harm and not on the survival, the resilience, and the recovery. From such testimony, we were inspired to create *A Body, Home*, a mobile performance and engagement project that explores themes of consent, trauma, toxic masculinity, and more, while celebrating the brilliance and resilience of survivors of sexual violence.

Why Use Art as a Primary Prevention Strategy?

Throughout the three-plus years of the CounterAct initiative, we and the other CounterAction creators tested varied approaches for addressing sexual violence through the arts. Artists created murals, pop-up installations, poetry, plays, dances, digital performances, arts-integrated courses, songs, mantras, and more. Through all this activity, we repeatedly came back to two approaches that seemed to have the deepest impact: storytelling and embodiment.

After a person has been sexually assaulted, people often ask questions about what the survivor may have done to deserve that harm. "Was he drunk?" "What were they wearing?" "Did she *really* say no?" These questions form a victim-blaming story that endures as such questions are repeated over time. Victim blaming penetrates the imaginations of both survivors and perpetrators of harm, creating a myth that any act, no matter what it is, causes a person to *deserve rape*. The victim-blaming story leads to severe underreporting of sexual assault, as many survivors think they will not be believed if they disclose it, and bystanders think the assault was the victim's fault entirely.

In CounterAct, we created an echo chamber for stories about healing from sexual assault, about instances of family and community support, and about what it means to come home to our bodies. We amplified these narratives through performances, murals that told compelling stories, and creative dialogues that helped rewrite dominant cultural scripts in the minds of ASU community members. Those scripts include stories about sexual assault told on cultural media platforms, which focus on questions of the victim's morality or otherwise paint an inaccurate, oversimplified picture and produce stereotypes that can lead to individual and collective violence. Through love-letter writing workshops, we helped survivors rewrite past stories told "about them, without them" with more accuracy and compassion. We helped survivors to revise assumptions written into the stories told about them, to see themselves as protagonists in their own stories, and to honor their own brilliant, resilient magic.

In addition to storytelling and narrative strategy, embodied practices were essential to CounterAct's success. The body is the site of harm in sexual violence. Sexual violence survivors often cope with their trauma through dissociation—the experience of being "out of body" and detached from reality. Dance is one way to reconnect survivors to their bodies—bodies that from the beginning of time have had the capacity to heal and regenerate. Theater and dance practices help participants to claim or reclaim agency over their bodies and to increase awareness of their three-dimensionality and place in space. Moving activates an incredible network of cells and bodily systems and helps individuals navigate gravity, maintain balance, and adjust for their size in relationship to others and to the space available.

To move is also to feel. Through an expanded capacity to feel and sense oneself through movement, people develop increased empathy for others. Humans are wired to connect. Mirror neurons are activated when we witness the movement of another. When someone smiles at us, we smile. When someone yawns, we yawn. When we see a diver on TV, our neurons react as though we were plunging into the water ourselves. Therefore, when people move, it increases their capacity for kinesthetic empathy. When empathy is present, physical boundaries can more easily be respected. We tune in and become physically able to listen to another. Thus, movement is a sexual violence prevention strategy: building the muscle of empathy protects us from violating another; we are better able to activate our mirror neurons in response to external stimuli. The more we are "in our bodies," the greater capacity we have to trust our intuition and gain clarity about physical desires and boundaries.

The Arts Promote Social Change

Through embodiment methods leading to feeling and empathy and through narrative processes for rewriting personal and collective stories, CounterAct changed ASU's sexual violence prevention approach by bringing the arts forward as a powerful tool for cultural change. After an early performance of

With Each Other in the first year of touring, one audience member explained during a post-performance talkback: "I used to think that if someone got sexually assaulted at a party and was drunk, that somehow they deserved it. I heard someone say that on stage today, and heard how stupid it sounded, and will never think that again." Because of the embodied story we told in that piece, that audience member is less likely to victim blame, deny the truth of a survivor, or perpetrate harm himself. The contributions to this volume speak to the power of storytelling, embodiment, and the arts in shifting public consciousness about sexual violence. We look forward to discovering what other "*never think that agains*" will develop from the artistic and critical work described in the pages that follow.

Preface
Art, Activism, and Sexual Violence

Sally L. Kitch

It is hard to miss the many headlines that remind readers, TV viewers, and internet users nearly every day of the scourge of sexual violence in the United States and around the world. Triggers for such violence apparently abound and intersect, from the frustrations of COVID-19 lockdowns to the emotions stirred by domestic arguments, the skewed morality of gang initiations and warfare, and the passions incited by sporting events and destructive storms. Much of this violence is inflicted on adult women by adult men, but gender-based violence also affects gay men, transgender people, children of all ages and sexes, and anyone perceived as vulnerable or powerless. As this book will demonstrate, the motivations for such violence have to do less with sexual desire or attraction than with the craving for power. In cases of sexual assault, sexual predation is the weapon, but humiliating, diminishing, or controlling another person is the goal, the impetus, and the purpose.

Art, Activism, and Sexual Violence constitutes an intervention in this cycle of violence through the creative expression of artists—as victims, survivors, and allies—in partnership with historians, anthropologists, journalists, gender scholars, and sociologists. Together contributors to the book explore the reasons such violence persists and model ways to expose, prevent, and combat it. Their doing so makes this the first book to bring together creative work, in multiple genres, with analyses of the historical and cultural contexts that illuminate the issue of sexual violence from intersectional feminist perspectives.

To achieve its goal, *Art, Activism, and Sexual Violence* is divided into four parts. After the foreword explaining the history of the project that inspired the book, the two chapters in part 1 discuss the power of the arts to address compelling, even deadly, social challenges such as sexual violence. The three chapters in part 2 provide historical and cultural background to the pervasiveness of sexual violence, both in the United States and across the world. One chapter in part 2 explains how sexual violence against women (as a social category) is built into key structures of US society. Another details the role of guns in the scourge of sexual violence, especially during COVID-19. A third explains the international activism, organized around performance, that preceded and paralleled the US-based #MeToo movement but also provided a critique of that movement's individualistic, star-studded focus.

Part 3 comprises twelve chapters devoted to art that addresses or responds to the disheartening juxtaposition of life's gifts of love and sexual pleasure with the harms of dominance, coercion, and assault. The chapters in part 3 discuss and present creative work in various genres: painting, sculpture, poetry, memoir, needlework, quilting, artistic performance, drawing, and social media images. Two chapters address the symbolism of clothing in its relationship to sexual violence and survivors' resistance.

Part 4 contains two chapters. One further contextualizes the sexual violence epidemic and discusses how the art featured in *Art, Activism, and Sexual Violence*, together with allyship by men, promotes resilience and resistance. The other, the book's last chapter, reviews who and what are missing from the book, what those absences might mean, and how future work on the topic of art, activism, and sexual violence might fill in current gaps.

In preparation for exploring this volume, we ask readers to recognize the complexities of sexual violence as a social and cultural issue and to appreciate its relationship to contentious ideas and assumptions about gender, class, and racial ideology both across and within cultures, including the United States. Even the terms used to discuss sexual violence in the United States are loaded—*men*, *women*, *male*, *female*, *victim*, *survivor*. Indeed, gender terms have taken on new meaning now that transgender people are more visible and better represented in the world. It is also necessary to understand the different gendered identities and life experiences entailed in different class, age, racial, ethnic, and ability-level social identities. As the diversity of the writers and artists in *Art, Activism, and Sexual Violence* reflects, to be victimized by sexual violence as a Black cisgender woman can be very different than to be targeted as a white lesbian or a trans female, especially regarding degrees of empathy for survivors and condemnation for the acts. Thus, it is not as clear-cut as it once may have seemed exactly who the women are against whom men commit approximately 90 percent of sexually violent acts, which are the focus of this book, or what the future of survivors may be.

In most cases, the authors in *Art, Activism, and Sexual Violence* understand gender categories as social rather than purely biological. Those categories entail anatomy, sexual behavior, and gender roles, but they are also powerful indicators of social engagement and status, as racialized gender and sexuality labeling can affect hiring decisions, pay scales, judgments about intelligence and capabilities, and social privilege or marginality, among other outcomes. In this volume, we consider *women* to include anyone who is perceived, treated, or judged to be female, regardless of physical characteristics under their clothes or their gender or sexual identity preferences. The book contains lesbian and transgender perspectives on sexual violence, and the gender terms used travel with the artists as they move through the contradictions of their social, emotional, and physiological transitions.

The term *victim* can also be contentious, as many women who have experienced sexual violence prefer the term *survivor*. We have settled that issue by using *victim* in discussing targets of sexually violent acts and their aftermaths and using *survivor* to denote victims' subsequent agency and empowerment, as in the creative work featured in this book.

There are many forms of sexual assault, including voyeurism, exhibitionism, unwelcome touching, and sexting others' private photos. There is also sexual harassment, defined as creating an intimidating, hostile, or offensive home or work environment, usually by an employer, teacher, spouse, partner or ex-partner, or other person who has or seeks power over the victim. Examples include everything from unwelcome sexual attentions to unwanted exposure to pornography. This book emphasizes assault, however, primarily to reflect the artists' concerns. Experiencing or witnessing violence has motivated most of the art included in *Art, Activism, and Sexual Violence*. Thus, the book focuses on coercive control, sometimes accompanied by threats of violence, as well as violent, even deadly, forms of sexual assault, including rape and attempted rape, child sexual abuse, and incest. Such acts are considered crimes in all US states, although they are not adjudicated uniformly across the country, nor are they taken equally seriously by law enforcement.[1] Coercive control without violence is rarely considered a crime in the United States.

Despite its ubiquity, sexual assault is the most underreported crime in the world because of the stigma, embarrassment, and mixed emotions victims face; the potential danger victims fear from perpetrators; and the mistreatment and misunderstanding victims have reason to expect from their communities or the legal system. Perhaps the crime's indeterminate, complicated, and unresolved status is what makes artists feel pressed to take matters into their own creative hands.

Art, Activism, and Sexual Violence is inclusive of many racial, class, and sexuality groups in its historical and cultural discussions and analyses. Such inclusion matters for understanding the disproportionate impacts of sexual violence according to social categories like race and class. But the art included in the book is not equally representative of all groups. The book's final chapter discusses in greater detail what is missing and why. We regard these absences as a challenge for future work designed to recognize and celebrate what artists contribute to the issue of sexual violence and its ultimate eradication.

The absence of artists whose work reflects the full range of racial or ethnic categories does not reflect the editors' preferences or intentions. It rather reflects the lack of discoverable creative work, focused explicitly on sexual violence, by artists in every social category we sought to incorporate in the book. It also reflects the deeply personal nature of the creative work that most artists produce around this topic. While racial and/or sexual identities are the focus of some works we did include, such as Stephanie Leigh Batiste's "Young Love Found and Lost: Six Poems in a Circle," Chloe Dzubilo's line drawings, and Sean Shannon's "Repressed," explicit identities are not prominent in others. Luzene Hill's "Retracing the Trace" sculpture and performance piece, for example, only indirectly invokes her Native American heritage. By the same token, Clarity Haynes's gigantic torso portraits are not explicitly the work of a lesbian artist, in contrast with Lucy Liu's paintings, which are.[2] Artists' purpose may or may not be to make a general social statement as they respond to their own experience or observations of sexual violence and resulting existential turmoil. Indeed, as Hill observes, the works' personal qualities may be what makes them most effective as mechanisms for addressing the issue. Particularities are, after all, the province of art.

Art, Activism, and Sexual Violence is intended to inspire readers to action, mutual recognition, resistance, and resilience. While not a blueprint for those responses, the book by its very nature advances social and personal change by shining a bright light on a subject that even today remains in the shadows. The data and analyses herein provide tools for understanding the depth and breadth of the suffering, injustice, and social and economic perils of this persistent scourge. The book's artworks allow readers to witness and experience those hazards on an emotional level and therefore to understand them more fully, even if they have experienced those hazards firsthand. Realizing that victims are not alone and sharing eloquent art-expressions of assault, resistance, and recovery from trauma can help break the silence.

Notes

1. "Is Sexual Assault a Crime? Here's What You Need to Know," Matt Alford Law, accessed May 29, 2023, https://mattalfordlaw.com/2020/12/29/is-sexual-assault-a-crime; Masey White, "Is Sexual Assault a Felony?," Felonies.org, December 24, 2019, https://felonies.org/is-sexual-assault-a-felony.

2. Because Liu's work does not focus on sexual violence, it is not included in *Art, Activism, and Sexual Violence*. Readers may see her work in Mey Rude, "Lucy Liu Paints Erotic Lesbian Portraits—and We Love It," *Out*, November 6, 2019, www.out.com/art/2019/11/06/lucy-liu-paints-erotic-lesbian-portraits-and-we-love-it. Haynes's portraits, in their acceptance of large female bodies and explicit delineation of breasts and nipples, might be considered sexualized. But Haynes's chapter reveals another motive for their work.

Part 1
The Transformative Power of the Arts

The relationship between art, activism, and sexual violence that forms the basis of this volume may not be immediately clear to many readers. Sexual violence is often approached as an individual-level problem, something that can be prevented through self-defense training or boundary setting, or a matter of how families raise their sons and daughters. Seeing it instead as a complex cultural issue clarifies why cultural approaches are necessary if there is any hope of reducing its pervasiveness. Art, with its inherent ability to connect with people emotionally and convey nuanced ideas, can be a powerful vehicle for tackling social change.

The chapters in part 1 of this volume lay the groundwork for what follows and help answer this foundational question: Why are we approaching the subject of sexual violence through art? Steven Tepper addresses that question in chapter 1 by emphasizing that contemplating culture is at least as important as making policy when seeking to combat this (or almost any other) issue. He quotes the anthropologist Clifford Geertz to point out that we humans are animals "'suspended in webs of significance' that we ourselves have spun." The webs of meaning through which we navigate the world are constructed through a variety of symbolic structures that together constitute a culture—including a culture of sexual violence.

The ways in which women, romantic relationships, gender roles, and families are represented in popular and news media, online, and in everyday conversations shape our views of what is normal, what is acceptable, what is inevitable. We form our ideas about what sexual violence looks like, where it happens, who perpetrates it (and why), and who is victimized by it (and why). Finally, it is only through imagining a world without sexual violence, again through systems of symbolic meaning, that we can begin to take steps toward realizing that vision through a combination of social and policy efforts.

Nicola Olsen continues the conversation about art's impact in chapter 2 by directly addressing why art is a powerful tool in processes of social change. The arts are, in essence, the most human form of communication: storytelling through movement, language, and images. Stories are an essential part of constituting culture and navigating meaning, as described by Tepper, but they also forge paths and offer models for imagining different futures. Every meaningful new policy or social movement begins with a story about how the world could be different. In human history, those stories began with art.

1

Responding to Sexual Violence with Art and Creative Expression

Steven Tepper

Most would agree that policy, procedure, education, and support services are critical levers for effecting change when it comes to sexual violence and harassment. On college campuses, in particular, where sexual violence continues at epidemic levels, universities are changing how to classify, report, and investigate sexual violence; they are increasing support services—counseling, peer-support, academic support—for those who experience violence; and they are investing in education and training so that students understand the causes and consequences of sexual violence, their role in reporting and intervening, and clear definitions and expectations around consent. But a more profound approach addresses both policy and culture. The anthropologist Clifford Geertz once wrote that we are animals "suspended in webs of significance" that we ourselves have spun.[1] No matter what policies or procedures we put in place to reduce sexual violence, if we fail to confront, appropriate, reuse, and remake our symbolic world, we will be trapped—like an insect caught in a web of meaning that we have not been part of spinning ourselves.

Sociologists and anthropologists have written extensively about "rape culture"—pointing out that people's actions are influenced not just by the legal and policy context, but, more importantly, by the ideas that shape their understanding of sexual violence—ideas that come from inherited notions of sexuality, gender, power, family, and more. So, how do we create a culture shift? How do we change the soil in which sexual violence grows?

Cultural change demands the ability to imagine a different future. It requires powerful stories to move people to action. It requires making the invisible visible so that we can address issues of equity and injustice that undermine our communities. Cultural change requires play, even when the issues and challenges are urgent and serious. Perhaps most importantly, cultural change requires reappropriating or reassembling symbols and narratives that perpetuate the dominant view of gender, sex, and power. Imagination, storytelling, play, and symbolic reassembly: these are the tools of the artist and designer. It is hard to imagine culture change without the arts at the center.

What does it mean to frame the problem of sexual violence as a cultural problem or one that requires a cultural solution? As a sociologist of culture, a central puzzle for me and for colleagues in my field is how culture is implicated in social life—from the beliefs, stories, rituals, and practices that support institutional arrangements (such as universities, our medical system, criminal justice, local government, and youth sports) to the language and symbols we use to erect social boundaries between groups and individuals and to the ways culture (art, music, theater, film, images, and story) can catalyze political action and social movements.

Culture is often invisible. It is different from policies, procedures, services—things that are visible, actionable, easily written down. Policy and procedures can be posted on websites, shared, enforced, adjudicated (consider the many policies, procedures, and services related to sexual violence prevention on a campus). But culture is harder to pinpoint, even as it is always present and always shaping us. Culture is the way we make sense of our world—it is shared meaning.

Here is an example: The word *mother* is a bit of culture that shapes so much of our understanding of family, of gender, even of our environment (think Mother Earth). *Mother* means different things to different people, derived from different sources and experiences, influenced by stories of motherhood, images from popular culture. Consider mothers who have been visible in history, politics, and religion and how each representation influences our understanding—Eve, the Virgin Mary, Mother Teresa, Mother Nature, Mother Goose. Motherhood is contested. Representations can value or devalue different ideas of motherhood. The political rhetoric around the "unwed mother" has been used to attack social policies aimed at protecting women and children. Or consider the idea of the teenage mom—a social category that has been used to diminish, demean, and shame. As a bachelor of fine arts undergraduate student at Arizona State University (ASU), Amanda Mollindo, who was born the daughter of a sixteen-year-old mother, set out with her photography to tell a different story: through interviews with and intimate photographic portraits of dozens of other mothers (current and once teenage mothers) and their children, she revealed the love, joy, care, and challenges of young motherhood. She writes, "I set out to create the representation of young motherhood that I searched for growing up."[2] Here we see how art, through its reassembly of our mental image of teenage motherhood, can turn social stigma into dignity and beauty.

While there are positive representations of motherhood in our culture, many of these ideas—from Eve to the "unwed mother"—advance notions of sexuality and gender that reinforce power and control within patriarchal society. In these instances, we can see how culture—for example, our understanding of motherhood—directly links to sexual violence. If mothers are vessels for reproduction, if their bodies are in service to their husbands or children, if their sexual desires are seen as deviant or subversive, then their full humanity is diminished and violence becomes more acceptable. At its root, sexual violence is cultural because the images, narratives, myths, and accounts that circulate at home and in the workplace, in social media and on television, and in dormitories and fraternities create notions of status, ideas of entitlement, and views of relationships and sex that lead people to act, or fail to act, in ways that cause harm.

The sociologist Ann Swidler describes culture as more than a set of worldviews and beliefs (e.g., patriarchy, or "the Protestant ethic," or meritocracy) and instead as a "'tool kit' of symbols, stories, rituals, and world-views, which people may use in varying configurations to solve different kinds of problems."[3] All too often, the tool kit that students on a college campus draw on when making decisions about intimacy, social drinking, and holding one another accountable contains dozens of "rape myths" (e.g., "Rape is usually violent and involves a stranger," or "Only certain type of women get raped," or "Hooking up is a socially desirable prize"), myths that are derived from other fragments of culture—media depictions, comments shared between friends or on social media, arguments in defense of Supreme Court nominees at congressional hearings, or the words of presidential candidates describing their freedom to grope women. How can we give students different tools to help them solve the difficult problems of belonging, social ease, intimacy, and status?

The scholar M. Candace Christensen draws from Michael Rohd's *Theatre for Community, Conflict and Dialogue* to show how theater can activate new cultural tools—narratives, stories, expressions, blueprints for interaction—to help communities of college students create an ethic of care. In her applied research, student actors perform short scenarios that depict situations students might confront every day related to sexual violence and unhealthy relationships.[4] Other students then actively rewrite the scripts, stopping the action in mid-dialogue and coming up with alternative scenarios that have different endings, different language, different responses. These reenactments and revisions create a new social reality for these students, where they feel empowered to act differently, stand up for each other, call out bad behavior, and create a newly imagined social order that values care over conquest, consent over coercion.

Sociologists of culture also look closely at how symbols (art, everyday objects, monuments, clothing) gain resonance in society—affirming ideas of power and prestige, signifying solidarity or difference, and communicating inclusion or exclusion.[5] National anthems and flags are symbols that bind people together around an idealized national identity.[6] Those symbols take on almost sacred power and can create extraordinary conflict and disagreement when they are challenged or undermined, as when professional football players, protesting racially biased police brutality, chose to kneel during the national anthem instead of standing with hands over their hearts.[7] Other symbols, such as corporate brands—Nike's swoosh or Ralph Lauren's polo horse—gain their power in part because global marketing campaigns create notions of affiliated status and lifestyle identity. A teen walking into a classroom wearing a Ralph Lauren shirt might be afforded different levels of respect by classmates than a teen wearing a generic shirt from Walmart. Whether a symbol—say a piece of public art or a book in the library—is celebrated or rejected might determine whether a person or a group who identifies with that symbol feels their own place in the community is valued. The ability to manipulate, enhance, activate, connect, and contest the meaning of the symbols that surround us every day is intricately connected to our sense of belonging, our self-confidence, and our capacity to act or react to the circumstances of our lives. As an example, in an interview with National Public Radio, teenage girls talked about their piercings and tattoos as symbolic strategies for taking control over their bodies during a time in adolescence when they felt others (parents, classmates, media, advertising) provided contradictory and harmful messages about how they were supposed to look, behave, and express themselves. These symbols—piercings and tattoos—became strategies for control, as one girl remarked: "Every time I look in the mirror and see my piercing, I think to myself . . . this is my body, I did that to myself."[8] Similarly, the sociologist Dick Hebdige discusses how subcultures—say of working-class British youth in the 1970s—reappropriate symbols to take something seen as negative about their lifestyle and turn it into a positive affirmation of identity. So, for example, British punks used safety pins as body piercings to take a common object symbolizing material deprivation (pins used to hang clothes on lines in the absence of expensive dryers) and turn it into a sign of rebellion, resistance, and anger.[9]

Consider the power of the symbol of the bedroom, the bed, the mattress. Bedrooms are private places. We like to think of the bedroom as a safe space. We paint it as a site of "domestic bliss," as when realtors use language such as "come buy a home in this quiet bedroom community." But Emma Sulkowicz, a Columbia University student whose alleged rapist was cleared by university authorities, experienced their bedroom, their mattress, as a place of danger, trauma, humiliation, shame, and loss. In response, Sulkowicz began *Mattress Performance (Carry That Weight)*—carrying a fifty-pound mattress on their back through campus to protest the university's handling of their case.[10] This art piece made the private bedroom a public spectacle. It turned a mattress—a site of comfort, rest, home, love—into a crucifix that Sulkowicz chose to bear on their back. It turned the symbol of a "safe space" into a crime scene. Sulkowicz used art and performance to give voice to their story and to make visible what is often invisible. They took a piece of culture (the "mattress") and shook it until it took on a new form, a new shape—a shape that could help us empathize and understand and feel something different and powerful and transformative. Gregory Sale, a faculty member in the School of Art at ASU, reappropriated this symbol once again, with the Open Air Mattress Talks—where students sat on blow-up mattresses arranged in a circle on the lawn of the main campus and engaged in artist-led dialogue about the issues of sexual violence on campus. The mattress now becomes a lifeboat, a stage, a conversation platform.

Another example of reappropriating symbols as an act of resistance comes from an art-based approach to sexual violence at a high school in Wales, United Kingdom. The researcher Emma Renold worked with a group of girls—through visual mind mapping and playful word association—to document their experiences of harassment and assault in school—from groping and catcalling to receiving sexually explicit texts and videos.[11] One common experience of all the girls involved boys lifting their skirts with rulers. Once the girls identified this common object of abuse, they began to play with its meaning, imagining different ways to write messages on the rulers and then assemble them into clothing, posters, chains, and other forms of expression. One girl noted the word *rule* in *ruler* and shouted "RULE HER"—acknowledging the deeper issues of power and patriarchy—the boys' attempt to rule them with their rules. Renold writes poetically about the transformational possibilities of this artistic process:

> From a ruler-poster to a ruler-monster to ruler-bunting, the girls' discussion turned to embodying and wearing the rulers: first a jacket, then a cape, the gladiator style ruler-skirt was born. What had once been a phallic object used to violate girls' bodies was now pulsating with the capacity to change and transform. Crafted from experience, the ruler-skirt became an [artifact] that in its multiplicity (there are over 20 rulers in the skirt), returned fluidity and movement to the stiff reality of enduring and normalized sexual violence. And with each step, as the rulers glisten in the light, and swish and slap together, they call us into action. The skirt . . . simultaneously tells the world something has happened/is happening.[12]

Sociologists of culture also explore the ways that creative expression, performance, and public storytelling can take personal experiences and individual stories and turn them into shared culture—public documentation, collective grief, shared responsibility, and, ultimately, political action. Sexual violence is too often internalized by survivors, who, because of many of the dominant myths, blame themselves, worry about being judged, feel embarrassed or ashamed, or feel dismissed and retraumatized by professionals in law enforcement and health care.[13] This in turn leads to underreporting and a lack of visibility of the prevalence and daily pervasiveness of sexual violence. This process is often referred to as stigmatization—creating a mark of disgrace associated with a person, circumstance, or quality. Stigma causes silence—as communities avoid a topic, an issue, or a group of people because of the discomfort and sense of shame associated with that issue or group.[14] For the past several decades, artists have used social practice art—working with communities of survivors of sexual violence—to build complex public art projects that convert personal experience into shared creative expression, thereby helping women and men overcome social isolation and build solidarity with other survivors and allies.

This type of public art making allows the community to "bear witness" to personal pain and trauma. Important to this process are feelings of public shame that come from witnessing something "unspeakable." The political philosopher Joel Feinberg argues that we feel ashamed by public spectacles—such as public mockery, bullying, or confronting a homeless family begging on the street—because we feel implicated in the scene, drawn into the humiliation and degradation of the person being exposed, and come to feel complicit in the "indecency" and larger moral failings of society.[15]

The author and Nobel Prize winner Elie Wiesel discussed the profound shame people feel at having done "nothing" in the face of atrocities.[16] "Bearing witness"—telling stories, erecting monuments, writing poetry, participating in a candlelight vigil—is a way to testify to injustice and condemn collective sin. The sociologist Michael P. Young describes Christian abolitionists participating in confessional "dramas" in the nineteenth century—public acts of prayer and personal confession—as a way to bear witness to the collective sin of slavery.[17] And, we find that feminist and activist artists, since the 1970s, have created public artworks that bear witness to the experiences of survivors and serve to break the cycles of silence and shame.

From May 7 to May 27 in 1977, the artist Suzanne Lacy staged a monumental public art project that made visible the alarming statistics that revealed Los Angeles to be among the most violent cities in the US in terms of sexual assault and rape. On twenty large maps throughout a shopping mall, Lacy stamped "rape" in red on the proximate locations in the city where rapes from the day before had been reported to the Los Angeles Police Department. Nine smaller stamped words were placed near each incident to signify all the unreported assaults as well. The maps served as backdrops for more than three dozen performances, including blindfolded women marching silently, holding signs exposing rape myths—"It could never happen to me"—juxtaposed with myth-busting statistics. Another performance included a men's group reenacting scenes from childhood that reinforce toxic masculinity. Finally, Lacy worked with survivors to document their experiences as testimonials printed on the walls of a public museum gallery, where visitors first walked past a flayed lamb cadaver with attached wings suspended from the ceiling and then proceeded below a ledge where four red-stained nude women crouched and observed passersby, reminding viewers that they were voyeurs to the pain of very real experiences. Lacy's work involved the coordination of dozens of artists, at least ten city agencies and nonprofits, workshops with government employees, significant coverage in the press, and thousands of active participants, from the survivors who contributed to the artworks to casual shoppers, passersby, and museum visitors.[18] For the first time, Lacy made rape a community-wide exploration, using art to make the invisible visible and to create public rituals and performances that bore witness to violence and turned personal shame into a shared social problem.

Bearing witness can also involve turning shame into declarations of love and support. The artist Tani Ikeda invited survivors of sexual violence to write a love letter to themselves, narrating their own stories of trauma and, importantly, resilience. Hundreds of these letters have been posted on Tumblr, Twitter, and Instagram, many incorporated into beautiful portraits painted by Ikeda.[19] Again, we see art and art making as an invitation to directly confront the stigma and private shame of sexual assault and to create new "webs of significance" that can be liberating for survivors while holding the rest of the community accountable for its complicity. Importantly, in these examples, as well as many others, artists humanize and contextualize data and statistics. The Indian sociologist and feminist legal scholar Pratiksha Baxi describes how publishing rape statistics—for example, in the United States, one in five women experience completed or attempted rape in their lifetime, and, nationally, every seventy-three seconds an assault occurs—can have the unintended impact of reinforcing the "risk society" frame of the modern liberal state, which argues that risk, from pollution to privacy to disease, is an inevitable part of daily life to which individuals must adjust their behaviors.[20] Rather than placing the responsibility on individuals to navigate risk, art and culture, as the examples provided attest, vividly reveal sexual violence as part of everyday life—embedded in larger patriarchal systems. Sexual assault is not a risk to be avoided but rather a condition to be confronted collectively.

If we are suspended in webs of meaning that we ourselves have spun, the silk strands of those webs are made of cultural "proteins"—bits and pieces of language, symbols, stories, and expression that can trap us, or support us, or provide new pathways from which to build new webs and new meanings. We are currently suspended in a web that supports daily acts of assault and violence, a web spun from patriarchy, toxic masculinity, victim blaming and shaming, silencing survivors, and propagating unhealthy views of sexuality, intimacy, and relationships. Artists are rebuilding this web through reappropriating and reusing symbols associated with trauma and violence. They are also using art to help survivors tell their stories through creative expression—driving solidarity, reducing isolation, and, importantly, helping the larger community bear witness to our collective transgression. Art can also help us imagine a future free of sexual intimidation and, through song, film, theater, and images, can begin to change what it means to be a survivor or how we see perpetrators or even where we look for the root causes of this problem.

Notes

1. Clifford Geertz, *The Interpretation of Cultures* (New York: Basic Books, 1973), 5.

2. See her powerful photographs at Amanda Mollindo, *Young Mothers*, accessed August 3, 2021, https://mollindo.com/art/young-mothers.

3. Ann Swidler, "Culture in Action: Symbols and Strategies," *American Sociological Review* 51, no. 2 (1986): 273.

4. M. Candace Christensen, "Engaging Theatre for Social Change to Address Sexual Violence on a College Campus: A Qualitative Investigation," *British Journal of Social Work* 44, no. 6 (2014): 1454–71; Michael Rohd, *Theatre for Community, Conflict and Dialogue: The Hope Is Vital Training Manual* (Portsmouth, NH: Heinemann, 1998).

5. Michael Schudson, "How Culture Works: Perspectives from Media Studies on the Efficacy of Symbols," *Theory and Society* 18, no. 2 (1989): 153–80.

6. Karen A. Cerulo, *Identity Designs: The Sights and Sounds of a Nation* (New Brunswick, NJ: Rutgers University Press, 1995).

7. Steven Tepper, *Not Here, Not Now, Not That! Protest over Art and Culture in America* (Chicago: University of Chicago Press, 2011).

8. Tepper, *Not Here, Not Now, Not That!*, 62.

9. Dick Hebdige, *Subculture: The Meaning of Style* (London: Routledge, 2013).

10. Roberta Smith, "In a Mattress, a Lever for Art and Political Protest," *New York Times*, September 21, 2014.

11. Emma Renold, "'Feel What I Feel': Making Da(r)ta with Teen Girls for Creative Activisms on How Sexual Violence Matters," *Journal of Gender Studies* 27, no. 1 (2018): 37–55.

12. Renold, "'Feel What I Feel,'" 45.

13. Christine Murray, Allison Crowe, and Whitney Akers, "How Can We End the Stigma Surrounding Domestic and Sexual Violence? A Modified Delphi Study with National Advocacy Leaders," *Journal of Family Violence* 31, no. 3 (2016): 271–87.

14. Peter Byrne, "Stigma of Mental Illness and Ways of Diminishing It," *Advances in Psychiatric Treatment* 6, no. 1 (2000): 65–72.

15. Joel Feinberg, *Offense to Others*, vol. 2 of *The Moral Limits of the Criminal Law* (New York: Oxford University Press on Demand, 1988).

16. Elie Wiesel, "Hope, Despair and Memory" (Nobel Lecture, Oslo, December 11, 1986), www.nobelprize.org/prizes/peace/1986/wiesel/lecture.

17. Michael P. Young, *Bearing Witness against Sin: The Evangelical Birth of the American Social Movement* (Chicago: University of Chicago Press, 2006).

18. Nancy Princenthal, "How Suzanne Lacy's Feminist Work about Sexual Assault in the 1970s Created a New Art Form," *ARTnews*, October 17, 2019.

19. #SurvivorLoveLetter, Tumblr, accessed January 15, 2022, https://survivorloveletter.tumblr.com.

20. Pratiksha Baxi, "Sexual Violence and Its Discontents," *Annual Review of Anthropology* 43 (2014): 139–54.

2

Mechanisms of Social Transformation in the Arts

Nicola Olsen

In discussing the transformative power of the arts to promote individual and community flourishing, scholars often employ the metaphor of a caterpillar's metamorphosis into a butterfly. A fuzzy, stumpy-legged caterpillar, perceived as a pest, saws the edges off leaves until it grows large enough to spin a cocoon; days or weeks later it emerges as a colorful-winged butterfly celebrated and protected around the globe. In human terms, this commonplace biological change represents the transformation of awareness, from surface comprehension or knowledge to new capacities and perceptions. The arts invite us to explore, make peace with, and express our ideas, emotions, relationships, and identities and lead to individual and community change.

Storytelling is a primary mechanism artists employ for facilitating such change. This chapter explores why humans tell stories about experience, how the arts facilitate meaningful storytelling, and why meaning making can be transformative.

The Arts and Storytelling

Human beings are storytellers. Indeed, F. Michael Connelly and D. Jean Clandinin note that "humans are storytelling organisms who, individually and collectively, lead storied lives."[1] Stories allow us to share our personal experience with others and represent "the primary scheme by means of which human existence is rendered meaningful."[2] Through shared stories, individual experiences transform from varied, incongruous, unexpected moments to meaningful tales, to collective understanding of what it means to feel, think, and be human.

The arts are a dynamic catalyst for communicating human experience through a variety of narrative types. Creative writing and poetry are obvious forms, but the arts also include visual narrative frames such as drawing, painting, sculpture, ceramics, and textile arts and physical forms of dance or theater, as well as musical genres that include vocal and instrumental music, just to name a few. As individuals and groups engage in the arts—in museums, theaters and concert halls, private homes, houses of worship, and parks or at community centers, schools, and local art fairs—they necessarily engage in meaning making. That process invites the transformation of perspectives, emotions, relationships, understandings, and possibilities. In short, art traditions and practices "provide critical opportunities for meaning-making, emotional connection, and expressions of creativity and imagination."[3]

Theories of Art's Transformative Capacities

This perspective on the arts has been developed in transformative learning theory, which focuses on how learners make meaning in their lives, moving beyond simply acquiring knowledge to determine how emotions and expression increase an individual's capacity for change. The educator and sociologist Jack Mezirow's theory of transformative learning asserts that the process by which students interpret and reinterpret their sense experience is key to making meaning and therefore to learning. Mezirow summarizes the focus of transformative learning theory as "how we learn to negotiate and act on our own purposes, values, feelings, and meanings rather than those we have uncritically assimilated from others." Students transform their "taken-for-granted" perspectives and mindsets to make them "more inclusive, discriminating, open, emotionally capable of change, and reflective" to increase constructive decision-making and effective action.[4] In short, transformative learning emphasizes meaning making as fundamental to human experience and identifies learning as a complex process requiring thoughts and feelings together designed to enable change.[5]

The authors of *Studio Thinking 2: The Real Benefits of Visual Arts Education* explore what the visual arts "actually teach" and what "art students actually learn."[6] Their findings align with Mezirow's transformative learning theory by identifying meaning making as a key aspect of arts education. Among the fundamental habits of mind taught by arts educators and learned by art students is one the authors identify as "express," defined as "actively pursuing meaning when making and viewing artworks." Express goes "beyond craft to convey meaning and feeling." Works of art use metaphor, symbolism, and representation to reveal deep meaning and feeling through line, color, tone, tempo, and shape that invite viewers to see beyond the literal work itself. As they look at an abstract painting, for example, viewers can experience melancholy based on the work's size, color, shape, or irregularity of line. A dancer might choose to use slow, long movements and body postures to convey a feeling of contentment and peace. Works of art are designed to reveal beyond physical art itself. Students of the arts are intentionally mentored to generate and search for purpose and significance within each creation and to experience emotions and connections. The arts utilize layered expression and metaphor to connect viewers, readers, and audiences with their feelings and identities.[7]

A Concrete Example: Arts and Culture in Public Health

The meaning-making, imaginative, and narrative strengths of the arts can be effective in addressing public health equities. Collaborations between the arts and public health institutions have tackled inequitable public health systems, structures, and policies and inspired new policies and systems starting at the community level to build a "culture of health."[8] Such systems employ arts related to identity, religion, ability, race, and ethnicity to shift perspectives and promote shared meaning that can produce individual and community behavioral change.

The role of art in transforming misconceptions about sexual violence, victims, and perpetrators fits into this public health framework. Because arts experiences transform the way people feel about a topic or an idea, they can shift assumptions and points of view about sexual abuse situations and the individuals involved. The safety and connection facilitated in arts activities encourages discussion even on difficult and divisive topics such as sexual violence. An arts and culture in public health framework directs attention to the vast capacity of the arts to adjust over time and meet individuals and communities where they are, within complex social systems. The arts can celebrate variety and change and build connections between individuals and groups.

A Caveat: Limitations of Arts Interventions

It is important to recognize that though the arts can be transformative, the transformations they engender can be helpful, harmful, or both, depending on the intents, ethics, and care taken by researchers and practitioners. The arts are not a magic serum that only requires application to be efficacious. Positive outcomes require thoughtful care and strategic planning.

A textbook of best practices recommends strategic planning of arts interventions that focus on inclusion, accessibility and universal design.[9] When designing a participatory arts experience, it is necessary to plan for a complete spectrum of human difference and provide access to full participation for all, as "inclusion" and "accessibility" indicate. Universal design highlights aspects of learning and participation, such as presenting content in a variety of ways, encouraging multiple ways for participants to engage, ensuring participant comfort, personalizing the art form, and thoughtfully considering the cultural appropriateness of the environment and the art.[10] Including voices of the participants in the design and implementation processes is essential, not just at the beginning but throughout the entire process.

Of particular importance is the person or group leading the intervention. The type of teacher, leader, or facilitator has a direct impact on how the intervention is delivered and how participants are cared for. Arts facilitators must have significant experience in their chosen art form (e.g., visual art, dance, or theater), but they also need to demonstrate specific qualities such as "empathy, compassion, intuitiveness, sensitivity, caring, and situational awareness," as well as an ability to be calm working with participants.[11] While teachers, leaders, or facilitators maintain high expectations around the art making and creativity in participatory arts experiences, they must also focus on the participants as the primary concern. An ability to be flexible with both the art form and how it can be taught allows facilitators to adapt to the needs of the participants. A balance between care and high expectations is necessary for positive outcomes.

Notes

1. F. Michael Connelly and D. Jean Clandinin, "Stories of Experience and Narrative Inquiry," *Educational Researcher* 19, no. 5 (1990): 2, https://doi.org/10.2307/1176100.

2. Donald Polkinghorne, *Narrative Knowing and the Human Sciences* (Albany: State University of New York Press, 1988), 11.

3. Jill Sonke, Tasha Golden, Samantha Francois, Jamie Hand, Anita Chandra, Lydia Clemmons, David Fakunle, et al., *Creating Healthy Communities through Cross-Sector Collaboration* (Gainesville: University of Florida Center for Arts in Medicine / ArtPlace America, 2019), 13.

4. Jack Mezirow and Associates, *Learning as Transformation: Critical Perspectives on a Theory in Progress* (San Francisco: Jossey-Bass, 2000), 7–8.

5. Lisa M. Baumgartner, "An Update on Transformational Learning," *New Directions for Adult and Continuing Education*, no. 89 (2001): 15–24.

6. Lois Hetland, Ellen Winner, Shirley Veenema, and Kimberly M. Sheridan, *Studio Thinking 2: The Real Benefits of Visual Arts Education* (New York: Teachers College Press, 2015), 1.

7. Hetland et al., *Studio Thinking 2*, 70–71.

8. Sonke et al., *Creating Healthy Communities*, 9.

9. Gay Hanna, Paula Cleggett, Niyati Dhokai, Grady Hillman, and Ermyn King, "Inclusion, Accessibility, and Specific Populations," in *Core Curriculum for Arts in Health Professionals*, ed. Ariadne Albright and Ferol P. Carytsas (San Diego, CA: National Organization for Arts in Health, 2021), 250–51.

10. Hanna et al., "Inclusion, Accessibility, and Specific Populations," 254.

11. Claire de Boer, Ariadne Albright, Ferol P. Carytsas, Ophelia Chambliss, Ping Ho, Sarah Hoover, and Kerry Royer, "Arts in Health Professionals," in Albright and Carytsas *Core Curriculum for Arts in Health Professionals*, 47.

Part 2
Situating Sexual Violence

Sexual violence is such a familiar phenomenon that is too often taken for granted. One legacy of the #MeToo movement has been to increase public awareness of the pervasiveness of gender-based harassment and violence throughout societies worldwide. Awareness has not necessarily produced widespread understanding of the underlying causes, however, or the systemic factors that contribute to maintaining the status quo. Without deeper reflection on these factors, it will be impossible to tackle the problem in any meaningful way.

Part 2 of this book invites readers to reflect on various facets of sexual violence, from its historical roots in the United States, to contemporary US gun culture, to a Latin American feminist performance movement that highlights the global nature of sexual violence. As well as providing a context for the persistence of sexual violence over time and throughout the world, these chapters focus specifically on the "violence" aspect of sexual violence and provide a bridge into part 3's exploration of art and activism.

Chapter 3 offers a deep dive into the struggle for gender-based power and dominance that underlies sexual violence in the United States. While it is generally understood that sexual violence is an expression of dominance and control rather than sexual desire gone awry, Sally Kitch's chapter explores the systemic structures that encourage, reward, and institutionalize the toxic power dynamics that underlie cultures of sexual violence. In a society built around those patriarchal traditions, sexual violence is bound to flourish.

According to a 2021 national gun survey, about one-third of adults in the United States own at least one firearm. Within the overall context of violence and patriarchy, it would be a serious omission not to address the role of guns in reinforcing power imbalances and conflicts and enabling domestic and other forms of abuse, sometimes with deadly consequences. The COVID-19 pandemic further exacerbated these tensions. In chapter 4, Dawn Gilpin examines the ways that the embodied nature of the Second Amendment, which has been interpreted by the US Supreme Court to define gun ownership as a natural right, implicitly condones the violation of physical space, boundaries, and personal sovereignty that characterizes sexual violence.

Chapter 5 extends this section's gaze beyond the United States. For historical, cultural, economic, and political reasons, femicide is a widespread issue throughout much of the global South, including South and Central America, frequently in tandem with sexual violence. As Deborah Martin and Deborah Shaw explain, the women of LasTesis, in creating the protest *Un violador en tu camino*, have combined gender theory with performance art in a movement that brings feminist action to public spaces and firmly identifies the root source of this violence as the state and its institutions, including law enforcement. In that way, *Un violador* shifts the focus from individual assailants, as in the #MeToo movement, to tacitly sanctioned cultures of sexual violence. The resonance of this performance, which has been localized and presented on nearly every continent since it first began in 2019 (including online performances during the pandemic), clearly illustrates that the message of part 2—sexual violence is institutionalized and reinforced through societal structures—is nearly universal.

3
Structures of Sexual Violence in the United States

Sally L. Kitch

Combating sexual violence by men against women in US society depends on understanding its causes and the reasons for its persistence. "Structures of Sexual Violence in the United States" addresses questions that speak to some of those issues: Why are women the primary targets of adult sexual abuse—on college campuses, in workplaces, and within marriages and domestic relationships?[1] Why is sexual violence against women, including transgender women, so prevalent, despite social advances for women?

Cultural lore has offered many inadequate answers to these questions over the years. Some people argue that women bring assault on themselves, through seductive behavior and clothing or by appearing weak and vulnerable. Others claim that women's assertive or confrontational behavior arouses male anger, so bitchy women get what they deserve. Still others claim that heterosexual men are not innately monogamous, so that the restrictions of marriage may drive them to sexual misconduct and assault. Or they argue that men become rapists to disseminate their seed, as nature intends. But none of these accounts really matches the offenses they are trying to explain. Rather, they leave many questions unanswered: If rape is natural to maleness, then why aren't all men sexual predators? If women "ask for it," through their behavior, then what explains prepubescent assaults or purely opportunistic attacks? If monogamy is anathema to cisgender men, then why do so many such men seek marriage or become enraged if a female lover or wife is not monogamous herself?

Better answers to the initial questions begin somewhere else—by recognizing that sexual violence is more about power than about sex. Many studies demonstrate that sexual violence inflicted by men against women has "more to do with keeping women 'in their place' and marking [male] turf than with sexual attraction or arousal."[2] As "Structures of Sexual Violence in the United States" explains, protecting assertions of male power is foundational to social institutions in most patriarchal societies—which are the dominant form across the globe.

"You're Only a Woman"

Sexual assault facilitates the assertion of and belief in men's innate power as a social principle. That act enables the male assailant to undermine his victim's sense of autonomy and agency by reducing her to a sexual object. An assailant's motivation has little to do with nature's plan for the sexes, the victim's age or sexual orientation, his own desire for sexual satisfaction, or the combativeness or attractiveness of victims. It has to do with the assailant's sense of himself and of the social order.

"Ensuring that women will be women and nothing else, pinning them down as women, can be seen as one of the core motives of rape" and other acts of sexual violence, according to the feminist psychoanalytic theorist Jacqueline Rose. Putting trans women in their place may include sending a violent message about power relations to those who have dared to violate gender boundaries as well as punishing them for revealing that the sexual identity some men fiercely protect "is not all it is cut out to be."[3] For many perpetrators of sexual violence, advances in women's social and economic successes only increases the motivation for sexual harassment and assault, as such female achievers have also breached traditional gender divides.

"Structures of Sexual Violence in the United States" takes such observations about the relationship between sexual violence and power a step further by demonstrating that rather than resisting sexual violence, many important social institutions, through their structures and practices, have actually—if indirectly—facilitated sexual violence by men, especially cisgender men, against persons perceived as women.[4] Such institutions have reinforced the concepts of male superiority and entitlement to women's bodies. They have given men permission to control the women in their lives, especially their sexual and reproductive behavior and agency. Contemporary societies are still haunted by this legacy. Some scholars have speculated that institutionalizing this gender hierarchy and reproductive power differential lies at the foundation of all patriarchal societies. Eclipsing women's reproductive advantage was men's way to give themselves a role and stake in the future, which women could otherwise control by simply walking away with their progeny.[5]

The significance of patriarchy's usurpation of reproductive agency is evident in the persistence of sexual violence against women as well as in repeated fights over abortion rights. Restrictions on women's reproductive choices threaten their capacity for economic independence and social participation. That threat may be precisely the point, if reducing women's viability as competitors with men for economic and social attainment is the goal. Reproductive restrictions also increase women's risk of bodily harm and death in childbirth.

This chapter of *Art, Activism, and Sexual Violence* focuses on two US institutions—law and religion—that have historically facilitated men's social and economic advantages over women by explicitly or implicitly legitimizing the sexualized violence considered necessary to enforce any claim to a superior male cultural role. Remnants of that history continue to support sexual violence today.

US Law: Coverture, Slavery, Colonialism, and Anti-miscegenation

Coverture

The coverture laws that controlled "free" (read: white) women's lives in the United States from colonial times until 1934 may seem like a sorry vestige of a misbegotten past. But in truth, those laws have contributed in various ways to maintaining cultural norms that support sexual violence by men against women, particularly within marriage, and perpetuate racialized myths about rape and rape victims.

Coverture was exported to the American colonies via British common law. US coverture laws codified the definition of all free women as property, first of their fathers and then of their husbands. Coverture's ostensible justification was protection, based on "a legal definition of womanhood as fragile and unsophisticated, thereby requiring protective cover." By judging women "unable to operate in society unaided," coverture laws mandated the dependency on men that came to define the female sex. Such mandated dependency effectively robbed a woman of her political, financial, and legal personhood and was touted in the United States as protection from the "dangerous snare" of gender equality.[6] That those very laws and the customs they generated prohibited women from obtaining the higher education or work experience and skills necessary to become independent did not strike US lawmakers as an absurdity for over a century.

Coverture had a devastating economic impact on women in this country. Before the state-by-state passage of Married Women's Property Acts in the United States from 1839 to 1913, women in many states were not allowed to keep or control their own wages, sign contracts or own businesses in their own names, inherit property, keep control of the property and worldly goods they brought into their marriages, or have custody of their children, who were considered marital property that men controlled.[7] The dependency principle of coverture, which defined husband and wife as one person (the husband), also restricted all US women's citizenship in various ways until the Equal Nationality Act was passed in 1934. Only then did a woman's citizenship finally become independent of her husband's.

An even more long-lasting and insidious aspect of coverture, however, was its implicit support for domestic violence and abuse under the guise of protecting women from themselves. Coverture entailed a husband's right to control and enjoy his wife's body and sexual and domestic services at will. That meant he had a right to rape or punish his wife if she did not comply with his wishes. This implicit right, justified on the grounds that women and society at large needed men's control and intervention against female weaknesses, irrationality, and undisciplined proclivities, became the basis of much jurisprudence and culture in the United States.[8]

Married women's continuing vulnerability to partner violence is a direct legacy of coverture's endorsement of male sexual privilege within marriage, reinforced by violence. As of 2018, 80 percent of people gunned down by intimate partners were women.[9] In 2019, one in two female murder victims (as compared with one in thirteen male murder victims) was killed by an intimate partner.[10] At the same time, defining women as marital property, subject to men's discipline, provided an indirect foundation for devaluing all women's personhood, agency, and bodily integrity. That conceptual heritage has undoubtedly contributed to today's gender-based sexual violence "problem of epidemic proportions."[11]

The Laws of Slavery and Colonialism

In the seventeenth century, colonial settlers introduced a unique version of chattel slavery into the world. For the first time, slavery was defined as perpetual and inheritable, and its continuation, especially after the importation of slaves was banned in the United States in 1807, depended on the sexual assault of enslaved women by their male masters. Many aspects of slavery were regulated by the laws of individual colonies and states, but the

US Constitution also tacitly supported the institution through eleven of its clauses.[12] Therefore, the sexual assaults and rapes that perpetuated slavery were implicitly endorsed by the nation's founders.

The earliest colonial laws promoting sexual violence against enslaved women were known as status-of-the-mother laws, which were first passed by the Virginia Assembly in 1662 and spread throughout many of the colonies by 1740.[13] The laws' official doctrine was *partus sequitur ventrem* (progeny follows the womb), and their effect was to make sexual violence against slaves by their masters (or their masters' friends, nephews, sons, and other associates) an economic prerogative. Because the progeny of such rapes shared the enslaved status of their mothers rather than the free status and white privilege of their fathers, those children could not claim a legitimate stake in white social status or property rights. For that reason, a plantation's slave population could grow without risk to white privilege and wealth and without the burden (or expense) of a purchase price.[14] Even more advantageous for white men, courts in the South ruled that the crime of rape did not exist for Black women, as they were inherently promiscuous.[15] Unlimited sexual access to winsome young women who were required to do their masters' bidding or suffer terrible consequences undoubtedly sweetened the deal for some slave owners by bolstering their belief in their own masculine prowess.

In addition to their support for mendacious, immoral, and violent behavior, status-of-the-mother laws violated the British custom of linking children's social and legal status to that of their fathers. Defining slavery via African women's violated bodies was also a precursor to racializing the "peculiar institution," which had heretofore been considered a noninheritable, frequently time-limited punishment inflicted on captives or on unfortunate debtors or miscreants of any race, including whites.[16] Importantly, as this racialized development became institutionalized in practice across the country, it stamped Black female bodies in general as symbols of sexual degradation long after slavery was abolished in the United States in 1863.

"The societal disregard for Black girls and women is an effect of a specific kind of racism and misogyny—an artifact from enslavement . . . [and its effects] prevail," writes Kimberlé Crenshaw, a law professor at the University of California, Los Angeles.[17] Those effects were evident in the vilification of "welfare queens" in the 1980s, more than one hundred years after emancipation. That campaign (falsely) painted a picture of sexually promiscuous and irresponsibly procreative Black mothers (often teenagers) who were overwhelming and gaming the welfare system and, therefore, unworthy of social support. The public and lawmakers eagerly bought into this racialized narrative, which coincided with their own prejudices, and supported Ronald Reagan's administration's elimination of benefits for households and communities.[18] What both groups failed to acknowledge, however, was that "white Americans are, and always have been, the biggest beneficiaries of welfare programs."[19]

Slavery's impact on contemporary Black women is also evident in myriad sexualized and animalized popular representations of Black female bodies, which undermine their claims of sexual violation. Often young Black women are blamed for their victimization in sexual assaults and ignored in sex-trafficking discussions, although they make up 40 percent of trafficking victims. It is the young white victims of that crime who are represented as the innocents that need saving. The sexualization of Black women also explains why the singer R. Kelly got away with sexual predation against scores of young girls for twenty years, argues Crenshaw. All his victims were Black.[20]

All women of color are more likely to become victims of sexual violence than white women, and Native American women are more likely to be assaulted than women of any other ethnic group. As with Black women, Native women's contemporary victimization has historical roots; in their case those roots were seeded and fertilized by colonization. After first contact, European colonizers considered themselves entitled to Indigenous women's bodies as the spoils of war and cultural domination. After 1776, the federal government sought to "civilize" the natives by establishing patriarchies within the tribes, frequently replacing matrilineal and matrilocal cultures and traditions of shared power between the sexes. That meant creating the conditions under which Native men joined white men in feeling entitled to Native women's bodies as they sought to achieve the control over women that patriarchy required. Marginalizing women under the US mandate, as among the Cherokees, resulted in the subjugation of women and the legitimation of violence against them. That stigma, coming both from within tribes and from white society, remains. One result is the unlikelihood that white assailants will be prosecuted for sexual assault, let alone punished.[21] Another is that the complicated relationships among federal, state, and tribal jurisdictions "make it hard to seek justice for victims," even when perpetrators are Native themselves.[22]

In addition to these institutionalized histories, women of color, in general, and Black women, in particular, fare differently in the legal system if they report sexual violence. "Prosecutors are less likely to pursue criminal charges against the assailant when the victim is black; and jurors are more likely to believe a white survivor's assailant is guilty than a black woman's." That is, if the case even makes it to court. In 2000, the *Philadelphia Inquirer* revealed that Philadelphia's Sex Crimes Unit, nicknamed "the Lying Bitches Unit," "bur[ied] nearly 2,000 cases of assault on low-income black women between 1995–2000." This outcome helps explain why only 17 percent of Black survivors report their assaults, compared to 44 percent of white survivors.[23]

Anti-miscegenation Laws

Anti-miscegenation laws, enacted in the American colonies starting in 1634, prohibited interracial marriages in many parts of the United States and were considered constitutional by the US Supreme Court until 1967.[24] Those laws, too, legally sanctioned sexual violence by men against women, as they fostered racialized views about acceptable and unacceptable rape victims and probable rapists, beliefs that live on to this day.

Anti-miscegenation laws targeted marriages in British colonies between persons of different races, primarily between Blacks and whites. (The laws focused on marriage rather than fornication—which slavery and racism made socially acceptable—in order to prevent the inheritance of white property across the races.) The laws became more plentiful after the US Civil War. By 1915, twenty-eight states barred and invalidated all marriages between Negroes and whites. In the 1920s, eugenicist fears of white "hypodescent" through racial dilution also led to prohibitions against white intermarriage with Asian immigrants and Native Americans. By the 1940s, forty-one out of forty-eight states had passed anti-miscegenation laws. In 1967, sixteen states still had anti-miscegenation laws on their books.[25]

US courts had declared anti-miscegenation laws constitutional before 1967 on the grounds that they applied equally to all races and to both sexes and were therefore not discriminatory.[26] But that was not really the case. The laws actually targeted two gendered racial groups—non-white men and white women—while leaving unpunished white men's rape or sexual coercion of non-white women.

The real purpose of anti-miscegenation laws, as the Supreme Court eventually acknowledged, was to maintain white supremacy, a doctrine predicated on the convenient principle, reinforced by status-of-the-mother laws, that women determined children's racial status. Thus, white women's relationships with Black men (presumed predators of white women) were vigorously policed, as those relationships represented the biggest threat to white racial purity, progeny, and property. Meanwhile, Black women could only produce Black children, according to the laws, even if the fathers were white.

Moreover, as Black women were considered hypersexual, they were presumed complicit in any rape. Eugenicists of the early twentieth century reinforced this gendered theory of racial transmission by declaring white women (but not white men) the "guardians" of white racial blood.[27]

In these ways, legalized white supremacy engendered the myth of the Black rapist and promoted white men's sexual privilege with and control of all women, especially those over whom they had the additional power advantage of alleged racial superiority. At the same time, the laws established white women as the primary victims of rape, while disregarding rapes committed against non-white women. Colonial and US law protected this racialized rape culture for over three hundred years.

Even decades after miscegenation laws ended, the myth of Black rapists preying on innocent white females persisted and distorted the realities of rape. That myth was evident in the "Central Park Five" rape case, adjudicated in 1989 but back in the news in 2019. Five Black teenagers were convicted of the brutal rape of a white female jogger, mostly because they were in the park at the time and fit the white police officers' and prosecutors' stereotypes of probable rapists. Despite the lack of forensic evidence, the five were convicted of the crime to varying degrees and served between six and thirteen years in prison before the real rapist confessed in 2002.

Donald Trump's remarks about the case over the years exemplify the myth's persistence, however. Trump publicly demanded that the death penalty be reinstated at the time and remarked to CNN host Larry King, "'Of course I hate these people and let's all hate these people because maybe hate is what we need if we're gonna get something done.'" Although the five men were later exonerated based on DNA evidence, Trump never backed down. In both 2014 and 2019, he refused to apologize for his original remarks or to retract his judgment that New York City's $41 million settlement with the falsely accused men was "a disgrace."[28]

US Religious Institutions

Religious institutions are perhaps the most effective—and most damaging—source of structural support for sexual violence in US society. Yet they are often slow to respond to its impact, in part because many religious organizations regard sexual violence as "a female social problem that some other agency will address." That, of course, is a mischaracterization. For one thing, victims of violence often need spiritual counsel. For another, religious institutions, especially conservative sects, promote the gender hierarchies (male dominance, female submission), "complementary" sex roles, and rape myths that feed a culture of sexual violence.[29] Some scholars even argue that religious institutions should acknowledge that the control of women's sexuality and reproduction form the core of their mission and purpose, especially if they vest religious power solely in male clergy who act and speak on behalf of a male God.[30]

Religious institutional support for or acceptance of sexual violence can be found on several levels: official documents and texts; adherents' and clergy's behavior and attitudes; and believers' experiences, as reflected in numerous studies and analyses.[31] Religious documents that support or promote sexual violence range from sacred texts and official edicts to sex education and dating guides. Among textual sources are Bible passages and stories that blame women for their own rapes (Dinah in Genesis) or identify womanhood (Eve) with original (sexual) sin and therefore consider all women rightly subject to sexual rule by husbands. Other stories suggest women should not reveal even an incestuous rape (Tamar) and accuse women of lying about rape (Potiphar's wife).

Biblical commentaries and theologians provide another source of support for sexual violence. For example, Saint Jerome used a rape metaphor to explain how pagan wisdom could be manipulated to serve Christian purposes—forcibly "take" a beautiful woman and discipline her to become "a matron of the true Israel." When confronted with actual rapes after the sack of Rome by Visigoths in 410 CE, Christian theologian Augustine was racked with doubts that contributed to enduring rape myths: Were raped sanctified virgins still pure? Can a woman really be raped against her will? Were rape victims being punished for their hidden sins? Did victims sin by feeling lust during the attacks?[32]

Following such theologians' lead, medieval European Christendom defined rape as a crime against men and treated victims harshly, including by execution. Women who did not resist or scream were considered complicit. Pregnancies resulting from rape were typically regarded as proof of consent.[33]

Fast forward to the United States in the twenty-first century and the legacy of those early texts and practices can still be found in some Christian religious doctrine, which maintains a male perspective on women's sexual purity and men's sexual privilege. The more fundamentalist the sect, the more likely it is to support rape mythology and to hold women responsible for maintaining their own and men's chastity, despite women's lack of power or authority and churches' explicit admonitions to women "to be submissive to men in their heterosexual interactions."[34] Such double messages enable men to exploit their religiously sanctioned authority over women, deny women agency in resisting unwanted sexual advances, and condemn or shun victims, particularly if they know their attackers or their behavior violates traditional gender expectations.[35]

Additional sources of support for sexual violence include religious educational materials. Abstinence-only sex education teaches girls to keep themselves "clean" for their eventual husbands and warns that women's (but not men's) sexual experience before marriage makes them disgusting, like "a dirty chocolate that has been passed around a classroom."[36] Dating books produced by conservative churches also focus on controlling the behavior of girls and women. The books tell young women that "men should control women's bodies and their sexuality." At the same time, boys are told that they cannot help their sexual urges and that it is up to girls to stop them. Thus, the books blame girls for becoming victims of sexual violence and tell kids of both sexes that abusive behavior from men is an acceptable way to control female sexuality. These messages shame women, normalize sexual violence, and "support rape culture and traditional toxic masculinity."[37]

The behavior and attitudes of rapacious male clergy also reinforce religious institutional support for sexual predation, even violence. Such clergy may "groom" (usually vulnerable) female targets by claiming that sex between them is God's will or that it will help the clergyman be a better minister to others. Given the religious framework for sex and gender norms they have learned, the female targets of such pressure are more likely to blame themselves than to condemn a clergyman's "use of his role as spiritual leader to manipulate her [into] intimacy she would never allow another man outside of . . . marriage." Having the power to define the situation, a predatory clergyman may convince his female target that sex between them has occurred by mutual consent. He may also blame her for their sexual congress, only furthering her sense of shame.[38] When such situations are exposed, church leaders often close ranks, deny women's claims, and spurn claimants, thereby tacitly enabling and condoning clerical sexual abuse.

Sexual abuse by male Christian clergy has even extended to nuns, as recently revealed by a suppressed 1995 report by Sister Maura O'Donohue. O'Donohue found cases in twenty-three countries, including the United States, of Catholic priests raping or otherwise forcing themselves on nuns and, in some instances, compelling them to have abortions. The report observes the same dynamic evident in most male clergy sexual abuse—religious women rendered powerless to refuse a man, especially an older man, and especially one designated as God's representative (as nuns are not).[39]

Clerical sexual abuse is a problem in some Muslim communities as well, including in the United States. Such sexual offenses affirm how unequal power relations between the sexes may lead to sexual abuse and reveal the level of "hypermasculinity still operating in certain contemporary Muslim . . . circles." The factors promoting Muslim clerical sexual predation resemble those in other conservative sects. Men are leaders; women are followers. Men have power; women submit. Communities protect clergy and impugn the integrity of accusers. Believers internalize notions about women's inherent weaknesses. Even if both sexes are admonished to avoid sexual sin, warnings imply that women are the tempters of men, thereby transforming men into women's victims.[40]

Some Muslim women are also subject to deadly violence from fathers and brothers as punishment for their presumed or actual sexual behaviors. Known as honor killing, such violence is rare and illegal in the United States. But the social structures behind it can exist in American Muslim communities. Patriarchal values, including male "ownership" of women's sexuality, huge gaps in men's and women's social power, and conservative religiosity combine to produce violence against women as sexual beings.[41] As with other religions, the proposed remedy for such offenses in Muslim practice includes reevaluating the underlying culture of hierarchical gender relations and inequality in religious institutions.[42]

Gendered Power, Powerlessness, and Guilt

In her poem "A Work of Artifice," Marge Piercy observes that a nine-inch-high bonsai tree "could have grown eighty feet tall on the side of a mountain." After the tree was split by lightning, however, a gardener pruned and potted it and now croons to his miniature creation: "It is your nature to be small and cozy, domestic and weak."[43]

Some US laws and religious institutions have acted like that gardener, systematically dwarfing the identities and reproductive power of women and girls, subjecting them to male control, and endorsing the myth of male superiority. Sexual violence by men against women is a structural element of that twisted power grab. Ironically, the virulence with which patriarchal dominance has persisted over the centuries and around the globe demonstrates the cultural significance of female sexuality and reproductive capacities. Humans must have recognized early on that nature had endowed fertile women with an extraordinary ability to shape society if they were free to exercise their sexual and reproductive powers. So, controlling that ability and the sexual behavior surrounding it became a primary motivation for creating social institutions that men would control and through which they could exercise control over and ownership of that astounding female reproductive power.

That patriarchal law and religion were established early among those institutions in Western countries and elsewhere cut off important avenues for redressing women's victimization and establishing gender parity. Those institutions have also fomented the collective delusion that males are naturally dominant and females naturally submissive. This myth is so powerful and well entrenched that transgender females—who may not even have female reproductive capacity—are targeted for sexual violence at greater rates than cisgender women.[44] Among other discriminatory messages, that violence conveys the idea that presenting as a female or bisexual from a born-male body necessarily offends the "natural" gender order and "deserves" punishment by it. That sexual assaults on transgender men also occur at high rates—including by intimate cisgender male partners—may convey a related message: "You may think you can escape your female biology, but I'll show you!"

This insidious loop, reinforced by the trope of essentialized maleness and male superiority, helps to justify institutionalized male dominance expressed through sexual violence. Disrupting the loop requires extracting that trope from global cultural DNA and exposing it as an insidious and destructive work of artifice.

Notes

1. A note on terminology: I recognize that the categories "men" and "women," "male" and "female" are problematic in the contemporary moment, when sexual identities are more fluid than the idea of opposite sexes allows and are increasingly matters of self-identification or self-selection. I use them here somewhat interchangeably, with *male* and *female* as indicators of physiological presumptions but also as the adjectival form of *men* and *women* as social categories that presume such physiology and infuse ideas about institutions, such as the laws and religious organizations discussed in this chapter, as well as about power discrepancies that continue to haunt hiring decisions, pay scales, prejudices about presidential and leadership fitness, and dozens of other forms of social engagement and status. By the same token, I use *victim* as well as *survivor* to describe those who have been targets of sexual assault, not as identities but as roles in assaults and their aftermath.

2. Heather Mclaughlin, Christopher Uggen, and Amy Blackstone, "Sexual Harassment, Workplace Authority, and the Paradox of Power," *American Sociological Review* 77, no. 4 (August 2012): 635.

3. Jacqueline Rose, *On Violence and Violence against Women* (New York: Farrar, Straus and Giroux, 2021), 18–19.

4. Addressing sexual violence committed by men against women does not capture all forms of sexual violence in US society. But that focus does exemplify the differential power relationships that constitute structures of sexual violence built into the US institutions discussed in this chapter. It also provides a framework for understanding power relationships entailed in other forms, such as female-to-female domestic violence or violence against transgender persons, as that framework was instituted by religious leaders and lawmakers centuries ago.

5. Monica A. Coleman, *The Dinah Project: A Handbook for Congregational Response to Sexual Violence* (Cleveland: Pilgrim Press, 2004), 68–71; James M. Smith, *Ireland's Magdalen Laundries and the Nation's Architecture of Containment* (Notre Dame, IN: University of Notre Dame Press, 2007), 50–51.

6. Maggie Cheu, "Now and Then: How Coverture Ideology Informs the Rhetoric of Abortion," *Texas Journal of Women and the Law* 22, no. 1 (Fall 2012): 116–17.

7. Unlike British women, American women under coverture did have the right to their husband's support and to protection from a husband's physical violence, if it went too far. They were also entitled to one-third of their husband's estate for life.

8. Janet Calvo, "A Decade of Spouse-Based Immigration Laws: Coverture's Diminishment, but Not Its Demise," *Northern Illinois University Law Review* 24 (Spring 2004): 160, 162–63.

9. Jenavieve Hatch, "11 Statistics That Remind Us Gun Violence Is a Women's Issue," *Huffington Post*, June 2, 2017, www.huffingtonpost.com/entry/gun-violence-women_us_5931668be4b0c242ca232990.

10. Allison Ertl, Kameron J. Sheats, Emiko Petrosky, Carter J. Betz, Keming Yuan, and Katherine A. Fowler, "Surveillance for Violent Deaths—National Violent Death Reporting System, 32 States, 2016," Surveillance Summaries, *Morbidity and Mortality Weekly Report* (Center for Disease Control and Prevention) 68, no. 9 (2019): 1–36, www.cdc.gov/mmwr/volumes/68/ss/ss6809a1.htm.

11. Rebecca M. Loya, "The Role of Sexual Violence in Creating and Maintaining Economic Insecurity among Asset-Poor Women of Color," *Violence against Women* 20, no. 11 (November 2014): 1299.

12. Although slavery is not explicitly mentioned in the Constitution, scholars identify eleven clauses that recognize its existence. The two most prominent are the "three-fifths" clause and the fugitive "servant" (read: "slave") clause. The first counted each slave as three-fifths of a person as a way to bolster Southern representation in the House of Representatives (despite slaveholders' claim that slavery was justified because slaves were not actually people). The second states, "No Person held to Service or Labour in one State, under the Laws thereof, escaping into another, shall, in Consequence of any Law or Regulation therein, be

discharged from such Service or Labour, but shall be delivered up on Claim of the Party to whom such Service or Labour may be due." Obviously, that clause helped to maintain slaveholders' ownership of their human chattel. Eric Burroughs, "The Constitution and Slavery," *The Odyssey Online* (blog), December 14, 2015, www.theodysseyonline.com/the-constitution-and-slavery.

13. Status-of-the-mother laws were passed in Maryland in 1688, Massachusetts in 1670, and South Carolina in 1740.

14. For more detail about status-of-the-mother laws, see Sally L. Kitch, *The Specter of Sex: Gendered Foundations of Racial Formation in the United States* (Albany: State University of New York Press, 2009).

15. Carolyn M. West and Kalimah Johnson, "Sexual Violence in the Lives of African American Women," National Online Research Center on Violence Against Women, March 2013, https://vawnet.org/material/sexual-violence-lives-african-american-women-risk-response-and-resilience.

16. Kitch, *The Specter of Sex*, 81. To understand this historical development, it is helpful to remember that the origin of the word *slave* is *Slav*, the white group the Greeks considered destined to serve them. It is also helpful to recall that the first slaves in the American colonies were the Pequot Indians.

17. Kimberlé Crenshaw, "How R. Kelly Got Away With It," *New York Times*, October 1, 2021.

18. Laura Briggs, *How All Politics Became Reproductive Politics* (Berkley: University of California Press, 2017), 71.

19. Economic Security Project, "A Killer Stereotype," June 8, 2020, https://economicsecurityproject.org/resource/a-killer-stereotype.

20. Crenshaw, "Got Away With It."

21. Martha Ann Bono, "Historicizing Sexual Violence against Native American Women: Colonization, Intracommunal Shifts, and Creative Forms of Discourse" (senior thesis, Scripps College, 2018), https://scholarship.claremont.edu/cgi/viewcontent.cgi?article=2297&context=scripps_theses.

22. Auburn Wilcox, "Sexual Violence Rates Double against Native American Women," *Daily Universe*, January 23, 2019, https://universe.byu.edu/2019/01/23/sexual-violence-rates-higher-against-native-women-in-america-1.

23. Sharon Folkenroth Hess, "The Stain of Slavery Is Silencing Sexual Violence against Black and Brown Women," *Nursing Clio* (blog), April 17, 2018, https://nursingclio.org/2018/04/17/the-stain-of-slavery-is-silencing-sexual-violence-against-black-and-brown-women.

24. Loving v. Virginia, 388 U.S. 1 (1967).

25. Kitch, *The Specter of Sex*, 137–38.

26. Peggy Pascoe, *What Comes Naturally: Miscegenation Law and the Making of Race in America* (New York: Oxford University Press, 2009), 3.

27. Kitch, *The Specter of Sex*, 137–38.

28. Devan Cole, "New Netflix Series Brings Attention to Trump's Call for

Death Penalty in 1989 during Central Park Five Case," CNN, June 8, 2019, www.cnn.com/2019/06/06/politics/donald-trump-central-park-five-death-penalty-comments/index.html; Jan Ransom, "Trump Will Not Apologize for Calling for Death Penalty over Central Park Five," *New York Times*, June 18, 2019.

29. Coleman, *The Dinah Project*, 39.

30. Joy A. Schroeder, *Dinah's Lament: The Biblical Legacy of Sexual Violence in Christian Interpretation* (Minneapolis: Fortress Press, 2007), 2–4.

31. Analise Barker and Renee V. Galliher, "A Mediation Model of Sexual Assault among Latter-Day Saints," *Journal of Aggression, Maltreatment and Trauma* 26, no. 3 (March 2017): 321.

32. Coleman, *The Dinah Project*, 4–5; Schroeder, *Dinah's Lament*, 1–3.

33. Schroeder, *Dinah's Lament*, 6–7, 9–10.

34. Barker and Galliher, "A Mediation Model of Sexual Assault," 328.

35. Thorayya Said Giovannelli and Latrelle Jackson, "Sexual Violence Perceptions among Christian College Students," *Mental Health, Religion and Culture* 16, no. 3 (March 2013): 257.

36. Barker and Galliher, "A Mediation Model of Sexual Assault," 317.

37. Kathryn R. Klement and Brad J. Sagarin, "Nobody Wants to Date a Whore: Rape-Supportive Messages in Women-Directed Christian Dating Books," *Sexuality and Culture* 21, no. 1 (2017): 206, 219.

38. Diana R. Garland, "When Wolves Wear Shepherds' Clothing," *Journal of Religion and Abuse* 8, no. 2 (November 2006): 32–36, 39.

39. Steve Pagani, "Some Priests Force Nuns to Have Sex, Report Says," *Globe and Mail* (Canada), March 2001.

40. Sally L. Kitch, "Epilogue: Gender, Peace, and War," in *Women and Peace in the Islamic World: Gender, Agency and Influence*, ed. Yasmin Saikia and Chad Haines (London: I. B. Tauris, 2015), 372–73.

41. Nuray Sakallı-Uğurlu, "Quantitative Empirical Studies on Women's Issues in Islamic Cultures: Introduction to Special Issue," *Sex Roles: A Journal of Research* 75, no. 11–12 (December 2016): 538.

42. Tasneem Chopra, "The Crisis of #MeToo in Muslim Communities," *SBS Life*, February 26, 2018, www.sbs.com.au/topics/life/culture/article/2018/02/23/crisis-metoo-muslim-communities; Garland, "When Wolves Wear Shepherds' Clothing," 47, 50. Little research has been done on structures of sexual abuse in Jewish theology or institutions. For more information on sexual assault and Judaism during the Holocaust, see Sonja M. Hedgepeth and Rochelle G. Saidel, eds., *Sexual Violence against Jewish Women during the Holocaust* (Waltham, MA: Brandeis University Press; Hanover, NH: University Press of New England, 2010). For more information on theological foundations of male roles in Judaism, see Daniel C. Maguire, and Sa'diyya Shaikh, eds., *Violence against Women in Contemporary World Religions: Roots and Cures* (Cleveland: Pilgrim Press, 2007).

43. Marge Piercy, *A Work of Artifice* (San Francisco: V. R. Leviathan Publications, 1970), 43.

44. According to 2018–19 data from the Williams Institute at the University of California, Los Angeles, School of Law, "transgender people are over four times more likely than cisgender people to experience violent victimization, including rape, sexual assault, and aggravated or simple assault." Whereas approximately 23.7 US cisgender women per 1,000 become victims of sexual assault, the statistic for transgender women is around 86 per 1,000. Williams Institute, "Transgender People over Four Times More Likely than Cisgender People to Be Victims of Violent Crime," press release, March 23, 2021, https://williamsinstitute.law.ucla.edu/press/ncvs-trans-press-release. More recent sources report that murder rates for transgender people have also gone up.

4

A Hostile Virus

Dawn R. Gilpin

It is impossible to have a meaningful discussion about sexual violence in the United States without addressing the topic of firearms. Pervasive gun ownership—according to a 2021 Pew Research Center study, 40 percent of adults report living in a household with at least one gun—cannot help but heighten tensions in power dynamics, whether among strangers or, more commonly, intimate partners.[1] A global crisis that exacerbates economic disparities, social isolation, and uncertainty about the future provides a setting tailor-made for social and domestic strife, with the potential for deadly consequences.

As the COVID-19 pandemic spread throughout the world, fears were raised from a number of quarters regarding the increased risk of sexual violence, in particular among intimate and domestic partners.[2] Early reports from China, Australia, Europe, and the United States all recorded a rise in domestic abuse incidents coinciding with lockdowns and other restrictive measures enacted to prevent the spread of disease.[3] One element that distinguishes the United States from most other places, however, and which increases the risks of gender-based and intimate partner violence (IPV), is the widespread access to guns, thanks to the Second Amendment and decades of policymaking in support of loosened restrictions on individual rights to purchase, own, and carry weapons, often without training or license. The Second Amendment encodes firearms as an extension of the person, who becomes a human-machine hybrid in perpetual conflict with the environment. In a pandemic setting characterized by immunological discourse of invasion and defense, the lines between Self and weapon are blurred still further, and the battle for sovereignty is often waged through exercises in control, intimidation, terror, physical attack, and even death. Women are most frequently the emotional or physical casualties of these battles, waged by their own current or former intimate partners. In chapter 18, Sally Kitch explains that one term for this trend is *silent pandemic*. This chapter argues that sexual violence, gun culture, and a viral pandemic all represent embodied phenomena and are worth examining as intertwined in their occurrence, in the measures taken to mitigate their negative impacts, and in the language used to describe them.

The Immunity Paradox

Immunity, from *immunitas*, originated etymologically as a term denoting freedom or exemption from legal or economic burdens; it was not until the discovery of the physiological defenses that became known as the *immune system*, in the late nineteenth century, that the word also took on biological connotations. These dual strands of meaning have since become interwoven, the legal and political and the immunological.[4]

Sexual violence of all kinds is a violation of personal sovereignty over one's own physical person, so it is important to consider the embodied nature of the act. The Enlightenment thinking that undergirds the structure of US government and the country's approach to democracy, however, is rooted in a Cartesian mind/body split, seeking to disembody reason and create a legal system that conceives of the body in a more abstract fashion. One of the most influential philosophers in Western political thought has been Thomas Hobbes. As the political theorist Mark Neocleous writes in *The Politics of Immunity: Security and the Policing of Bodies*, Hobbes mapped contemporary mechanical understandings of the body onto the body politic: "Conceptualized as a machine, sovereignty is truly impersonal, while as a body it retains some of the 'human' features characteristic of an age of personal power."[5]

Nowhere is this line of thinking more evident than in the Second Amendment to the US Constitution, which states in its entirety that "a well regulated Militia, being necessary to the security of a free State, the right of the people to keep and bear Arms, shall not be infringed." Of all the Bill of Rights, this amendment stands out because it is the only one that is not intrinsic to the human condition, but involves a mechanical device. Weapons are therefore inscribed into the worldview of the United States as an extension of the Self, a technological augmentation of the physical and political body.

Hobbes was also known for his worldview that the natural state of humankind is to live an existence that is one of "continual fear, and danger of violent death" as well as "solitary, poor, nasty, brutish, and short."[6] Government is a defense for the body politic against this state. Similar language has historically been employed to describe the immune system and the body, the need to repel a siege of invaders (such as, for instance, a deadly virus) by mobilizing armies of antibodies, either acquired naturally or enhanced by man-made weapons, vaccines. To protect the physical person against COVID-19, we were urged to observe a careful regimen of isolation, handwashing, testing, and, when possible, vaccination to fend off and kill the marauders. As Neocleous writes, "The *care of the self* leaves one at *war with the world*. The message is clear: *You are by nature a war machine*."[7] While these measures were certainly necessary from a public health standpoint, the militant framing amplified the combative tendencies of a nation already armed and trigger-happy.

Immunity, in both its legal sense of exemption from consequences and the microbiological meaning, can be seen as rooted in the notion of the Self as one's individual property, for which each person is responsible for establishing and policing the perimeter as well as its overall integrity. Neocleous writes, "To put it bluntly, wherever one looks in immunology one gets the same message: 'The story of immunity is the story of the self.'"[8] As conceptualizations of the Self are deeply rooted in culture as well as biological and political discourse, it is worth reflecting on the implications of this proprietary approach to self-sovereignty.

Sovereignty, property ownership, and control are thus inherent in the Enlightenment notion of the Self. If we think through the ramifications, historical laws that prohibited women from owning property in essence represented a restriction of their selfhood; today's debates over reproductive rights can be seen as a continuation of the ongoing debate over where the boundaries of sovereignty lie when it comes to women's bodies—and their Selves. What does it mean when, as in American culture, that Self-identity includes a firearm as a quasi-natural extension? In many gun communities, women without guns are viewed as incomplete and deserving of any attacks that might befall them, because they have neglected to exercise their "empowerment," incomplete in their mechanized Self without having acquired and wielded a firearm. They have failed to understand that their body is a war zone and have left it open to incursion.

If immunity is about the perceived boundaries of the Self, both the physical body and one's personal autonomy, IPV and domestic violence (DV) may be conceived of as an autoimmune disease: when the Self's defenses are turned against one's own domestic unit. The defensive mechanism that may have originated as a means of protecting hearth and home becomes instead the tool of aggression and self-destruction. Coercive control, which is often exercised with the aid of a firearm (even though it may never be deployed), has been described as "fundamentally a highly nuanced attack on the victim's sense of self, their perception of reality and freedom, which is intended to grant perpetrators control and power over victims."[9] It is also profoundly gendered within intimate partner relationships, with women overwhelmingly victimized, and it meets the definition of DV because it constitutes not an individual act of abuse but an ongoing pattern of behaviors.[10]

This phenomenon was especially heightened during the pandemic, when the notion of immunity became interwoven into everyday existence and the tools intended to protect the collective created the conditions to put many people in increased danger, in particular when in the presence of firearms.

IPV and DV

In the popular imagination, sexual assault is largely perpetrated by violent strangers. Statistics paint a different picture, though: the National Intimate Partner and Sexual Violence Survey indicates that more than ten million men and women experience violence at the hands of a current or former intimate partner each year. Not all of that violence is sexual in nature, but nearly one out of every eleven women reports having been raped by a current or former intimate partner. According to the most recently compiled data, from 2011, approximately 9.2 percent of women and 2.5 percent of men have experienced stalking by a current or former intimate partner.[11] We also know that only a fraction of IPV cases are reported, suggesting that the actual figures are much higher than these—a 2017 study by the Bureau of Justice Statistics estimated that more than 40 percent of DV cases are never reported to authorities.[12]

IPV refers to "physical, sexual, or psychological harm by a current or former intimate partner or spouse."[13] Nearly a third of women worldwide are affected by IPV, threatening their physical and mental well-being, exposing them to sexually transmitted infections, and even placing them at risk of death.[14]

Not everyone is equally vulnerable to intimate partner sexual violence (IPSV). There is considerable evidence that poverty, housing instability, and food insecurity correspond to increased IPV victimization and sexual violence overall.[15] In one study, women with recent IPV experience were found to be nearly four times as likely to suffer housing instability, even after adjusting for socioeconomic factors.[16] The reasons for this relationship appear to be bidirectional, with housing insecurity and other poverty indicators making people (especially women) more vulnerable to violence of all kinds, but also with the volatility of abusive relationships increasing the likelihood of financial hardship.[17]

Researchers have found that overall IPV rates are fairly consistent across urban, suburban, and rural settings. However, rates for IPSV and homicide tend to be higher in rural areas, and the cases may be more chronic and severe. Geographically, community response is also lower in these regions. With homes located farther apart, distance contributing to longer emergency response times to reported incidents, poorly funded services, and social norms making it less acceptable to seek intervention in domestic affairs, the risk of severe injury or death is greater than in more densely populated locales. Higher incidences of alcoholism, drug addiction, and unemployment may also be factors in these increased risks.[18]

The culture of gun ownership may also vary between population centers. Even service providers in rural areas may downplay the risks associated with gun ownership in DV situations, given the ubiquity of guns used for hunting and sport as well as home defense in more rural regions. These communities also tend to be poorer, and, with fewer resources, victim advocates, services, and law enforcement are often stretched thin to cover a large geographical territory.[19] There is considerably less research on the IPV impacts of the COVID-19 pandemic in rural regions compared to urban centers, making it difficult to estimate the effects of containment measures in these areas.

The Pandemic and IPV

Shelter-in-place measures and school closures, intended to limit the spread of the virus to protect individuals and communities, paradoxically created conditions that exacerbated the dangers for those already (knowingly or unknowingly) at risk for gender-based violence in general and intimate partner gun violence in particular.[20] In addition to the increased dangers at home, it also became more difficult to deliver services to victims isolated with or in proximity to their abusers. Rural areas suffered from limited resources and sometimes reduced access to technology, as chat lines and online systems were often preferred means of requesting help to avoid alerting abusers by making a voice call. Without the ability to speak to service providers in person, victims found themselves trapped in dangerous households.

A study comparing calls reporting DV to law enforcement in major US cities before and after social distancing measures were implemented found an overall 7.5 percent increase during the first three months of the pandemic, with a 9.7 percent spike in the first five weeks. Most notably, there was a statistically significant increase in DV reports from city blocks without a recent history of such calls, "suggesting COVID-19 ha[d] led to an extensive margin increase with new households placing calls."[21] Interviews with victim service providers for gender-based violence in both rural and urban areas found that nearly half reported an increase in abusers who threatened to shoot victims, as well as homicides involving firearms.[22]

In the United States, the effects of the pandemic on DV reports specifically involving firearms were uneven: dire predictions became reality in some locales, while others saw rates remain stable or even decrease. The reasons for this patchwork are not yet fully understood and likely complex.[23] Teasing apart the distinctions between differences in incidence and in reports to authorities or other services, for instance, remains difficult without reliable data. Many studies rely on the Gun Violence Archive (GVA), which tracks news reports of shootings and classifies them by state.[24] A 2021 *Frontline* reportage based on GVA data found that between 2019 and 2020 domestic shooting fatalities in Georgia actually decreased—but increased by 67 percent in Missouri, 69 percent in Texas, 93 percent in Maryland, and 160 percent in Utah.[25]

Factors that may have contributed to these increases include financial stress and unemployment, as well as confinement due to lockdowns, along with the spike in gun sales. Court closures in some places may also have delayed trials for domestic assault, possibly placing victims at greater risk. The strain and uncertainty of the pandemic also exacerbated mental health issues, such as depression and anxiety.[26]

Most studies of the impact of the pandemic on IPV have focused on readily available measures of violence, such as reported injuries or deaths. The emphasis on outcomes makes it difficult to accurately estimate other patterns of abuse such as coercive control or general psychological and emotional abuse (with or without the aid of firearms or other weapons), although these tactics may be at least as damaging to their victims over time.[27] Even friends or family members may fail to recognize the tactics of coercive control and not report incidents or provide support to those experiencing it.[28]

Firearms and the Violation of Immunity

As the pandemic spread, many Americans turned to their Second Amendment rights to exercise a sense of control and attempt to assert some form of immunity even while a biological vaccine remained elusive. Accurate, comprehensive firearm and ammunition ownership and purchasing data are difficult to obtain, as there are no official centralized databases and record-keeping practices vary widely, but a nationally representative survey found that approximately 6 percent of US adults reported purchasing a gun during the early months of the pandemic (from March to mid-July 2020); 34 percent of those indicated they were first-time gun purchasers.[29] Background checks are often used as a proxy for firearm sales, however incomplete, but even these figures increased 39 percent from 2019 to 2020 nationwide.[30] The National Shooting Sports Foundation reported that first-time gun purchases soared in the first seven months of 2020, with a 71 percent increase over the same period in 2019.[31] Most of these weapons were reportedly purchased to protect against other people as fear and uncertainty rose during the early weeks of the pandemic, but these trends continued through 2021.

The rise in gun purchases, perhaps unsurprisingly, has been accompanied by an increase in the incidence of gun violence. There is a well-documented association between surges in gun purchases, which typically take place at moments of heightened political turmoil or in the wake of mass shootings, and ensuing increases in gun violence.[32] The pandemic surge therefore fits into an established cycle of escalating violence, especially given the social and political unrest that accompanied the pandemic, such as the George Floyd murder in the spring of 2020, the 2020 US elections, and the insurrection at the US Capitol on January 6, 2021. Even before those polarizing events, researchers found that the risk of gun violence was up 30 percent in March 2020 over March 2019. That same 30 percent increase characterized the period between March 2020 and March 2021 compared to the previous thirteen-month period. Only Alaska was exempt from this increased risk of pandemic gun violence.[33]

The role of firearm ownership in IPV has been well established. However, little research has been carried out to investigate the impact of the pandemic on firearm abuse behaviors.[34] A 2021 *PBS NewsHour* report highlighted the increases in DV, gun violence, and homicide during the pandemic.[35] Similarly, *Frontline* cited 2021 statistics indicating that domestic homicides constituted nearly a quarter of all killings in the United States, over half of which involved firearms. Women represent a disproportionate percentage of DV fatalities: current or former male partners are responsible for almost half of all female homicide victims.[36] Fifty-seven women are killed each month by an intimate partner, on average, and these rates are even higher for Black, Latina, and Indigenous women; LGBTQ individuals are also at increased risk of intimate partner homicide.[37] After controlling for other risk factors, access to firearms has been found to produce an eightfold increase in femicide risk. Previous use of a gun (even brandished as a threat) in domestic disputes was found to be associated with a forty-one-fold increase in risk.[38] More than 50 percent of intimate partner homicides are committed using a gun, and when guns are used in a domestic killing there is nearly double the likelihood of multiple victims.[39] Medical providers are typically urged to determine whether a reported abuser has access to guns and to inform women of the risks these present.[40] Although there are federal laws prohibiting the purchase and possession of firearms by those convicted of DV, enforcement of these laws varies greatly by state and locale, and there are a number of gaps in legal protection—such as the "boyfriend loophole"—that limit the effectiveness of these laws.[41] This term refers to the fact that most laws restricting firearm purchases cover only current or former spouses, co-parents, or live-in partners, not other kinds of dating partners or even confirmed stalkers.[42]

Suicide rates in the United States have risen significantly over the past two decades, in particular among white males aged twenty-five to thirty-four. The steepest increases, including among teens and young adults, have taken place in rural areas.[43] One potential contributing factor is the rising number of guns, also through the growing population of veterans in those geographical regions. The association between relationship problems and suicide (in particular intimate partner homicide-suicide) is strong, especially in households containing firearms.[44]

The Insidiousness of Coercive Control in DV and IPV

According to the US Department of Justice, DV refers to "a pattern of abusive behavior in any relationship that is used by one partner to gain or maintain power and control over another intimate partner."[45] Guns are commonly employed in the United States as a tool to intimidate and terrorize victims, but firing a weapon is not the only way to employ guns in DV and IPV.[46] Growing evidence reveals the power of coercive control, where displaying or brandishing a gun, threatening to shoot, or even just the victim's awareness of the presence of an accessible firearm can be used to intimidate, control, and inflict psychological abuse.[47] Coercive control is said to exist when three conditions—cognitive, behavioral, and physiological—exist: a victim perceives a credible risk from a coercive threat, complies with or resists the threat, and experiences fear.[48] The risk of coercive control is considerably greater than the risk of suffering fatal or nonfatal physical gun violence.

However, less is known about the nonfatal use of guns against women by intimate partners than about homicide cases, due to the lack of reporting and limited data from agencies. Coercive control, in particular, is especially "difficult to operationalize, measure and action in law, policy and frontline interventions."[49] What we do know from extant research is that around four and a half million women alive today in the United States say that they have had an intimate partner threaten them with a gun; nearly one million have been shot or shot at by a partner. Since coercive control with a legally owned weapon is not against the law in the United States, the conditions are created for chronic abuse that can (and is likely to) escalate.[50] Reporting systems that focus on outcomes such as injury and death can therefore obscure a multitude of tactics for control, intimidation, terror, and coercion that rely on firearms to oppress intimate partners.

COVID-19 had a number of impacts on the rate of physical as well as psychological IPV in the United States. One study found that, early on, those who had experienced symptoms or tested positive for the novel coronavirus were two to three times more likely to be victims or perpetrators of IPV; those who suffered pandemic-induced unemployment were found to be three to four times more likely to commit IPV compared to their employed counterparts.[51] A *Time* magazine story from March 2020 reported that abusive partners leveraged the pandemic to intimidate and further isolate their victims: forbidding them from leaving under penalty of being locked outside, threatening to throw them out if they became sick, or, conversely, threatening to deliberately throw them into the street to infect them.[52] Regardless of the absolute number of cases, it is likely that lockdowns exposed those in already abusive situations to more extreme violence with no opportunity for relief through the workplace or social activities with friends and family, also for fear of infecting vulnerable loved ones.

The pandemic caused widespread disruption that proved difficult for many people to navigate with any degree of equanimity. As Katie Ray-Jones, chief executive officer of the National Domestic Violence Hotline, pointed out, "We know that domestic violence is rooted in power and control. Right now, we are all feeling a lack of control over our lives and an individual who cannot manage that will take it out on their victim."[53] Stress and uncertainty about the future, loss of employment, or pivots to remote work, especially paired with home schooling and extended confinement with family members, can all create stressors that can push relationships to a breaking point.[54]

Around 20 percent of victim services workers in rural, suburban, and urban areas stated in interviews that threats to shoot others increased markedly during the pandemic. Given the link between DV and mass shootings, these threats may constitute an early warning sign for an increase in these incidents even as pandemic containment measures ease.[55] Indeed, most mass shootings are connected to DV, especially those with higher case fatality rates.[56] While these represent a minuscule fraction of gun deaths in the United States, they receive considerable media attention and often prompt public discourse and attempts at policy change.

Conclusion: When Safety Is Not Safe

The COVID-19 pandemic exacerbated previously existing tensions within the notion of "safety," namely, the contrast between the romanticized Second Amendment ideal of guns as a protective tool for self-defense against tyrants or invaders, a symbol of "freedom," and the reality of a world in which the presence of a firearm within a household leads to increased likelihood of IPV, accidental death, or suicide. These tensions echo those within the virology field with regard to the notion of "immunity" and its characterization as a system of defense against invasion that may cause paradoxically greater harm than the outside threat. Discourse surrounding immunity and protection from a deadly virus thus intertwines with that of guns as a tool for safety, self-defense, and deadly violence.

While all violence involves invading boundaries, bullets physically penetrate the body in a way that has frequently been compared to sexual intercourse. Conversely, guns can be used as tools of sexual violence without firing a shot, through coercive control. There is evidence that the combination of lockdown restrictions and economic distress exacerbated the incidence of IPV of all kinds, particularly in rural parts of the country, where gun ownership is also more widespread. With guns inscribed in the United States Constitution as an extension of the Self and of the physical body, firearm violence is a profoundly embodied phenomenon even when no physical contact occurs. Intimate partner and domestic gun violence may therefore be seen as a sort of autoimmune disease of a system gone awry, mechanisms that turn on the body, personal or political, and destroy it from within.

Notes

1. Ted Van Green, "Wide Differences on Most Gun Policies between Gun Owners and Non-owners, but Also Some Agreement," Pew Research Center, August 4, 2021, www.pewresearch.org/fact-tank/2021/08/04/wide-differences-on-most-gun-policies-between-gun-owners-and-non-owners-but-also-some-agreement.

2. See, e.g., Caroline Bradbury-Jones and Louise Isham, "The Pandemic Paradox: The Consequences of COVID-19 on Domestic Violence," *Journal of Clinical Nursing* 29, no. 13–14 (2020): 2047; Lisa Geller and Lauren Footman, "Guns, Domestic Violence and COVID-19 Are a Lethal Combination," *Morning Consult*, October 27, 2020, https://morningconsult.com/opinions/guns-domestic-violence-and-covid-19-are-a-lethal-combination.

3. Kim Usher, Navjot Bhullar, Joanne Durkin, Naomi Gyamfi, and Debra Jackson, "Family Violence and COVID-19: Increased Vulnerability and Reduced Options for Support," *International Journal of Mental Health Nursing* 29, no. 4 (2020): 549.

4. Mark Neocleous, *The Politics of Immunity: Security and the Policing of Bodies* (London: Verso, 2022), 2.

5. Neocleous, *The Politics of Immunity*, 6–7.

6. Thomas Hobbes, *Leviathan* (Baltimore: Penguin Books, 1968), chap. 13, para. 9.

7. Neocleous, *The Politics of Immunity*, 38.

8. Neocleous, *The Politics of Immunity*, 82.

9. Ciara Smyth, Patricia Cullen, Jan Breckenridge, Natasha Cortis, and Kylie Valentine, "COVID-19 Lockdowns, Intimate Partner Violence and Coercive Control," *Australian Journal of Social Issues* 56, no. 3 (2021): 360.

10. Smyth et al., "Coercive Control."

11. See, e.g., Matthew J. Breiding, Sharon G. Smith, Kathleen C. Basile, Mikel L. Walters, Jieru Chen, and Melissa T. Merrick, "Prevalence and Characteristics of Sexual Violence, Stalking, and Intimate Partner Violence Victimization—National Intimate Partner and Sexual Violence Survey, United States, 2011," Surveillance Summaries, *Morbidity and Mortality Weekly Report* (Center for Disease Control and Prevention) 63 no. 8 (2014): 1.

12. Brian A. Reaves, *Police Response to Domestic Violence, 2006–2015* (Washington, DC: Bureau of Justice Statistics, Department of Justice, 2017), https://bjs.ojp.gov/content/pub/pdf/prdv0615.pdf.

13. Alexandria Goodyear, Michael Rodriguez, and Deborah Glik, "The Role of Firearms in Intimate Partner Violence: Policy and Research Considerations," *Journal of Public Health Policy* 41, no. 2 (2019): 185.

14. Goodyear, Rodriguez, and Glik, "Firearms in Intimate Partner Violence."

15. Matthew J. Breiding, Kathleen C. Basile, Joanne Klevens, and Sharon G. Smith, "Economic Insecurity and Intimate Partner and Sexual Violence Victimization," *American Journal of Preventive Medicine* 53, no. 4 (2017): 457–58.

16. Joanne Pavao, Jennifer Alvarez, Nikki Baumrind, Marta Induni, and Rachel Kimerling, "Intimate Partner Violence and Housing Instability," *American Journal of Preventive Medicine* 32, no. 2 (2007): 143.

17. Breiding et al., "Economic Insecurity," 461.

18. Katie M. Edwards, "Intimate Partner Violence and the Rural-Urban-

Suburban Divide: Myth or Reality? A Critical Review of the Literature," *Trauma, Violence and Abuse* 16, no. 3 (2015): 359.

19. Kellie R. Lynch and T. K. Logan, "'Always Know Where the Gun Is': Service Providers Perceptions of Firearm Access, Violence, and Safety Planning during the COVID-19 Pandemic," *Journal of Interpersonal Violence* 37, no. 21–22 (October 2021): NP19827–NP19856.

20. Lynch and Logan, "Service Providers' Perceptions."

21. Emily Leslie and Riley Wilson, "Sheltering in Place and Domestic Violence: Evidence from Calls for Service during COVID-19," *Journal of Public Economics* 189 (September 2020): 2, 104241, https://doi.org/10.1016/j.jpubeco.2020.104241.

22. Lynch and Logan, "Service Providers' Perceptions," NP19827.

23. Dan Glaun, "A Handful of States Fueled a National Increase in Domestic Violence Shooting Deaths as COVID-19 Spread," *Frontline*, June 2, 2021, www.pbs.org/wgbh/frontline/article/national-increase-domestic-violence-shooting-deaths-during-covid-19.

24. The GVA has its limitations, as it tracks only shootings that are reported in the media, and classifications regarding the involvement of intimate or domestic partners depend on how the incidents are recorded by local agencies.

25. Glaun, "Domestic Violence Shooting Deaths."

26. See Glaun, "Domestic Violence Shooting Deaths"; Lynch and Logan, "Service Providers Perceptions."

27. Smyth et al., "Coercive Control."

28. Smyth et al., "Coercive Control."

29. Cassandra K. Crifasi, Julie A. Ward, Emma E. McGinty, Daniel Webster, and Colleen L. Barry, "Gun Purchasing Behaviours during the Initial Phase of the COVID-19 Pandemic, March to Mid-July 2020," *International Review of Psychiatry* 33, no. 7 (2021): 594.

30. Glaun, "Domestic Violence Shooting Deaths."

31. National Shooting Sports Foundation, "First-Time Gun Buyers Grow to Nearly 5 Million," August 24, 2020, www.nssf.org/articles/first-time-gun-buyers-grow-to-nearly-5-million-in-2020.

32. Julia P. Schleimer, Christopher D. McCort, Aaron B. Shev, Veronica A. Pear, Elizabeth Tomsich, Alaina De Biasi, Shani Buggs, Hannah S. Laqueur, and Garen J. Wintemute, "Firearm Purchasing and Firearm Violence during the Coronavirus Pandemic in the United States: A Cross-Sectional Study," *Injury Epidemiology* 8, no. 43 (2021): 2.

33. Paddy Ssentongo, Claudio Fronterre, Anna E. Ssentongo, Shailesh Advani, Emily S. Heilbrunn, Joshua P. Hazelton, John S. Oh, Jennifer S. McCall-Hosenfeld, and Vernon M. Chinchilli, "Gun Violence Incidence during the COVID-19 Pandemic Is Higher than before the Pandemic in the United States," *Scientific Reports* 11 (2021): 1, 4, 20654, https://doi.org/10.1038/s41598-021-98813-z.

34. Lynch and Logan, "Service Providers' Perceptions."

35. Corey Meador, "Domestic Violence Shelters Are Swamped: Experts Worry Surging Gun Sales Could Make Things Worse," *PBS NewsHour*, July 14, 2021, www.pbs.org/newshour/health/domestic-violence-shelters-are-swamped-experts-worry-surging-gun-sales-could-make-things-worse.

36. Glaun, "Domestic Violence Shooting Deaths."

37. Meador, "Domestic Violence Shelters."

38. Jacquelyn C. Campbell, Daniel Webster, Jane Koziol-McLain, Carolyn Block, Doris Campbell, Mary Ann Curry, Faye Gary, et al., "Risk Factors for Femicide in Abusive Relationships: Results from a Multisite Case Control Study," *American Journal of Public Health* 93, no. 7 (2003): 1092.

39. Lisa Geller, Marisa Booty, and Cassandra K. Crifasi, "The Role of Domestic Violence in Fatal Mass Shootings in the United States, 2014–2019," *Injury Epidemiology* 8, no. 38 (2021): 2.

40. Campbell et al., "Risk Factors for Femicide."

41. On these laws, see Geller, Booty, and Crifasi, "Fatal Mass Shootings."

42. Geller and Footman, "Guns, Domestic Violence and COVID-19."

43. Sabrina Brown and Donna L. Schuman, "Suicide in the Time of COVID-19: A Perfect Storm," *Journal of Rural Health* 37, no. 1 (2021): 211–12.

44. Brown and Schuman, "Suicide," 213.

45. US Department of Justice, Office on Violence Against Women, "Domestic Violence," June 20, 2022, www.justice.gov/ovw/domestic-violence.

46. April M. Zeoli, *Non-fatal Firearm Uses in Domestic Violence* (Minneapolis: Battered Women's Justice Project, 2017), www.preventdvgunviolence.org/nonfatal-gun-dv-zeoli-.pdf.

47. See Lynch and Logan, "Service Providers Perceptions," NP19829–NP19830; Zeoli, *Non-fatal Firearm Uses*, 2.

48. Mary Ann Dutton and Lisa A. Goodman, "Coercion in Intimate Partner Violence: Toward a New Conceptualization," *Sex Roles: A Journal of Research* 52, no. 11–12 (2005): 751.

49. Smyth et al., "Coercive Control," 359.

50. Susan B. Sorenson and Rebecca A. Schut, "Nonfatal Gun Use in Intimate Partner Violence: A Systematic Review of the Literature," *Trauma, Violence and Abuse* 19, no. 4 (2018): 431.

51. Maxine Davis, Ohad Gilbar, and Diana M. Padilla-Medina, "Intimate Partner Violence Victimization and Perpetration among U.S. Adults during the Earliest Stage of the COVID-19 Pandemic," *Violence and Victims* 36, no. 5 (2021): 583.

52. Melissa Godin, "As Cities around the World Go on Lockdown, Victims of Domestic Violence Look for a Way Out," *Time*, March 18, 2020, https://time.com/5803887/coronavirus-domestic-violence-victims.

53. Quoted in Godin, "Lockdown."

54. Leslie and Wilson, "Sheltering in Place," 5.

55. About one in five participants reported that threatening to shoot others in public increased during the pandemic and the role of DV in mass shootings cannot be ignored. Everytown for Gun Safety, "Guns and Violence against Women: America's Uniquely Lethal Intimate Partner Violence Problem," October 17, 2019, https://everytownresearch.org/report/guns-and-violence-against-women-americas-uniquely-lethal-intimate-partner-violence-problem; Jackie Gu, "Deadliest Mass Shooters Have a History of Domestic Violence," Bloomberg, June 30, 2020, www.bloomberg.com/graphics/2020-mass-shootings-domestic-violence-connection. It is critical to recognize the overlap of domestic abuse and gun violence and do a better job of assessing and managing these threats to mitigate the potential risk of devastating homicides.

56. The term *mass shooting* conventionally refers to gun violence incidents with four or more victims, not including the perpetrator, although sources are inconsistent about whether to count only fatalities or include injuries as well. See Geller, Booty, and Crifasi, "Fatal Mass Shootings," 3, 6.

5

Transnational Performances of Disobedience to Cultures of Sexual Violence

Deborah Martin and Deborah Shaw

On November 20, 2019, the Chilean feminist theater collective LasTesis staged a powerful street performance, *Un violador en tu camino* (A rapist in your path), in Valparaíso, calling out rape culture and indicting the state and wider society for women's oppression. The performance went on to be shared and restaged in other Spanish-speaking countries, including Argentina, Colombia, the Dominican Republic, Ecuador, Mexico, Nicaragua, Paraguay, Peru, and Spain, and it has been reinterpreted in over two hundred locations around the world.[1] The original piece incorporates a powerful and catchy chant, references to Chilean national songs, and accusations of rape against the instruments of the state, including the president. The opening lyrics were pointed:

The patriarchy is a judge
that judges us for being born
and our punishment
is the violence you don't see
The patriarchy is a judge
that judges us for being born
and our punishment
is the violence you now see
It's femicide
Impunity for my killer
It's disappearance
It's rape

And it wasn't my fault, not where I was nor what I wore
[Repeat refrain four times]
The rapist was you
the rapist is you
the police
the judges
the State
the president
The oppressive state is a macho rapist. [Repeat refrain twice][2]

LasTesis is an interdisciplinary, intersectional, and trans-inclusive feminist collective. Interviews with LasTesis members indicate that their performance was inspired by the writings of the Argentine feminist anthropologist and decolonial thinker Rita Segato and that it was conceived as an attempt to translate her theories into a format that would be accessible to those who would not ordinarily encounter them.[3]

After the Valparaíso interventions on November 20, 2019, performances of *Un violador en tu camino* were staged in Santiago on November 25, the International Day for the Elimination of Violence against Women. Performances, in fact, had been planned for October 2019 but were postponed due to the massive protests that swept the country that month against the inequality and privatization fostered by the current Chilean Constitution (inherited from Augusto Pinochet) and the government of Sebastián Piñera (2018–22). The organization Human Rights Watch reported on excessive force used by Chile's police (*carabineros*) and human rights violations. A Human Rights Watch report in 2020 noted credible testimony that police forced detainees, especially women and girls, to undress and squat fully naked, a practice banned by police protocols. (*Un violador* dance moves represent this form of police malpractice.) *Un violador* is, then, intimately bound up with these protests, known as the "Chilean social outbreak" (*estallido social chileno*) in its timing, its response to the police abuse of protesters, and its ideological alignment.

The original performances in Chile can be seen as a way for women to reassert their visibility at a moment of heightened tensions and violence. The title *Un violador* is a sarcastic rewording of the 1990s Chilean police slogan: *Un amigo en tu camino* (A friend in your path), and the LasTesis performances incorporated a verse from the *Himno de los carabineros de Chile* (Chilean police anthem):

Sleep tight, innocent girl
With no fear of outlaws
For your *carabinero* lover
Watches over your sweet and happy dreams.[4]

As Dafne Valdés of LasTesis explained in an interview, this citation is directed at the police who use sexual violence to intimidate women protesters, and who claim to protect women while doing the opposite.[5] More broadly, the protest takes place within the context of other mass protests responding to the ascendancy of the new Right at the time of the protests.

Piñera's cabinet was male-dominated and criticized for its anti-women policies, especially its opposition to the legalization of abortion.[6] Throughout the Americas, an emphasis on the ideal of the family, defined as the locus of rights to be defended at all costs, has galvanized efforts to demonize and punish what is called "the ideology of gender" and gender theory.[7] Feminist movements in Latin America have called into question the sanctity of the traditional family unit and the conservative patriarchal state as its self-proclaimed protector by highlighting the abuses and violence committed against women within the family and by the state and agents of its institutions: judges, state security forces, police, politicians—all groups explicitly named and denounced by *Un violador*.

In Chile, two recent political protests stand out as important precedents for *Un violador*: those against the reform of the education system in 2011, which saw the increase of art, performance, and dance, including flash mobs, and the Mayo Feminista protests of May 2018, in which feminist student groups took over universities to protest the male-oriented and misogynist nature of education and research.

This chapter considers the ways LasTesis's performance contributes to the relocation of art and theory, moving them from academic, theater, and museum settings to the streets: *El arte fuera de sala* (Art outside the classroom)—as one placard held up by a male ally, during the first performance, put it. In addition, as we discuss, the performance was shared globally and digitally, further decentering any authorship associated with the original performances and thus contributing to a radically de-hierarchized form of art activism.

We examine the performance's impressive transnational circulation and the cultural moment this responds to by discussing case studies of restagings in Chile, Mexico, Turkey, and India, all countries led by men with poor records of tackling gender-based violence, and focusing on commonalities and local specificities illustrated by the adaptations. With its origins in Chile and its widespread transnational adoption, *Un violador* reverses the neocolonial direction of travel of more individualistic cultural moments such as #MeToo, with its choice of the first-person pronoun and its roots in the Hollywood star system. In contrast, the theory and practice of *Un violador* highlights a systemic form of patriarchal, state-sanctioned rape culture and effectively challenges it by breaking with regimes that consign certain bodies to specific spaces and positions and by inventing new subjects and new forms of collective, disobedient, performative enunciation.

Un violador en tu camino: Theory, Politics, and Aesthetics

LasTesis's performance transforms feminist theoretical knowledge and discourse into embodied street activism and, in taking theory to the street, counters public and populist conservative attacks on gender theory. An example of the latter was the hostility faced by queer theorist Judith Butler during a visit to Brazil in 2017, when an effigy of her was burned by right-wing protesters.[8] LasTesis's name expresses their aim, which is to deploy catchy and simple performance methods to share feminist theories with those who may not have had the opportunity to read or analyze them.[9]

For *Un violador*, the group drew on Segato's analyses of rape culture and violence against women. Segato argues that the patriarchal myth of female disobedience and punishment is universal in the sense that it occurs as a foundational narrative in cultures found on all five continents and that it is a pillar of rape culture.[10] LasTesis represents this idea with the first words of their chant: within patriarchy all women/girls are at birth "judged" as disobedient and thus deemed deserving of punishment. For Segato, the lack of importance given by the state (here she speaks in global terms) to the crime of rape has to do with the fact that it is considered a minor crime; it is associated with desire, passion, and what is private. Crimes against men, by contrast, are seen as crimes against what is public, given the equivalency between the masculine and the universal subject.[11]

By naming the state as perpetrator ("el estado opresor es un macho violador") and pointing the finger (literally, through the dance moves, as well as figuratively) at the judges, the state, and the president ("los jueces, el estado, el presidente"), the performance draws attention to the unacknowledged continuities between so-called private acts of violence and public institutions.

When the song denounces the rapist as "you"—in past and present tenses—and names the pillars of the patriarchal state, it does not refer to one woman raped by one man in any one country, but rather presents a systemic abuse of women's bodies by a patriarchal apparatus.[12] In *Un violador*, groups of women come together to perform in high-profile, highly symbolic state- and judiciary-linked locations, thus situating the crime of rape as a major, a general, and a public phenomenon, rather than a minor, particular, and private one; it constitutes a making-public of rape and establishes the female body / female subject as something collective and public and thus rape as a crime against *lo público*.

Feminism in the Southern Cone has been predominantly a lettered feminism (*feminismo letrado*), an elite and therefore a Eurocentric feminism—by contrast, Central American feminism has its origin in armed struggles and rural communities.[13] LasTesis's performance is a product of these historical circumstances in the sense that, like the May 2018 protests, it originates in the university (LasTesis's members are graduates of the University of Valparaíso, where they are employed as researchers and lecturers at the Escuela de Teatro), but it also acts to counter the elite tendency of Southern Cone feminism, bringing it to audiences and participants who have historically been excluded from the feminism of this region through their exclusion from universities and letters.

The performance can thus be understood as a means of decolonizing and de-hierarchizing elements of feminist theory and knowledge surrounding rape and violence against women. This is especially the case when we consider some of the contexts in which the performance has been restaged, for example, by the Indigenous women of the Escuela Antisuyu Warmikuna (an Indigenous women's center for gender equality and environmental sustainability in Puyo, Ecuador). This broad adoption of *Un violador* does include some performances in academic settings, however, such as the University College of Cork (UCC), Ireland (February 10, 2020), thus completing the circle.[14]

To counter the patriarchal judgment of women as "disobedient," *Un violador* embraces and performs a "vital intensity of disobedience." Indeed, disobedience is central to the new aesthetics of feminist rebellion throughout Chile, including those of the Yeguada Latinoamericana performances also staged to protest violence against women, in which female performers appear naked from the waist down except for horse tails, and of the bare breasts and adorned balaclavas of Chile's feminist protesters of 2018, in "collective aesthetic rebellions" that left their mark on Chilean social memory.[15] Such performances can be seen as forerunners of the approach of LasTesis.

Un violador en tu camino is also intentionally in clear contravention of the rules of polite society, especially as these rules are bound up with gender norms and expectations of women and their behavior and movement in public spaces. The assembly of large groups of women, the parodic appropriation of state slogans, and the use of forceful chanting and in-your-face physical movements to call attention to what is censored in dominant culture all constitute "disobedient" acts. They are not "civil disobedience" in the tradition of Gandhi or Martin Luther King Jr., as they do not peacefully break the law; rather, they break symbolic and unwritten rules, particularly those that govern the behavior and expectations of women. In patriarchal culture, the manifestation of female rage is a disobedient act and a marginalized phenomenon, as women are denied "emotions as political as rage" in countries such as Chile.[16] While *Un violador* is physically nonviolent, its response to violence is one of rage, and LasTesis refers to "la rabia" as a condition of their work.[17] The rage constituted and channeled by *Un violador*, therefore, breaks the pact of acquiescence that upholds rape culture.

In addition, the performance plays on a central juxtaposition of rape culture, that of invisibility, on the one hand, and spectacle or performance, on the other. Rape often takes place in domestic and private settings and is a taboo subject that women are discouraged from talking about, sometimes through threats to their life; the high rate of femicide in Latin America cannot be separated from rape.[18] Segato defines rape, however, as an act perpetrated not out of sexual desire, but out of a desire for power and the need to demonstrate one's power both for oneself and for others; it is therefore inherently a demonstration or performance.[19]

There is thus a tension around rape as both hidden/silenced and shown/performed, compounded by the ways the hidden realities of such violence are displaced and displayed, glamorized and spectacularized as part of popular culture, as the raped and mutilated bodies of women fill our image world, from cinema (e.g., *El secreto de sus ojos* [The secret in their eyes], directed by Juan José Campanella, 2009) to the sensationalist tabloid press, whose practices, Segato argues, make the phenomenon "contagious."[20] This interplay of visibility and invisibility is woven into the semiotics of *Un violador*, in which the use of blindfolds and the lyrics ("the violence you don't see" and "the violence you now see") combine with the effective visual spectacle that is the performance itself: it is a loud and eye-catching effort to combat the forces of censorship and erasure.

Un violador further revolves around the juxtaposition of female bodies as both subjects and objects, both resistant and subjugated. It refers to the trappings of femininity both for direct protest and as a means of "staging" femininity in order to think about and critique gender norms. Dance moves and chanting that explicitly posit women's bodies as powerful, accusatory, and enraged are combined with moves that represent the humiliating poses required of women detained by the police. Costume is also central here: participants are invited to come in "party" clothes, which are "traditionally perceived as signifying a heightened sexual availability."[21] Through costume, the performance protests victim blaming that often centers around styles of dress ("it wasn't my fault, not where I was nor what I wore"). It asserts women's right to presence in the street, however they are dressed, and foregrounds the historical construction and positioning of the female body. In this sense, *Un violador* can be understood as part of a history of feminist performance/protest in which the performers "use their bodies beside themselves, as if for a second time, as a means of making explicit the historical staging of that body."[22] This theme is evident in other transnational feminist performance activism, such as SlutWalks, which also protest rape culture and victim blaming.

Un violador can be understood as a "political act" in the sense that the philosopher Jacques Rancière defines it: "inventing new ways of making sense of the sensible, new configurations between the visible and the invisible, and between the audible and the inaudible, new distributions of space and time—in short, new bodily capacities."[23] Political performances can, therefore, interfere in and reconfigure what is visible and audible, making public that which is socially deemed to be private, combating erasure and silencing.

Locations for *Un Violador* have been selected to highlight such politics by exposing the complicity of state institutions with rape culture. *Un violador* has been staged at Santiago's Palacio de la Moneda, Quebec's Parliament, London's Chilean Consulate, Thessaloniki's Police Headquarters, Santo Domingo's Procuraduría General de la Nación (Office of the Inspector General), and the Eiffel Tower.[24] High-profile, state-linked locations magnify the assertion of the "right to appear" made by these performances associated with the coming together of bodies in the street.[25] The body has long been central to artistic and performance-based protest culture in Chile, during both the 2011 protests and the Mayo Feminista of 2018. In such protests, "the body becomes a resource for staging catastrophe, because of the way it is imbued with the fragility of human existence."[26]

Not only does *Un violador* take aspects of feminist theory from the academy to the street, then, but it also transforms it into a kind of embodied thinking not accommodated within written or verbal discourse. It creates space for the transformation of individuals into collectives and (potentially) docile bodies into resistant ones, as humiliation is reenacted momentarily before bodies shift to positions of accusation and empowerment. *Un violador* is performative in the same way the cultural theorist Nelly Richard argues that the 2018 occupations of Chilean universities were. Its participants begin to experience what they are fighting for: "They both announce—and enunciate—change."[27] The performance thereby produces an "embodied sense of agency among performers and participants."[28]

Individualism, Collectivism, and Transnationalism

The United States and its #MeToo movement should not be taken as the single origin point of global women's activism against sexual violence. This spotlight on *Un violador*, and thus on the transnational impact of Latin American feminist activism, including Ni Una Menos (Not One Less), is also part of a decolonizing project. As Segato has noted, "Let's remember that there is a form of coloniality within social movements as well. That coloniality is deceptive and disorienting. #MeToo, with its roots in North American pilgrim-Puritan feminism, is directed towards and appeals to the paternity of the State, a third party as an indispensable arbiter of relations, a lawyer in the sheets, possibly as the only tool available in that ultra-individualist world. While #MeToo speaks to the state, Ni Una Menos speaks to all of us, men and women, it speaks to a society."[29]

Un violador critiques the state as the site of patriarchal violence. Members of LasTesis have also rejected working with the government or declaring an affiliation with any political party, writing on their Instagram account on February 3, 2020, "Institutional politics will NEVER be our home."[30] Yet, despite differences in expressions of feminist activism, in the transnational world of social media few high-profile movements are constrained by national borders, reductive meanings, or singular affiliations to any one hashtag or performance of political resistance. Indeed, #MeToo activists have embraced *Un violador*, while Latin American feminists have adopted and adapted the denunciatory power of #MeToo. US #MeToo activist groups have in fact used performances of *Un violador* to highlight allegations of sexual predation against two high-profile US figures: Harvey Weinstein and Donald Trump.[31] *Un violador* was performed outside the courtroom in New York at Weinstein's trial in January 2020, and activists followed this with performances on the same day on the subway and outside the Trump Hotel.[32] In turn, #MeToo was adopted in Mexico by profession-specific #MeToo Twitter accounts that denounced sexual violence in a way that protected individuals too fearful to speak out without guaranteed anonymity.[33] Argentinean activists were also instrumental in importing but adapting #MeToo, substituting the primary message—the sexual assault and harassment of actresses—with the Argentine feminist agenda of abortion, by framing this issue as a form of discrimination and violence against women. Indeed, #MeToo "was preceded by the #NiUnaMenos movement from 2015."[34] Nonetheless, it seems clear that the global reach of *Un violador* and its multilingual performances have disrupted the neocolonial power structures of social movements, including Anglo and Hollywood-centric iterations of protest and resistance dominating the anti–sexual violence narrative.

#MeToo has faced criticisms for "efforts to construct a 'universal' account of sexual violence" and for an "overt focus on white women's experiences of sexual victimization in anti–sexual violence politics and activism."[35] Transnationalism in this case works both with and against universalism, as each performance of *Un Violador* speaks to the pervasiveness of rape cultures yet is adapted for each specific context. The performers give their own voices to words that they make their own—there is no fixed lineup or dominant story of rape; there are no stars or soloists; each performer has equal value. The addressee of the song—linked to the state but also anonymous, and potentially everywhere—denotes a systemic abuse of women's bodies by a patriarchal apparatus that is collective, transnational, and transhistorical, an idea that gathers force with each repetition, each new location. These are multiple bodies in the performance, and the fact that not all women have been raped and not all men are rapists is not the point; the insistent use of the second-person singular (*El violador eres tú* [You are the rapist]) situates this performance in the accusatory mode. This is not victimhood, it is abuser-hood—it is not MeToo, it is WeToo and YouToo. While #MeToo builds a collection of individual stories that shines a light on the scale of sexual violence against women, *Un violador* and Ni Una Menos understand a priori that rape and femicide are rooted in misogynistic cultures, rather than in individual men.

Un violador en tu camino Goes (Almost) Global

The difficult task of tracking the global performances of *Un violador* has been facilitated by Geochicas, a group of geographers, cartographers, sociologists, and anthropologists working "to close the gender gap in the OpenStreetMap community."[36] The mapping of *Un violador* ("Map about the Performance"), their principal project of 2019, comprehensively pinpoints the locations of protests globally, as well as linking to further information including press coverage and video clips. Geochicas's map reveals that there were performances in two hundred cities in 2019, with the main concentration in Latin America, North America, and Europe.[37] But there were also adaptations in Mexico, Turkey, and India, which highlight a shared experience of rape culture as a central pillar of patriarchy, as well as culturally and geographically diverse experiences of oppression.

Chile and LasTesis Senior

LasTesis Senior consists of older women inspired by their younger compatriots to stage their own performance. This took place on December 4, 2019, opposite the Estadio Nacional de Chile, a notorious center of detention and torture for over forty thousand political detainees of Pinochet's regime (1973–90).[38]

The LasTesis Senior performance—organized by ten women's groups and attended by ten thousand women—was prompted by the academic Marcela Betancourt's humorous tweet, calling for a staging of the dance specifically for women over forty, but without the physically demanding squats.[39] LasTesis Senior stuck closely to the words of the original performance, but participants wore black and red in homage to women who were raped or murdered during the dictatorship.[40] The 2004 Valech Truth Commission report, based on extensive interviews with those detained by the regime, concluded that "sexual torture had been practiced in the whole country, in practically all police detention centers," which gives a historical context to the lyrics that accuse the police of being rapists. One infamous site of rape and torture in Santiago was known as the Venda Sexy (Sexy Blindfold) or the Discotheque, as the guards would blindfold the women detainees and play loud music as they were raped and tortured.[41] The references to impunity and disappearances, and the wearing of blindfolds, in *Un violador* acquired a new resonance when performed by the older generation.[42]

Mexico

A Mexico City performance took place on November 29, 2019, in the Zócalo, the main public square opposite the Palacio Nacional. The largest of many performances throughout the country, its scale is an illustration of an intensification of protests against gender-based violence and femicide in Mexico.[43] At the same time, certain elements of its staging highlight transregional Latin

American concerns and alliances. It included women of all social classes, ages, sexual orientations, and ethnic origins, with thousands in attendance, filling the Zócalo.[44] That many women at this event wore the green bandanas associated initially with Argentinian calls for abortion rights highlights the transregional spread of feminist activist concerns in Latin America.

In most ways, the Mexican rendition reproduced the original Chilean performance, pointing to shared feminist concerns across the two countries. As is the case in many Latin American countries, the staging of *Un violador* in Mexico City is one in a series of many instances of feminist protest. On March 8, 2020, International Women's Day, more than eighty thousand women marched in the capital to protest sexual violence and femicide, followed the next day by a twenty-four-hour mass strike by Mexican women.[45] This march ended in the Zócalo with the femicide protest song "Canción sin miedo" (Fearless song), performed by its (Mexican) composer, Vivir Quintana, and the Chilean singer Mon Laferte, a further example of Chilean and transnational performances of disobedience by feminist artist-activists collaborating across the two countries to demand an end to gender-based violence.

Turkey

Two performances in Turkey in December 2019 stand out for their resistance to state repression of women's rights and general brutality toward women. In 2019 alone, for example, a total of 405 women were killed by men in Turkey.[46] The Kadın Cinayetlerini Durduracağız Platformu (We Will Stop Femicide Platform) organized a street performance of *Un violador* on December 8, 2019, in the Kadiköy neighborhood of Istanbul. About three hundred mainly young women congregated to perform *Un violador* in Turkish, dressed casually, but with no uniformity, although they wore the black blindfolds of the original performance. As the women began a second rendition in Spanish, they were corralled by riot police; at least seven were arrested and two allegedly severely beaten for the crime of insulting the president and disrespecting state institutions.[47]

Under Recep Tayyip Erdogan's conservative regime, Turkey is the only country where parliamentary immunity is required for a foreign song to be sung. In solidarity with the protesters, female parliamentarians took up part of the chant, while banging on tables and holding up photographs of twenty murdered women.[48] Turkish feminist politicians thereby lent their voices to the activists prevented from completing their street performance by repressive policing. Transcultural and transnational adaptation took place through linguistic translation, with language repurposed to fit the concerns of Turkish feminists and their demand for better implementation of laws protecting women from violence.[49]

India

Performances in India also illustrate strategies of local adaptation to focus on urgent domestic issues. A performance in Delhi on December 8, 2019, connected sexual violence and femicide to the social inequities of the caste structure. The performance in Hindi added the following lyrics:

In the name of the caste
In the name of religion
We disappear
We are exploited
We carry the worst part of rape
And violence on our bodies.[50]

The performance was in response to the murder four days earlier of a twenty-three-year-old woman who was burned alive by five men while she was on her way to testify in her rape trial.[51] The case drew attention to the fact that India is considered "the world's most dangerous country for women due to the high risk of sexual violence and being forced into slave labor."[52] Jyotsna Siddharth, an organizer, observed that her group decided to adapt *Un violador* in this way for the Indian context because the response to sexual violence varies according to caste, with crimes against lower-caste women receiving little attention.[53]

LasTesis: New Ventures and Collaborations

Most performances of *Un violador* took place between October and December 2019, but performances continue, and LasTesis moved their activism online during the COVID-19 lockdown restrictions. They have forged new collaborations, most notably with the (mainly) Russian anti–Vladimir Putin punk collective Pussy Riot. On May 27, 2020, LasTesis and Pussy Riot released a video manifesto featuring LasTesis and the Mexican Wendy Moira, who is a member of Pussy Riot and the director of Teatro Lúcido.[54] In it, the groups denounce police violence and highlight the pandemic's exacerbation of the problems of hunger, poverty, domestic violence, and inadequate health care, in an example of intersectional feminist activism. They connect police repression with patriarchy and "savage capitalism," ending with the words: "The police don't look after me, my friends do." Subsequently, the Chilean police called for LasTesis to be brought to trial, for intimidation of the police—the video features LasTesis standing outside a Valparaíso police station and the words *Fuego a los pacos* (Set fire to the police). They also accused LasTesis of fomenting acts of violence committed by protesters in November and December 2020, which they link to performances of *Un violador*.[55]

These responses represent a failure by the police to accept responsibility for documented crimes that they have committed and to which the performance of *Un violador* was responding.[56] This case has only succeeded in bringing LasTesis increased support, including a petition addressed to Piñera's administration sent by leading Hollywood actresses, demanding that the police charges be dropped—an example of the high-profile celebrity feminism associated with #MeToo using its platform for transnational solidarity. An all-women list of signatories included America Ferrera, Ashley Judd, Eva Longoria, Julianne Moore, Rosie Pérez, Natalie Portman, Zoe Saldana, Marisa Tomei, and Michelle Williams.[57] LasTesis was also recognized in *Time* magazine's "100 Most Influential People of 2020" list, with an entry written by Pussy Riot member Nadya Tolokonnikova.[58]

Although it may be too soon to fully understand the significance and legacy of *Un violador en tu camino*, this chapter makes clear that LasTesis's performance has been significant in its translation of feminist theory for a nonacademic setting and in its shifting of the location of knowledge production. Confronting and condemning cultures of rape and sexual violence through new forms of collective, bodily enunciation, its nonhierarchical, empowering format has created opportunities for self-transformation among participants and audiences. The power of *Un violador* is evidenced by the fact that it has taken on a transnational life of its own, with its message and impact gathering force as it has been adopted in and adapted to multiple global locations, reversing and resisting the US-centrism of other recent forms of feminist protest. It has traveled far beyond what LasTesis had foreseen, making manifest the global pervasiveness of rape culture, and women's resistance to it, and launching LasTesis themselves into radical transnational partnerships of feminist activist art creation. *Un violador en tu camino* has given voice to a new recognition of the ways in which sexual violence against women is systemic and structural in many cultures and has enabled a new coming together of women who draw strength from each other across borders.

Notes

This chapter is a revised version of an article originally published in the *Bulletin of Latin American Research* 40, no. 5 (2021): 712–29, under the title "Chilean and Transnational Performances of Disobedience: LasTesis and the Phenomenon of *Un violador en tu camino*," https://onlinelibrary.wiley.com/doi/epdf/10.1111/blar.13215.

1. Sandra Cuffe, "Chile's 'A Rapist in Your Path' Chant Hits 200 Cities: Map," *Al Jazeera*, December 20, 2019, www.aljazeera.com/news/2019/12/20/chiles-a-rapist-in-your-path-chant-hits-200-cities-map.

2. Translation by the authors.

3. Paula J. Huenchumil, "Las mujeres chilenas detrás de la performance 'Un violador en tu camino,'" *Interferencia*, November 28, 2019, https://interferencia.cl/articulos/las-mujeres-chilenas-detras-de-la-performance-un-violador-en-tu-camino.

4. Translation by the authors.

5. Huenchumil, "Las mujeres chilenas detrás de la performance."

6. José M. Vivanco, "A Backward Step for Reproductive Rights in Chile," Human Rights Watch, April 16, 2018, www.hrw.org/news/2018/04/16/backward-step-reproductive-rights-chile.

7. Rita Segato and Ramsey McGlazer, "A Manifesto in Four Themes," *Critical Times* 1, no. 1 (2018): 198–211, https://doi.org/10.1215/26410478-1.1.198.

8. Masha Gessen, "Judith Butler Wants Us to Reshape Our Rage," *New Yorker*, February 9, 2020, www.newyorker.com/culture/the-new-yorker-interview/judith-butler-wants-us-to-reshape-our-rage.

9. See Dafne Valdés in Huenchumil, "Las mujeres chilenas detrás de la performance."

10. Segato and McGlazer, "A Manifesto in Four Themes"; Rita Segato, "Seventh Disobedience," Rosa Luxemburg Stiftung, July 2019, www.rosalux.de/en/publication/id/40778.

11. Mariana Carbajal, "Entrevista a Rita Segato, antropóloga y feminista Argentina," *Nodal: Noticias de América Látina y el Caribe*, July 1, 2019, www.nodal.am/2019/01/rita-segato-antropologa-el-de-genero-es-un-crimen-de-exceso-de-poder.

12. For photos of these performances, see Martin and Shaw, "Chilean and Transnational Performances of Disobedience"; and "Las Tesis y el Festival de Artes Cielos del Infinito estrenan pusta en escena en torno a la histórica-subalternidad de las mujeres colonizadas," *El Mostrador*, August 27, 2020, www.elmostrador.cl/braga/2020/08/27/las-tesis-y-el-festival-de-artes-cielos-del-infinito-estrenan-puesta-en-escena-en-torno-a-la-historica-subalternidad-de-las-mujeres-colonizadas.

13. Carbajal, "Entrevista a Rita Segato."

14. UCC, Ireland, "Flashmob Edit," YouTube video, 1:14, February 13, 2020, www.youtube.com/watch?v=etfGjw2IXiQ.

15. Vanessa Vargas Rojas, "El grito de Cheril Linett, la artista que sacó a la yeguada latinoamericana a denunciar la violencia a la calle," *El Desconcierto*, September 11, 2018, www.eldesconcierto.cl/tendencias/2018/11/09/el-grito-de-cheril-linett-la-artista-que-saco-a-la-yeguada-latinoamericana-a-denunciar-la-violencia-a-la-calle.html; Olga Grau, "Un cardo en la mano," in *Mayo Feminista: La rebelión contra el patriarcado*, ed. Faride Zerán (Santiago: LOM Ediciones, 2018), 91–97.

16. Alia Trabucco Zerán, "Imaginar," in Zerán, *Mayo Feminista*, 154.

17. LasTesis and Pussy Riot, "Manifesto against Police Violence," YouTube video, May 27, 2020, www.youtube.com/watch?v=UPfcb9aTclo.

18. Gender Equality Observatory for Latin America and the Caribbean, "Femicide or Feminicide," accessed June 1, 2021, https://oig.cepal.org/en/indicators/femicide-or-feminicide.

19. Segato, "Seventh Disobedience."

20. L. M. Neuquén, "Rita Segato: 'Los femicidios se repiten porque se muestran como un espectáculo,'" YouTube video, 12:48, September 7, 2019, www.youtube.com/watch?v=sUoJ28QFFyk.

21. Maggie B. Gale, "Resolute Presence, Fugitive Moments, and the Body in Women's Protest Performance," *Contemporary Theatre Review* 25, no. 3 (2015): 319, https://doi.org/10.1080/10486801.2015.1049819.

22. Rebecca Schneider, quoted in Gale, "Resolute Presence," 316.

23. Jacques Rancière, *Dissensus: On Politics and Aesthetics* (London: Bloomsbury, 2010), 147.

24. "Map about the Performance 'A Rapist in Your Path' from #LasTesis," OpenStreetMap, 2019, https://umap.openstreetmap.fr/es/map/un-violador-en-tu-camino-20192021-actualizado-2905_394247#2/16.8/11.4.

25. Judith Butler, *Notes toward a Performative Power of Assembly* (Cambridge, MA: Harvard University Press, 2015), 81.

26. Consuelo Banda and Valeska Navea, "Comunidades en pugna: Desplazamiento de los métodos de protesta hacia una nueva producción de sentido," in *En Marcha: Ensayos sobre arte, violencia y cuerpo en la manifestación social* (Santiago: Adrede Editora, 2013), 23.

27. Nelly Richard, "La insurgencia feminista de mayo 2018," in Zerán, *Mayo Feminista*, 115.

28. Paula Serafini, *Performance Action: The Politics of Art Activism* (London: Routledge, 2018), 15.

29. Segato, "Seventh Disobedience."

30. Colectivo LasTesis, "Intervención Colectivo LasTesis (Un violador en tu camino)," YouTube video, 3:49, November 20, 2019, www.youtube.com/watch?v=9sbcUopmViM.

31. Barry Levine and Monique El-Faizy, *All the President's Women: Donald Trump and the Making of a Predator* (New York: Hachette Books, 2019).

32. Emma Gray, "Women Stage Flash Mob Protest outside Harvey Weinstein Trial," *Huffington Post*, January 10, 2020, www.huffingtonpost.co.uk/entry/protest-harvey-weinsteintrial-chilean-anthem_n_5e1758ffc5b61f70194b7e57?ri18n=true.

33. Deborah Shaw, "#MeToo in Mexico: Women Finding Their Voice as Campaign Gathers Force," *Conversation*, April 9, 2019, https://theconversation.com/metoo-in-mexico-womenfinding-their-voice-as-campaign-gathers-force-114927.

34. María C. Garibotti and Cecilia M. Hopp, "Substitution Activism: The Impact of #MeToo in Argentina," in *#MeToo and the Politics of Social Change*, ed. Bianca Fileborn and Rachel Loney-Howes (London: Palgrave Macmillan, 2020), 185–99.

35. Fileborn and Loney-Howes, *#MeToo and the Politics of Social Change*, 6; Lauren Rosewarne, "#MeToo and the Reasons to Be Cautious," in Fileborn and Loney-Howes, *#MeToo and the Politics of Social Change*, 178.

36. Cuffe, "'A Rapist in Your Path' Chant"; "Geochicas," OpenStreetMap Wiki, last modified April 17, 2022, https://wiki.openstreetmap.org/wiki/GeoChicas.

37. Cuffe, "'A Rapist in Your Path' Chant"; "Map about the Performance."

38. David Wood, "General Pinochet's Long Shadow Still Hangs over Chile's National Stadium," *Conversation*, December 19, 2016, https://theconversation.com/general-pinochets-long-shadowstill-hangs-over-chiles-national-stadium-70305.

39. Simona Paranhos, "Vocera de LasTesis Senior: 'La performance es perfecta,'" *Vergara240*, January 30, 2020, https://vergara240.udp.cl/especiales/vocera-de-lastesis-senior-la-performance-es-perfecta.

40. Jonathan Flores, "Las Tesis Seniors: Miles de mujeres se tomaron el frontis del Estadio Nacional," *Bio Bio Chile*, December 4, 2019, www.biobiochile.cl/noticias/nacional/region-metropolitana/2019/12/04/las-tesis-senior-intervencion-feminista-post-40-se-toma-avenida-grecia-frente-al-estadio-nacional.shtml.

41. Mariana Joffily, "Sexual Violence in the Military Dictatorships of Latin America: Who Wants to Know?," *SUR: International Journal on Human Rights* 13, no. 24 (2016): 165–76, https://sur.conectas.org/en/who-wants-to-know.

42. For a photo of the Estadio Nacional de Chile performance organized by LasTesis Senior, see Mónica Rincón Gonzále (@tv_monica), "Alguien se pregunta qué es sororidad? Esto: Solidaridad con otras. Nunca más solas," Twitter, December 4, 2019, https://twitter.com/tv_monica/status/1202410159169048576.

43. See "Map about the Performance."

44. R. Aída Hernández Castillo, "*Un violador en tu camino* y las masculinidades tóxicas," *La Jornada*, December 5, 2019, www.jornada.com.mx/2019/12/05/opinion/024a2pol.

45. Amanda Petersen and Deborah Shaw, "Mexican Women Aren't Just Fighting for Equality—but Survival," *Globe Post*, March 25, 2020, https://theglobepost.com/2020/03/25/mexico-femicides.

46. We Will Stop Femicide Platform, accessed July 21, 2000, www.kadincinayetlerinidurduracagiz.net.

47. "'Un violador en tu camino' de Las Tesis: La policía en Turquía reprime una representación del himno feminista Chileno que le ha dado la vuelta al mundo," *BBC News Mundo*, December 9, 2019, www.bbc.com/mundo/noticias-internacional-50715146.

48. Irem Koca and Jonathan Spicer, "Legisladoras Turcas protestan entonando tema de Chilenas Las Tesis contra la violación," *Infobae*, December 15, 2019, www.infobae.com/america/agencias/2019/12/15/legisladoras-turcas-protestan-entonando-tema-de-chilenas-las-tesis-contra-la-violacion.

49. Barçin Yinanç, "Turkey Needs an Integrated Policy to Fight Violence against Women," *Hurriyet Daily News*, December 1, 2019, www.hurriyetdailynews.com/turkey-needs-an-integrated-policy-to-fight-violence-against-women-149069.

50. David Noriega, "'Un violador en tu camino' llega a India: 'En el nombre de la casta, somos explotadas,'" *elDiario.es*, December 8, 2019, www.eldiario.es/internacional/violadorIndia-respondiendo-violencia-cotidiana_0_971852881.html.

51. Hannah Ellis-Petersen, "India: Woman Set on Fire on Way to Testify against Alleged Rapists," *Guardian*, December 5, 2019, www.theguardian.com/world/2019/dec/05/india-woman-set-on-fire-on-way-to-testify-against-alleged-rapists; Noriega, "'Un violador en tu camino' llega a India."

52. Belinda Goldsmith and Meka Beresford, "India Most Dangerous Country for Women with Sexual Violence Rife," Reuters, June 25, 2018, www.reuters.com/article/us-women-dangerous-poll-exclusive/exclusive-india-most-dangerous-country-forwomen-with-sexual-violence-rife-global-poll-idUSKBN1JM01X.

53. "El himno viral, 'El violador eres tú' llega a una India conmocionada por las últimas violaciones," *El Periódico*, December 8, 2019, www.elperiodico.com/es/internacional/20191208/himno-viral-antimachistael-violador-eres-tu-india-conmocion-violaciones-mujeres-7766618.

54. Charis McGowan, "Pussy Riot and Chilean Group Join Forces against State Repression," *Guardian*, May 29, 2020, www.theguardian.com/world/2020/may/29/pussy-riot-lastesis-chilean-group-release-manifesto-against-state-repression; LasTesis and Pussy Riot, "Manifesto against Police Violence."

55. Víctor Rivera, "La ofensiva de carabineros contra 'Lastesis' ante la Fiscalía: Acusa incitación de acciones violentas contra la institución," *La Tercera*, June 16, 2020, www.latercera.com/la-tercera-pm/noticia/la-ofensiva-de-carabineros-contra-lastesis-ante-la-fiscalia-acusa-incitacion-de-acciones-violentas-contra-la-institucion/NBEWW526ZBCNFBSAQQ5LCT52W4. This case was

subsequently dismissed by Valparaíso's Court of Guarantee. Front Line Defenders, "Judicial Threat against Feminist Collective LasTesis," June 24, 2020, www.frontlinedefenders.org/en/case/judicial-threat-against-feminist-collective-lastesis.

56. Human Rights Watch, "Chile: Events of 2019," 2020, www.hrw.org/world-report/2020/country-chapters/chile.

57. "US Stars Sign Petition against LasTesis Criminal Case in Chile," La Prensa Latina, July 22, 2020, www.laprensalatina.com/us-stars-sign-petition-against-lastesis-criminal-case-in-chile.

58. Nadya Tolokonnikova, "The 100 Most Influential People of 2020: LasTesis," *Time*, September 22, 2020, https://time.com/collection/100-most-influential-people-2020/5888485/lastesis.

Part 3
Art as Advocacy

The scourge of sexual violence in societies across the globe is symptomatic of a deep wound at the heart of human societies. Such violence persists regardless of a society's form of government or social organization. It flourishes whether women have political and social rights or live in abjection. It continues despite religious or legal opposition to it, possibly because social institutions, including law and religion, implicitly support it, as discussed in part 2. As an abstraction, the looming possibility of sexual violence produces anger and frustration among all potential victims, especially those who must organize their lives to decrease their vulnerability or walk on eggshells to avoid accusations of provocation. As an experience, sexual violence is uniformly devastating. Victims' feelings of trust and safety shatter, both in public and at home. Their sense of identity and agency may collapse in the face of violent physical coercion, especially if family or authorities cast blame on them for their anguish. The requisite journey from victim-without-agency to survivor-with-purpose is usually a long and painful one. For artists, that journey to healing and resistance often passes through their creative work.

The art forms and artists featured in part 3 of *Art, Activism, and Sexual Violence* demonstrate the power of the arts to express and engage with the emotional turmoil that the experience of sexual violence induces. They exemplify evocative and impactful ways to transform harm into powerful representations of resistance and resilience. In most cases, the artworks also evoke those same transformational responses in viewers and participants. The examples in part 3 bring to life claims in part 1 about art's impact on social issues and public attitudes. Part 3 makes clear not only *that* art works but *how* art works, through creative products that expose and contest social and personal injury, break cycles of silence and shame, and invalidate attitudes of coercion and conquest. Some artworks in part 3 also create new social realities and postulate what salubrious forms of community support, gendered relationships, and personal healing could look like.

The chapters in part 3 include descriptions, depictions, statements, and analyses by the artists themselves, as in chapters written by Stephanie Leigh Batiste, Sean Shannon, Clarity Haynes, Jennifer Patterson, Luzene Hill, and Susanne Slavick. The work of these artists, illustrated both within a few chapters and among the book's colorplates, spans artistic genres, including drama (Batiste), poetry (Shannon), painting (Haynes), needlework (Patterson), performance art (Hill), and sculpture (Slavick). These artist-writers bring their own pain to the project of recognition and transformation.

Other chapters in part 3 explain and describe performances or artworks and introduce additional genres, such as T De Long's discussion of the late Chloe Dzubilo's scathing line drawings and Sydney Burrows's discussion of professional dance that produces reconciliation and revival out of torment, despite the dance community's long-standing resistance to depicting the horror of sexual violence onstage. Jennifer Karash-Eastman's chapter reveals the power of Ruta Butkus Marino's discomforting, graphic, and spine-chilling quilts, while Emily Bonistall Postel, Elaina Behounek, and Alesha Durfee describe impactful community art projects that protest all forms of sexual violence through T-shirts. Jasmin Goodman and Wei Sun explore the presumed role of clothing in inviting sexual assault, as revealed in art projects and exhibitions debunking that role. Leslie-Jean Thornton transports readers to the world of the internet, where sexual violence survivors illustrate their rage and resistance in visual and narrative form.

Some of the art and performances featured in *Art, Activism, and Sexual Violence* are designed to shock. We hope readers will agree that shock is what a world too willing to normalize the scourge of sexual violence truly needs.

6

Young Love Found and Lost

Six Poems in a Circle

Stephanie Leigh Batiste

This play in poems traces the emotional shifts of young women in and out and in and out of romantic love and lust. These young women erroneously look for themselves through romantic love. They search for and mostly lose the connections so powerfully sought, so present, so advertised during young adulthood.

The performance piece is intended for rendering in theatrical jazz form, pioneered by Laurie Carlos and Ntozake Shange and practiced and theorized by Omi Osun Joni L. Jones, Sharon Bridgforth, Daniel Alexander Jones, and Grisha Coleman.

The impact of sexual violence is insidious and not obvious. In *Young Love Found and Lost* some poems are not counted, not yet fully accounting for experience and intimating the obscurity of self-knowing. Repression, shame, secrecy, and self-destruction are more common than triumphant declarations of intact healing and restored identity. The piece performs the embeddedness of the violence through repression and dysfunction as the women try to deal with and make their way through their everyday lives, their own yearning for love, and their insistence on sexual fulfillment. The process of healing is long and uneven, painful and not foregone. But as a woman lives, pain is not always, not always thorough, and not (always) total. This piece moves only slightly toward new states of sexual embodiment and emotional satisfaction in its recursive battles with the experience and memory of violence alongside emergent sensuality, sex, and desire. Yet it mostly stays stuck in the maladaptive repetitions of slow change.

Performance Notes

There are six poems noted. They are the show. They go round and round. Then there are secret ones. These others are embedded, unspeakable, on a different track—off the cycle, not counted and unaccounted for, cataclysmic, confused, and pending.

The poems in italics are algebraic unknowns, an x, y, or z refusing an end, dislocating, and always going back to a beginning. They are the "xyz," in the vernacular, "and such and so" of all that unspeakable-ment that happens.

Each poem considers relationships that have passed. The losses are very present for the speakers. There is melodrama, irony, and pathos in their yearnings. The first poem might repeat at the end. Two or more women each perform all of the poems in tandem or together to emphasize the repetition of a cycle of romantic hope and its failures.

At least one is the wind, blue and purple, capricious and grabbing, pursuing in escape and slippage. She draws her lovers on the wisp of a breeze, carries them on the crest of a gale. Another is hunger, orange and red, ravenous and devouring, spitting out the bones with shards stuck between her teeth. They move with eager desire—for sex, love, and life. They make mistakes. And they suffer.

The entire piece should be delivered by no fewer than two Black women, who perform the poems choreographed in "a round," like the same song sung at different times in different tempos. The poems may appear in different orders, and sometimes simultaneously. A cello or bass accompanies. There should be at least one dancer.

x. Tasty

the innermost swirl
of a cinnamon bun
is tight and warm.
smug confidence holding joy tender
in self-satisfied pleasure sticky fingers preface the bite

One: Retrospective Romance

(From a feeling of rejection comes a new relationship in memory as the speaker sees a sensibility of connection played out in others. She realizes an acceptance she couldn't feel at the time.)

I saw him
hold her at her elbows,
look
into her eyes and
finally
kiss her
and saw
in them
the way you held me,
softly almost not at all,
gazed gently,
expectantly
into my face
before
we kissed.

My eyes stung
overflowed
as I thought
maybe
you actually
did
want me.

Two: Just Friends

(This slamming into the joy of the brand-new is full of pleasure, generosity, and excitement. The admiration is at a distance and unconfessed. The eroticism is queer, homo, and het.)

I was falling
for you.
The softness in the tips of your fingers,
your palms
and the hidden center of your spirit—
the treble moan
in your voice
and excited tension in your stance
as you taste the forever newness of the world,
swirl it over your tongue
and raise your lashes in amusement.
Smiling with you,
learning your ways, sharing mine,
crush
crash
falling. . . .

y. Wanting

Is love a speaking in tongues,
language uninterpretable, inaccessible
except by the ears of heaven?

And passion rich and burning
that consumes
with emptiness and ashes its remains?
Is it power all its own
without respect of persons

demanding worship
punishing impatience
withholding its face?

Four: Dead Sea

(It is difficult to tell if one speaker is disgusted with herself or "the game." Another might feel the drain. In the rules of exchange, a giver seems to lose.)

Too Much Love
too freely given
flows (from me)
like blood.
I drown in it

Choke in it
Sputter and
Float
Belly-up
in abjection.

Five: Chimera

(The stages of moving on are out of order. To miss a feeling of missing someone, the passing of feeling becomes the loss. Here distance is physical and emotional.)

Even the soul ache
of missing you would be something
to hold onto

But your substance dissipates
And my grasp on you dissolves

I am left
in love
with a figment of my imagination

Three: Ways

(This is funny and fun. It sounds like hip-hop or Lauryn Hill's "Lost Ones" from "Miseducation.")

Met a Brotha turned my head, all up on my nip
Words of beauty from his lips
Shinin' smiles, holdin' hands but that lovin' is like sand
Runnin' through the fingers of infatua-shan
as his goodness turns cold and he jockeys for control
of my actions, thoughts and soul
seemed deep, but all shallow, he was just huntin' gold

Why can't I get a man
Who'll see me as a persan
Who can love me for who I am
Black, white, Asian, tan
All y'all pull is the same
Yanking my chain and runnin' game

I can call you but one time
while you text a hundred-nine,
I write your punkass back
And you play a silent track
And you're the one whose thru 'cause I'm buggin' you
Seems you get a million chances to my some
Time to find another lover to have some fun
Maybe someday I'll find the one

Why can't I get a man
Who'll see me as a persan
Who can love me for who I am
Black, white, Asian, tan
All y'all pull is the same
Yanking my chain and runnin' game

Are you interested or not?
No word from you—then the clock
chimes 2—a.m. and there you are
suddenly my friend, wantin' some lovin,'
tryin' to pet the kitty, I think thas pretty shitty
Call me t'marr' if you think you can
Show me some dressed up, daylight hugg-an'

Why can't I get a man
Who'll see me as a persan
Who can love me for who I am
Black, white, Asian, tan
All y'all pull is the same
Yanking my chain and runnin' game

Forcing me to do the same

Girlfriendz don't get to carin',
'Cause Brothas get to scarin',
Thinkin' you're a prison term
Maybe someday they'll learn
In the meantime don't get burned
Learn to love the game and try not to let it change
Your golden giving ways

q. fugue

fleshly external
external layer flab
skin and fat and fat
wet armor
thick thicker slim
slim to bone skeletal

ravening

hunger
mucosal tear
rend to vaginal
sac

none of it tells how to find the way back

(There is quiet—and quiet in the sounds that punctuate the women dancing in transition to becoming something else. One performer stays with emotional states found in "fugue," while another begins the next piece. Performer one finds witness to her alter ego's story. She participates, and both move together through its final stand. "Up" is performed only once.)

z. Up

I don't want you.

So . . . I don't care
if you want to feel my soft lips
on your bristled face
or if you want tosmash yoursagainst thenape of myneck.
"Kiss me" you say

I don't care

ifyourunyourspindle fingers
along my backfrommyshouldertomytoesdownmytoastedskin
"You're soft" you say

And I don't care

ifyouscrapeyourlizardtonguealongthebackofmyearssmelltheCreamofNatureinmyhair
"smell nice" you drool

And I certainly don't care

ifyoufeel thedampwarmthof me whileyougrabfrombehindpushmeflatandsweat.
I guess I don't count
'cause you did it anyway.

But let me tell you something,
you good for nothin', deranged,
Slick game runnin', overconfident,
greedy, nothin' assed . . .

I'm too deep for your reach
too high
if you held the hand of Jesus on your right, Satan on your left

I get up from this.

You stay
empty alone,
no matter
how many women you run through run in to.
You touch nothin'
fla t c erv i x acorp se not l ife not lo v e not for you

i may d ie, we
rise again

and still . . .
don't nobody want you.

Six: Changing Same: A Blues Poem

(This poem uses sensuality to consider love as sound and repetition.
The performer does not give in to the sex of it.)

You soar
through my mind
assaulting my nerves
with incessant penetrating massage
saying

feel me
accept me
into your soul
and caress me.

But you slip
through my fingers
and expand
beyond the walls
of my being
evading my embrace
and eluding my comprehension.

I can't ignore
the beauty of your touch
that turns teasingly soft
and kisses my eyelids—
traces the curve of my nose and my ears—
enters my mind
with the wet gentle prodding
of the tip of your tongue.

I surrender
and let you surround me
titillate me
knowing that you'll simply leave me
when you're done
playing around my memory
like some kind of familiar dream
I can't say or share—
like some lonely traveler
that wants the warmth of my regard—
but cannot help but go
like—
some kind of blues.

You soar through the air
with the rhythm
of my heartbeat
using my pulse
to urge you along.

Taking what's mine
and etching
it into a finite infinity
lasting a moment
but lingering ethereal mine.

I am rested
and spent I stay
agitated and calm
project in my eyes
the love we've made
full and
unsatisfied
like—
this kind of blues.

Note

An early version of this play was performed by Towne Street Theater: LA's Premier African-American Theatre Company, as part of the production *In Response: Year of the Woman* (2018, 2019), under the direction of Nancy Cheryll Davis.

7

Voicing Trauma through Dance

Sydney Burrows

Their spotlit faces turn upward with hopeful looks. They wave signs as if they are protesting. They sit with their backs to the audience and gradually stand up. They move together in harmony or sink to the floor alone in fear. They pretend to hold guns. They encourage the audience to break their silence and join them onstage. These are dancers tackling an uncomfortable subject in their profession. They take risks, but they help themselves and others reclaim their power after sexual assault.

Introduction

Dance is a unique art form in that it uses the body as its instrument for expression. That is why dance is naturally intimate. As dancers, we portray emotions, stories, and characters all with only our bodies as the focal point. The audience members sit in a dark auditorium, hidden from our view, but we feel their gaze. We create movement specifically for their gaze, to make them feel the same emotions we experience as we move under the hot lights onstage. It is the audience that makes a performance real; they give choreography a life beyond the dancer. To perform, to bare our bodies and souls, can be difficult, exhilarating, and therapeutic.

There is also a healing component to the choreography process that precedes a performance. It is here that dancers must dig deep into our personal experiences and emotions to guide the movement for the work. Even if we are not choreographing, we must give the movement created by another an artistic spin of our own, which makes it personal. We escape the world outside when we enter the studio and pull from the difficulties we face in our daily lives to inspire the movement for the stage. It is not surprising that dance and movement therapy is growing steadily. Movement in and of itself is healing. There is something freeing about jumping, pressing in and out of the floor, and taking up space. Professional dancers and choreographers take this restorative process one step further and invite the audience to join in with them.

For this reason, professional dance offers a unique opportunity for choreographers to explore the topic of sexual assault and use the performance as a form of healing for both the artists and the viewers. In addition, dance gives artists the ability to reclaim their bodies as their own, which is especially powerful to victims of sexual assault. In 2017, the #MeToo movement, a social media campaign in which users shared their stories about sexual assault accompanied by the hashtag #MeToo in their tweet or social media posts, continued a stalled but much-needed conversation worldwide about the common experience of sexual assault. Celebrities, artists, and women and men everywhere started using the hashtag to acknowledge that they had experienced sexual assault. In the dance world, the movement led to dancers speaking up against abuse and demanding recognition of their experiences. Choreographers began to consider it a topic to explore within their work. The subject that was once very much off-limits was now a potential inspiration for creative work.

Before the past decade, sexual trauma was rarely explored in dance pieces. Even today, it is still somewhat taboo, and choreographers who tackle it are considered brave for bringing sensitive stories to the stage. In the past, artists used dance to make statements about political justice and oppression, as in La Revue Nègre in 1925, in which a pas de deux performed by Josephine Baker and Joe Alex showed the horror of colonization. Baker is an example of an artist who fully embraced her sexuality and used it to show her own power onstage. Kiara Kinghorn writes in her essay "Dance in the Era of #MeToo": "Baker's unique talent to move her body in opposing directions, using multiple rhythms and tempos, can be seen as contributing to interpretations of Baker as someone who has sexual agency and control over her own body."[1] Today, dancers are again fully embracing their bodies and sexuality, using movement onstage to make a statement. Like Baker, they are not shying away from current controversial topics. For some dancers, to distinguish between sexual expression and sexual exploitation, they demonstrate their agency over their own individual bodies with movement that is fully independent of others. Choreographers may use partnering to illustrate sexual abuse and power dynamics, with the dancers reclaiming their bodies by dancing on their own.

Sexual assault became a topic of conversation within the dance world when the #MeToo movement exposed sexual assault occurring directly within dance companies. The ballet world came under scrutiny when Peter Martins, the director of the New York City Ballet, retired in January 2018, after allegations of sexual harassment and verbal and sexual abuse came to light. In addition, a School of American Ballet dance student, Alexandra Waterbury, filed a lawsuit against three male dancers in the City Ballet company.[2] To many dancers and those familiar with their training and culture, this was not entirely a surprise. Dance is an art form in which the body is the vehicle of expression and perfection is expected. Because of the focus on the body, dancers are hyperaware of their appearance. Teachers will suggest certain diets, cross-training, and potentially even a career shift, depending on a dancer's build. They also may correct a dancer by touching him or her to demonstrate which muscle the dancer needs to engage or where the dancer needs to focus his or her attention. The nature of this kind of teaching can lead to blurred boundaries, and predators in powerful positions have the opportunity to take advantage of the gray area.

In addition to the focus on the body, dance also has a history of male choreographers and directors holding power over young female dancers. Dancers are often taught that they are replaceable, and therefore they are unlikely to speak up if those who are in power are guilty of assault or inappropriate behavior. Kinghorn addresses the hierarchy that has been in place for many years: "The field of dance had also been susceptible to sexual abuse due to the patriarchal culture and authoritarian pedagogical methods in which it develops."[3] The dance world is now starting to acknowledge the need for a change in its culture, and the power dynamic is starting to shift. For example, teachers are having conversations with students to determine what feels appropriate to them for physical corrections in the studio. Some modern companies, including those featured in this chapter, focus on collaboration in their creative processes, encouraging dancers to speak up and share their own ideas, rather than leaving the choreography to a single person.

While the dance world began to change slowly and to reflect on the policies and hierarchies in place, the #MeToo movement inspired the artists Jamie Minkus and Kevin Lee-Y Green to work finally on the piece that each felt needed to be made. Minkus was given the opportunity to choreograph a piece within a larger show, which she realized was her chance to dive into a process of pain, growth, and healing from sexual assault. Green, who is currently creating his work, realized that the Black community's voice needed to be heard surrounding sexual assault. Collaborating with other artists and engaging his community, Green is now choreographing a piece that will feature Black dancers and will use a combination of gestural, technical, and athletic movement, designed to end that silence. While the piece is still in progress, Green's choreography includes a mixture of modern and jazz techniques. He is planning to draw inspiration from anonymous survivor stories to create movement vignettes for his work.

Although the #MeToo movement helped to push their work further, the choreographers Jinah Parker and Beth Braun were already tackling the topic of sexual assault in their work before the hashtag found its platform. They had felt the need to begin conversations and help others heal in 2017 and 2011, respectively, inspired by their own experiences and those they witnessed. Braun focused on teaching high school students that it was okay to speak up, while Parker produced an entire evening-length performance that led audience members to confront their own biases and hidden trauma. All four of these artists, each with a different story and choreographic journey, hope to contribute to the conversation surrounding sexual assault and healing by sharing their stories through dance.

Jinah Parker: *SHE, a Choreoplay*

With beautiful lines and expansive gestures, Jinah Parker, a dancer and the choreographer of *SHE, a Choreoplay*, projects both confidence and determination onstage. The work opens with Parker dancing alone, dressed in a tight black crop top that allows the audience to see her stomach muscles clench and expand with her movement. A long, flowing black skirt completes her outfit, showing off her long legs, which are accentuated by the stage lighting. Other dancers, dressed in the same attire as Parker but in white, join her onstage. They dance fluidly, partnering with one another easily and frequently as they turn their faces upward with hopeful looks. The dancers move in sync with one another, shifting through deep pliés, showing a sense of grounding strength. They take up space on the stage, jumping, twirling, and embracing the joy of dancing together.

In stark contrast to the hopeful and supportive environment of the opening piece, the dancers later physically embody a story of rape and abuse. An actor stands in the center of the stage and begins the story: "There once was a good little girl who went to live with her uncle." While the actor describes the terrible things that occurred to that "good little girl," the dancers, wearing pale-colored nightgowns, dance violently. They move in and out of the ground quickly and run back and forth across the stage. They grab one

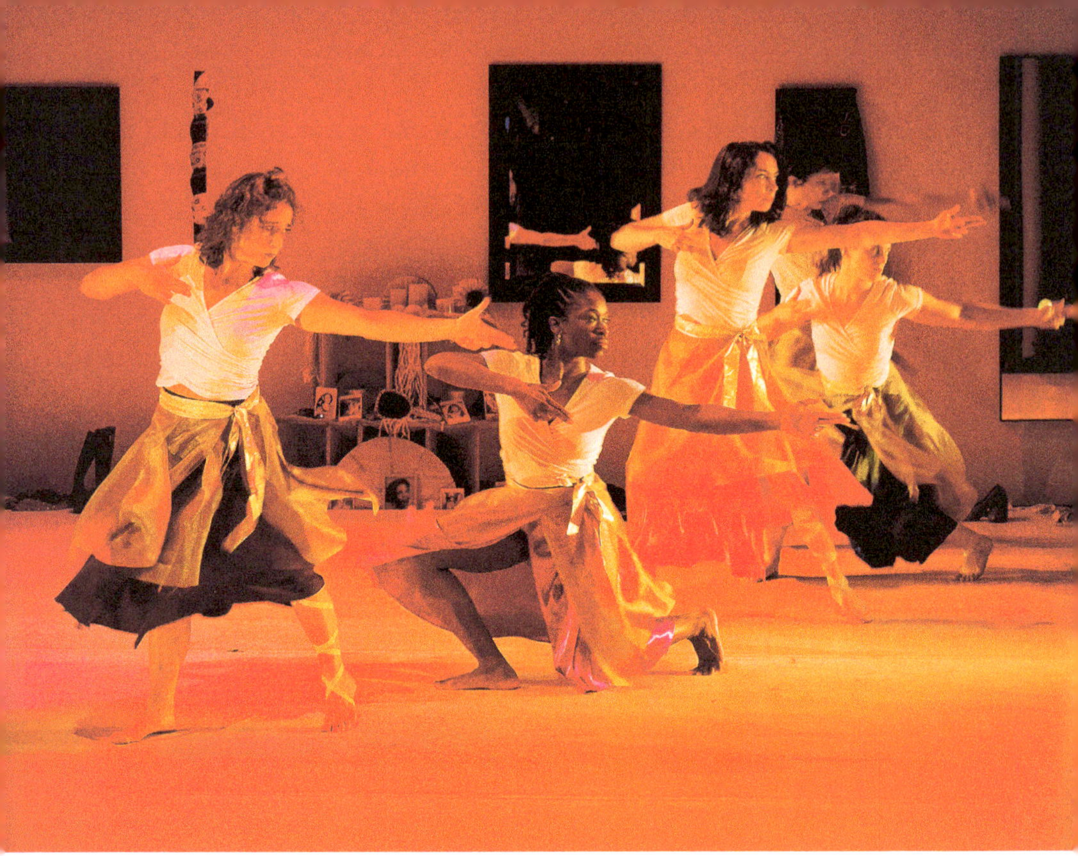

SHE, a Choreoplay performance. Choreographed by Jinah Parker. Photo by Mickey Hoelscher.

another, some reaching up toward the sky before falling brutally back to the ground. The dancers contract into their bodies, making themselves smaller, pausing in fetal positions, lying on the ground. They roll and shift their bodies in a way that is broken and messy, with jerking motions and flailing limbs. The choreography is fast and repetitive, exuding panic and trauma, while the actor concludes, "The nightmares in the tiny dark space became a part of her."

When Parker, a dancer and choreographer based in New York City, decided to create an evening-length piece surrounding the topic of sexual assault, she realized that it was a story for both dancers and nondancers to share. Initially, the piece featured a cast of six female dancers and four women whose stories were told throughout the work. Now, the revised stories are told by four actors, accompanied by six professional dancers. The cast tells true stories of sexual assault with dance, multimedia projections, music, and the spoken word. The projections include imagery of protests, complemented by the dancers using props of signs and demonstrating as if they were protesting as well. The music ranges from Aretha Franklin to Madonna, depending on the setting presented by the performers and the projections. The choreography is a mixture of impressive modern technique and gestures that help demonstrate the words of the actors, who tell chilling stories of sexual assault and abuse. With *SHE, a Choreoplay*, Parker aims to build awareness of sexual assault and violence and to give the cast and audience members an outlet to release their personal pain.

After the first Off-Off-Broadway performance in 2017 at HERE Arts Center, an audience member came up to Parker and said, "I am 'SHE,' and I've never told anybody else that." It was in this moment that Parker realized the premiere was only the beginning, and that *SHE* needed to continue its journey. In 2018, *SHE* was slated for its Off-Broadway production and, since then, has been presented at HERE Arts Center, the Brooklyn Museum, and the New York City Ethical Society and at several universities across the United States, with a series of workshops and classes offered to students and

SHE, a Choreoplay performance. Choreographed by Jinah Parker.
Photo by Mickey Hoelscher.

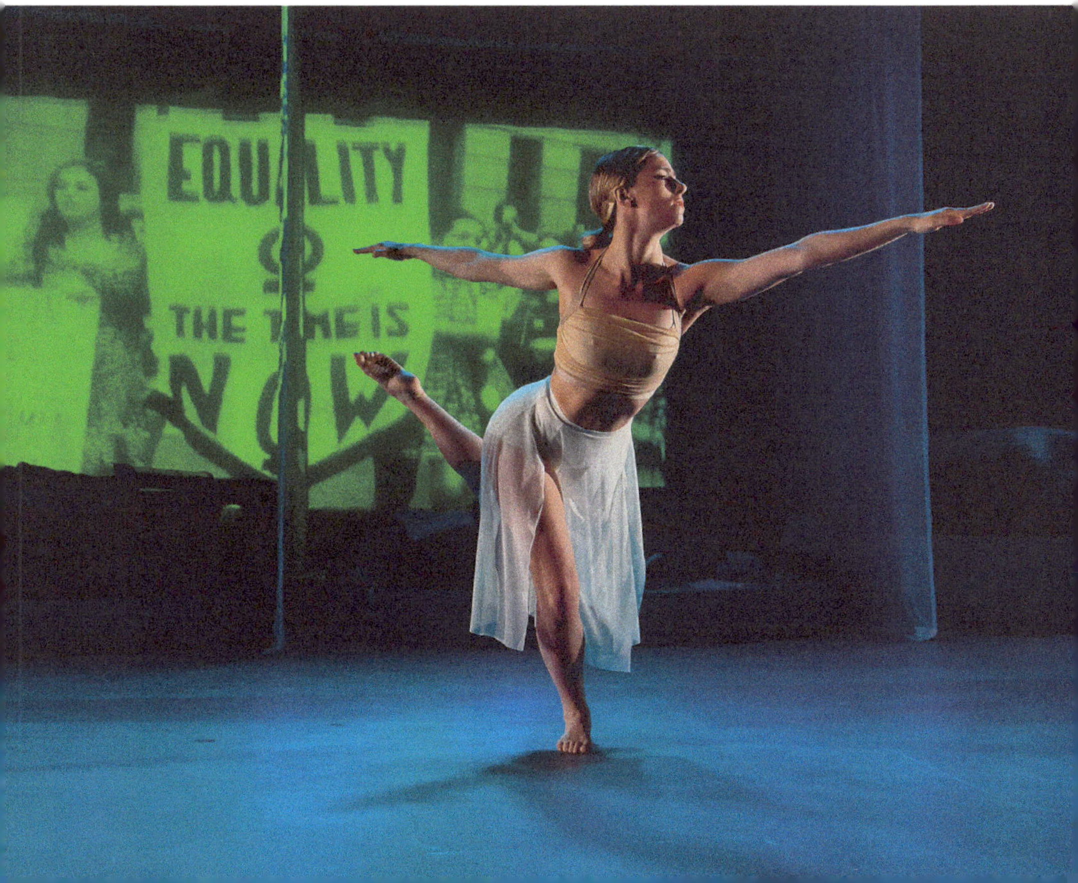

faculty. After each performance, the cast holds a talkback with the audience. They create a safe space in which audience members have shared their own personal stories, including some who had never vocalized their experience.

In addition to offering moments for discussion and reflection with the audience, Parker created a safe space in her studio with the dancers during the creation of *SHE*. Parker used a combination of directly choreographed material and collaboration and experimentation in her choreographic process. She also encouraged her dancers to look to their own lives and internal struggles to guide their art. Because of the deeply personal stories they were using to inspire movement, which often included choreography that directly demonstrated a traumatic event, the process was emotional. "It was finding that balance of not triggering but having people dig deep enough to pull out the pain when they needed it," Parker says.[4]

Together, the cast experienced a sense of release and began a journey of healing that many had not realized they needed. Parker personally had hoped that the artistic process would be healing for her dancers and the women whose stories were being told. What she did not expect was to begin a healing journey herself. She reflects, "I didn't realize I had a story of my own until rehearsals for this show. I had buried it for years. It made me wonder, if I had buried my story, how many other women are walking around with their own buried stories?" With *SHE*, Parker hopes to help others reveal and reflect on their own experiences, using dance and art to begin the first steps of healing.

Beth Braun: Esperanza Dance Project

Rather than telling individual stories, the performances by the Esperanza Dance Project use dance to portray a wide array of feelings and emotions, most of which survivors experience. They open with a piece titled "I Don't Pray Anymore." The dancers are dressed in plain white T-shirts and jeans, presented against a blue backdrop. They pause between fast-paced movements of jumps, quick turns, and brief handstands to hug one another or to help another dancer off the ground. They dance in duets, lifting and supporting one another by sharing weight and shifting through positions. In one moment, the dancers come together to lift one dancer high above their heads. She reaches toward the audience, her back arching against the hands of her fellow dancers. A motif that repeats throughout the work is of the dancers sitting on the floor with their backs facing the audience, and gradually they shift from sitting to standing. In the late moments of the performance, the dancers stand in a line facing the audience, before shifting quickly into individual shapes. The piece concludes with the dancer lifted up again, this time with her hands reaching away from the audience as the other dancers walk her upstage and the lights fade. “I Don’t Pray Anymore” exists to introduce the audience to the company. Before the dancers take the stage, narrators give the audience facts about sexual violence, such as that 93 percent of childhood sexual assault and abuse victims know their abuser.[5]

In a later piece, “Hurt,” the dancers use chairs to demonstrate feelings of stress, depression, and hopelessness. The chairs also are reminiscent of the desk chairs in which students sit each day; showing the audience that if they are experiencing or have experienced assault, they are not alone. They dance to the song “Hurt” by Nine Inch Nails and are dressed in red tops with black bottoms. The stage is flooded in red lighting, emphasizing the intensity of the trauma victims experience. Solos and duets are featured throughout the piece, while other dancers sit upright in the chairs placed upstage. In this way, the individual dancers are highlighted, demonstrating different emotions, which vary based on individual experiences with sexual assault. In this section, anxiety and depression are key emotions that come across from the choreography.

Beth Braun, the executive director of the Esperanza Dance Project, has a very personal experience with these emotions and the trauma of sexual assault. Well into her career as a high school modern dance teacher in Tucson, Arizona, Braun’s daughter revealed that she had been sexually assaulted by a close family member. Before she came forward with the story of her assault, which occurred when she was a young child and continued for many years, she had suffered from depression, anxiety, chronic migraines, and, eventually, drug abuse. At one point, she did not want to continue living, and it was then that she finally spoke up. Unfortunately, these are all very common experiences for survivors of child sexual abuse.

Braun witnessed her daughter’s struggle, and, in particular, she saw how hard it was for her to talk about the experience. Realizing that her daughter was not the only teenager who needed help, Braun decided to start a company that used dance to connect with high school students who had similar stories. She says, “It’s such a vulnerable age and it’s so critical to support teenagers, create safe spaces and to try to empower them and get them to talk.”[6] The Esperanza Dance Project exists to give them the encouragement to speak up about their experiences.

While creating the Esperanza Dance Project, Braun realized that although she had the background in dance and teaching, she needed help from others with different expertise. She reached out to friends in the behavioral health field and worked closely with them to develop a script for a performance that encouraged conversations about sexual assault. The cast of the performance, which shifts each year, includes a large range of artists, from high school students to adults with professional dance experience. Initially, Braun planned to find survivors who were willing to share their stories through the work. However, after an initial workshop with her dancers during which they revealed their own stories, she realized that they had more than enough material from which to pull inspiration.

In addition to the dance piece, there is a curriculum that accompanies the performance. All the performers, interns, and board members of the Esperanza Dance Project must participate in advocate training so that they are prepared for conversations with survivors. The high school–aged students who perform also act as peer advocates, alongside the adult advocates. The curriculum guides students and counselors through much-needed conversations after they watch the piece. "One of our main intentions is to break the silence of all of this and make it okay for people to stand up and say, 'I was abused,'" Braun explains. "That has been the most profound part of the project."

Jamie Minkus, *When I Dare to Be Powerful*, and Kevin Lee-Y Green, *Quiet as It's Kept*

Jamie Minkus, a dancer and choreographer with the company Rejoice! Diaspora Dance Theater, based in Portland, Oregon, created the work *When I Dare to Be Powerful* to begin her own healing process from sexual assault. Her piece explores female sexuality and empowerment, as well as the experience of being a survivor of domestic and sexual violence. She uses choreography to show both the strength of the female body and the trauma experienced after a sexual assault. One gesture she uses is the gun mimic, in which the dancers demonstrate a gun with the shape of their hands. Minkus chose to use this gesture to show the battle that women confront every day, fighting against a society that blames the victim. The choreography emphasizes the power of the dancers, showing the audience that despite the adversity women face and the trauma that comes with sexual abuse, women are strong and resilient, and they will triumph.

When the piece premiered, she felt a sense of relief to have her story and her experiences out in front of the world. She reflects, "After putting that piece out, I was able to claim my whole life and more of my whole being, and I don't get afraid to say it anymore. I get to be an advocate for sexual liberation

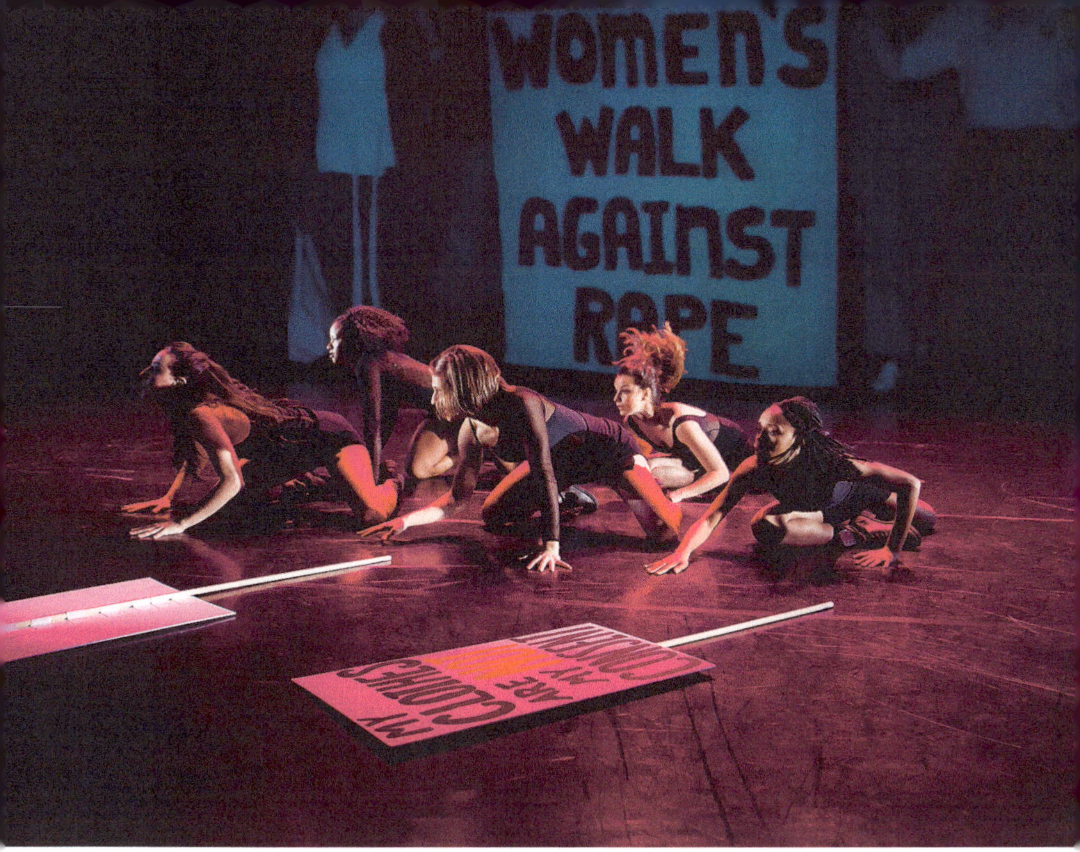

Rejoice! Diaspora Dance Theater. Courtesy of Diaspora Dance Theater. Photo by Cameron Ousley.

and humanization." Minkus decided that she would reclaim her own power and sexual liberation through movement. She realized that dance, with its unique ability to evoke emotion without words, was a powerful medium with which to bring awareness to sexual assault. "The emotional response can be a very personal journey to the onlooker. Dance still gets to be a little bit masked. We're not saying anything, we're not telling you what it is. Rather, we are showing you. That gives the individual the space to take it personally."[7]

In addition to giving Minkus a personal release, the piece also helped others begin their own healing journeys. Each night after the performance, audience members came up to Minkus and told her their own stories. Many had never voiced them before that night. She says, "I realized that I did this process because I needed to, but I also needed to for everyone else. Because it is way too common. We don't talk about it, and that means we don't expose it. And that means it gets to keep happening."

Kevin Lee-Y Green's company, Techmoja, (pronounced *Tech mo jé*), is a dance and theater company that blends modern and jazz techniques. Green first created the company with his mother in 2009, when they realized there were no arts organizations in his area led by Black artists. He says, "We wanted a space where people felt valued and important and felt like they had ownership." In addition to its emphasis on Black leadership in the arts, Techmoja also aims to share the stories of the coastal region of North Carolina with more urban areas and communities. Green feels that it is important to highlight the stories of those who live in this region because "it brings visibility to an area that is often overlooked."[8]

With Techmoja's piece *Quiet as It's Kept*, Green is working to acknowledge the voices of the Black community. Specifically, he is addressing the silence in the Black community surrounding sexual trauma. Green noticed that throughout the #MeToo movement, many more white survivors were speaking out and being featured in the media than Black survivors, even though the creator of the movement, Tarana Burke, is a Black woman. He says, "I couldn't understand why our stories weren't being brought forward." Green decided that he would use dance and his company to share his own story and give space to others in his community to share or reflect on their experiences.

The title of the piece *Quiet as It's Kept* comes directly from the Southern vernacular used in Black communities.[9] Green chose this title because the piece aims to address both sexual trauma and the silence in the Black community. He says, "I see it as a reconciliation and revival process. Art has that ability to get people in a certain place that they wouldn't otherwise go to. I hope not to sensationalize these stories but to treat them with the integrity and the respect that they're due and to inform people on this, that there is help, there is a way through. Because I wish someone would have told me that."

Conclusion

Artists across art forms are raising awareness and promoting healing from sexual assault by exploring the topic in their work. However, despite the increase of conversations and artwork, the dance world is still trailing behind other genres in this area. In the dance community, there are still very few choreographers who are tackling this subject. Dance is already a vulnerable art, in which a dancer's body is on display and available for criticism. It is understandable that a topic that is so very personal is difficult for both choreographers, whose names will be attached to the piece, and dancers, whose bodies and faces will be directly associated with the traumatizing stories they are reflecting. The four artists highlighted in this chapter are taking important steps for the dance community, demonstrating the power of putting this topic onstage.

Despite the forward progress made from the #MeToo movement, conversations surrounding sexual assault and violence still feel unwelcome. Dancers are fighting a culture in which stories are questioned and victims are blamed. By having the important discussions and putting experiences out in the open, artists can help one another heal and raise awareness. While there is still much work to be done in the field of dance in terms of culture and power dynamics, the ambition and determination of these choreographers who are putting their bodies and souls behind such an important and personal statement gives hope for more much-needed discussion and change in the future.

Notes

1. Kiara Kinghorn, "Dance in the Era of #MeToo" (master's thesis, University of California, Irvine, 2020), 35, https://escholarship.org/uc/item/3f45r3nf.

2. Gia Kourlas and Siobhan Burke, "Two Critics Reflect on Ballet's #MeToo Moment," *New York Times*, October 18, 2018.

3. Kinghorn, "Dance in the Era of #MeToo," 6.

4. Jinah Parker, interview with the author, April 26, 2021.

5. US Department of Justice, Office of Justice Programs, Bureau of Justice Statistics, National Crime Victimization Survey, 2005.

6. Beth Braun, interview with the author, April 28, 2021.

7. Jamie Minkus, interview with the author, April 23, 2021.

8. This and the following quotations from Kevin Lee-Y Green are from an interview with the author, May 7, 2021.

9. "Quiet as it's kept, there were no marigolds in the fall of 1941" is also the first line of the 1970 novel *The Bluest Eye* by Toni Morrison.

8 Retracing the Trace

Luzene Hill

On January 4, 1994, I was attacked, beaten, and raped, in Piedmont Park in Atlanta. Rape is not about sex, it's about power and rage. A woman is made powerless and she is silenced. The rapist grabbed me from behind by the hood of my jacket and strangled me with the cords tied around my neck. Those traces of violence remained on my neck for six months. I thought they would be there forever, constant reminders of the assault, permanent reminders of being silenced.

Silence shrouds the experience of sexual assault. A woman is often strangled to silence and control her, and the aftermath is characterized by a different kind of enveloping disquiet.

Prologue

Retracing the Trace is an imprint of rape and an exposition of the number of unreported sexual assaults that occur within a twenty-four-hour period in the United States. The foundation for this work derived from the original marks of my own trauma and was realized by inserting myself (my body) into the process of making an imprint, as well as my presence in the gallery each day.

This installation had three components. Numbers, indicating each hour in a day, were stenciled in a line around the gallery walls. Material volume, knotted cords, was pooled on the floor around the outline of my body and re-presented the traces of violence left in the leaves and mud where I was attacked. Each cord signified a specific number between 1 and 3,780, the estimated number of unreported rapes that occur in the United States each day. I borrowed principles of the Inka *khipu*, an ancient cord knotting system used for accounting and storytelling, to count and give voice to those women who remain silent. The third element was my daily ritual of moving a portion of the cords from the floor to the walls. These three parts merged into one visual image by the end of the exhibit. The body trace of violence slowly diminished, then disappeared, through my ritual. The counting cords that had been on the floor encircled the gallery walls in a unified, reckoning *re*trace of the marks left on my neck.

Prior to creating *Retracing the Trace*, I addressed the issue of violence toward women in an abstract and personally detached way. *Retracing the Trace* marked a shift in my approach to making work about this issue. Each aspect of this work reflected my identity and involvement, from making the body imprint to removing the last cord from the floor and attaching it to the wall. The gallery was a metaphor for my body, as I drew attention to the number of sexual assaults that go unreported and renounced the traces of my own trauma.

As a Native American woman, I often reference precontact culture in my work. The *khipu* was pertinent to this work, as a device made from cords and as an endangered Native American language. I metaphorically connected the silencing I experienced when I was raped to the silencing of Native American culture and voices.

Installation

Retracing the Trace surrounded the viewer with material volume to provoke engagement, with the work and with the issue of sexual assault. It placed the visitor between the material on the floor and the material on the walls; they were *in* the work, rather than standing apart from it and looking on. I expressed the temporal nature of installation art through my daily relocation of the knotted cords, presenting the gallery visitor with a momentary presence and experience. The focus of *Retracing the Trace* is simple: material volume and its relocation through ritual.

Although ritualized action was not in my mind when I began this work, it became an important part of it. In my use of ritual (relocation of material volume) I sought to maintain a quality of unrelenting, repetitive energy.

Material Volume—the Cords

In developing *Retracing the Trace*, I returned again and again to the idea of cords. The original cords on my jacket had silenced me, and traces of that

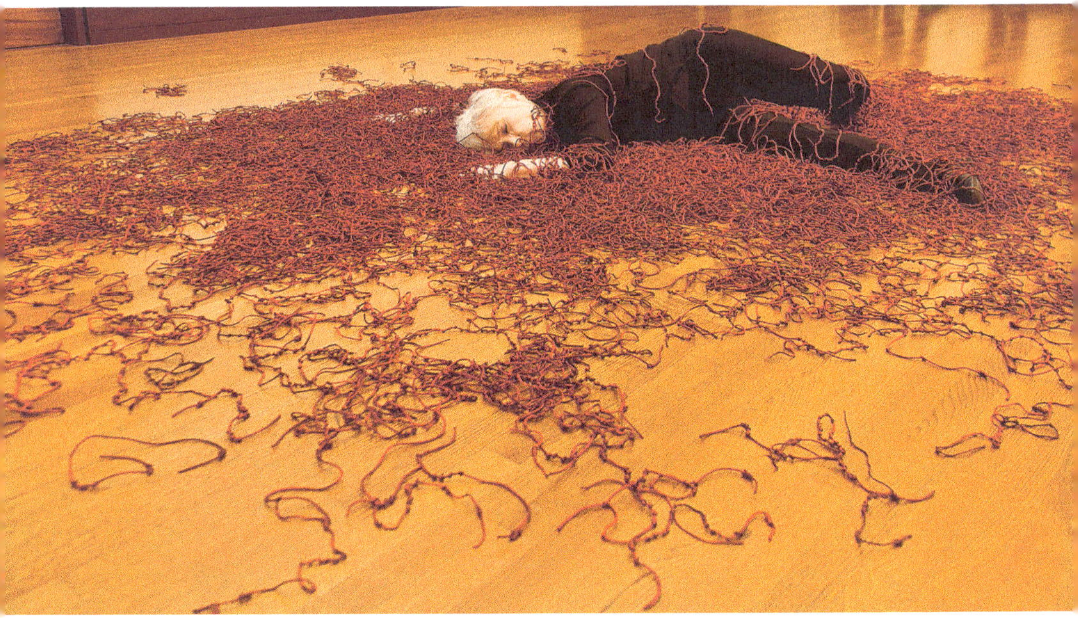

Luzene Hill, *Retracing the Trace*, 2015. Artist performance with knotted cords. Eiteljorg Museum of American Indians and Western Art, Indianapolis. Photo courtesy of the Eiteljorg Museum.

silencing haunted me each day as I looked in the mirror. The streaks on my neck were the visual evidence of being strangled, silenced, and controlled. I wanted to turn that around and use cords for tracing a voice that would break the silence. The *khipu* gave me a device to do that.

Each of the knotted cords in my installation was a specific number designation, 1 through 3,780. Only about 16 percent of sexual assaults are reported in the United States. Statistically, these reported assaults occur every two minutes, or 720 times a day. If 720 represents the reported rapes, the unreported number of assaults would be 3,780. According to the Rape, Abuse and Incest National Network (RAINN), sexual assault is the most underreported violent crime. My goal was not to create replicas of the *khipu*, but to use that system of counting to represent each woman who would be attacked, and remain silent, during a twenty-four-hour period. These statistics are those available when I initially created *Retracing the Trace* in 2012.

I used three diameters of satin cord, which were similar to the size of the cords that strangled me. These commercially dyed cords were two shades of medium red and shiny. I wanted a deep, dark red that suggested blood.

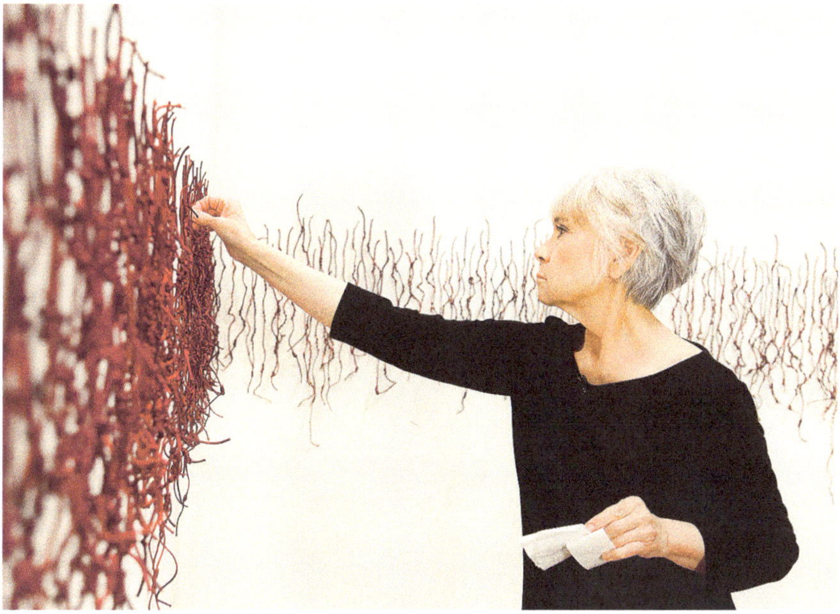

Luzene Hill, *Retracing the Trace*, 2015. Artist hanging knotted cords on museum wall. Eiteljorg Museum of American Indians and Western Art, Indianapolis. Photo courtesy of the Eiteljorg Museum.

Staining and dying the cords gave more depth of color and a matte finish. I began what would become a four-month process of making the knotted cords. After knotting, I dyed the cords, soaking them in combinations of ink, acrylic paint, tea, and walnut stain. Sometimes I dyed and dried a batch (forty or fifty cords) two or three times to get added depth and variation in shades.

At the beginning of this production, I carefully hung each knotted cord on a rack, so that it remained straight. My initial idea was to have all the cords hanging in an orderly display, possibly even in sequential order. As the number of knotted cords waiting to be dyed and dried mounted, I began to take a handful of cords from the dye bath and pile them over the drying racks. I looked at those clumps, with their ragged, bent tendrils hanging down, for several weeks. The twisted, irregular cords were more expressive than the neat, straight ones, as they denoted the damage and abjection of sexual violation.

In the *khipu* system, there are three basic counting knots: a simple overhand knot, a knot tied to create a figure-eight pattern, and a *long* knot, made by wrapping the cord around itself from two to nine times. The knotted cords

I created followed that system in order to make each cord unique, specific, and countable.

The Khipu

When I began to research the *khipu*, I discovered new theories pointing to a narrative language within this system, previously considered to have been used only for accounting. Spanish chronicles, made at first contact, indicate that the Inka, and even earlier people in South America, did indeed have a method of communication equivalent to a *written* language. However, these theories may never be proved, because most of the *khipu*, like Aztec codices, were destroyed five hundred years ago. Ignorance and fear dictated destruction of the *khipu*, as one group assumed power over another through the systematic silencing of language and culture.

The Imprint

The impetus for making this trace came from my exploration of bodywork printmaking and was influenced by Ana Mendieta's *Body Tracks* and her *Siluetas* series. The body, as an art-making tool in the manner of Mendieta, is how I approached the floor piece in this installation. Mendieta's direct and personal process in making *Body Tracks* reminded me of the red-smeared drawings and paintings I had made, then destroyed, in the months immediately after being raped. My goal was not to create a permanent image through photography, as Mendieta had done with the *Siluetas*. Most of those female silhouettes were made by pressing her body into mud, leaves, flowers, sand, and other soft surfaces in nature and photographing the imprints. I wanted to re-present a trace of violence that I would transform through ritual action. A few of the *Siluetas* involved Mendieta being covered with flowers, grasses, or snow. I used that model to create the floor piece by lying on the floor and having the 3,780 knotted cords scattered on and around me. I then got up, allowing the cords on top of me to fall around the space. After I repeated this process, in different positions, the result was an image of the cords pooling around the imprint of my body slumped on the ground.[1]

My initial response to Mendieta's work had been personal and literal, rather than symbolic. The *Siluetas* brought back memories of the crime scene and the ensuing days when the police failed to catch the rapist. Only a small percentage of rapists are caught, few are ever prosecuted, and fewer

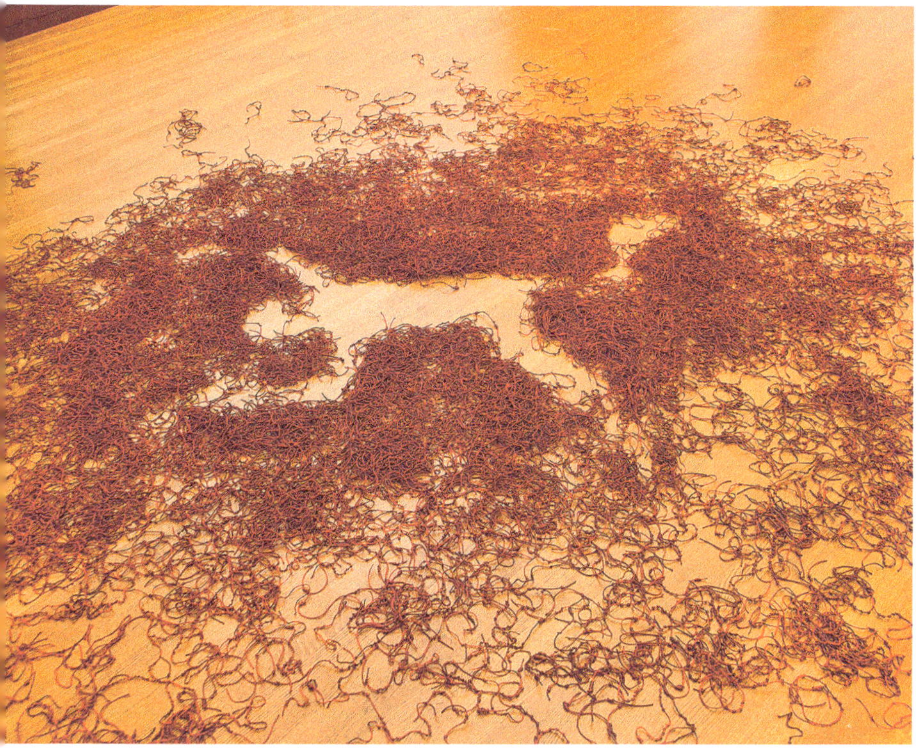

Luzene Hill, *Retracing the Trace*, 2015. Artist's body shape outlined by cords. Eiteljorg Museum of American Indians and Western Art, Indianapolis. Photo courtesy of the Eiteljorg Museum.

still actually spend time in jail. The day after I was attacked, I returned to the scene of the crime. Rape trauma syndrome explains the counterintuitive actions that victims often exhibit after being sexually assaulted. By returning, I was attempting to gain back the power I had lost at that place. Re-creating that scene by imprinting the cords with my own body empowered me, over the scene and over the trauma.

Trauma

I had not planned this work to be so focused on my personal experience. But, through the evolution of the art-making process, I realized this work *is* about my experience. I resisted this because I thought making work about my personal trauma would put it in the category of confessional/victim art. My way of examining a very private experience had previously been in personally detached terms, using images of dolls and paper dolls that were damaged and scarred.

I began by making body prints that were executed by lying down on my ink-smeared back and then peeling myself off the paper to get a clear imprint. I progressed to making some prints in which I mimicked actions of struggling. Although these initial body prints were not included in this installation, they were important to my development of this work. These prints were the result of a conscious decision to insert myself, as art tool, into work that addressed the physical violation of women and, specifically, the sexual violation of my own body. I identified with the process and the resulting artifact. In those prints, I was claiming, for the first time, both the trauma and my expression of it.

As my thinking about the expression of trauma shifted, I searched for other contemporary female artists addressing the issue of sexual assault, but found few. Now, almost ten years later, many more artists are creating work about sexual assault. Their voices are raising the volume of this conversation.

Ritual

My action/ritual in the gallery gradually diminished the imprint on the floor, as it increased the volume of material encircling the walls. On the first day, the empty walls, with subtle hour numbers stenciled with gray pastel, suggested an expectation of something about to happen.

I placed the first group of knotted cords on the wall between the 7:00 and 8:00 a.m. hours because that is the time of day I was attacked. After those first cords, my placement of the cords each day was made instinctively, but always returned to that morning hour. As I relocated more of the knotted cords, the space between the hours became filled with red "marks" and with shadows of the hanging cords tracing behind them. The increasing number of cords on the wall, and layer of shadows, implied even larger numbers of assaults that remain in the background, unreported.

I had anticipated that my daily time in the gallery, relocating the cords, would take about two hours each day for the ten days of the exhibit. I underestimated the time required for this process, due to the time I spent talking with visitors, and because I performed the relocation in a much slower and more deliberate way than I had planned. Preparing the knotted cords, making the imprint, and stenciling the numbers set the stage and provided the props. The execution of the performance/ritual was open to variations, in response to visitor activity in the gallery and to my energy/intent. By the midway point, the cords on the walls were slowly gaining importance as the floor piece diminished.

By the last two or three days of the exhibit, the floor imprint had been diminished in depth and volume. The remaining individual cords were more scattered and separated. Each cord configuration and knot pattern was more apparent, and the imprint displayed an increasingly delicate figure.

By the tenth day, the walls were encircled with a solid and intense trace, above the vacant gallery floor.

Conclusion

This installation involved a new exploration for me, being in the gallery every day and performing an action. People who came into the gallery talked with me, sometimes at length, about the issue of sexual assault, and often about their own experience. Some remarked on the impact of seeing the shifting material volume day after day. Others did not speak to me as I was working, but wrote a comment in the gallery book. At one point in the planning I worried that talking with people in the space would be disruptive or bring the atmosphere down to a "social" level. It did not. Each time I entered the space I felt a sense of quiet and calm. The lighting was subdued, and the mounting number of red cords on the walls conveyed an intense, but serene, presence.

On the last day of the exhibit, when all the cords were on the wall, the installation looked exactly as I had envisioned it. The unknown factor was my action each day in the gallery. I had hoped that action would be a ritual of acknowledging and honoring those women who remain silent. It *was* that to some extent. However, after being in the gallery moving the cords from the floor to the wall every day, I became aware of a shift in my energy and in the way I performed the action. I doubt that it was apparent to a visitor, but possibly it was. The process became very focused for me, as I felt the weight of the increasing numbers getting stronger, building the visual volume.

My movements became more emphatic, as I pressed the cords against the wall. Moving the cords off the floor became more about my own experience of having been silenced and powerless. With each cord I attached to the wall, I was making my mark—marking, noting, announcing the increasing numbers as my visual voice became more pronounced.

I had resisted my personal experience being the primary focus because I believed it would put the spotlight on me, rather than the issue of sexual assault. Through conversations I had during this exhibit, and from comments in my gallery book, I realize that my speaking out in a personal way was important for the effectiveness of the work. My own response to Mendieta's *Siluetas* had been a personal recollection of the ground where I had been attacked. I made a connection between the imprint she had made with *her* body and the imprint of *my* body I had seen on the ground.

One person wrote in my gallery book, "This makes me realize how much I've healed and helps me feel connected to others going through the same thing." Another wrote, "There is one [cord] for me." Those women felt they were not alone, that other women, *many* other women had experienced this too. They felt a connection to a larger company and in that gallery space were empowered to write and talk about their experiences. Talking about sexual assault is not something women do readily. It is easier to remain silent, thinking no one else knows what it feels like to experience this trauma. There was action and conversation during this exhibit. The silence was broken through visual image, and through words, written and spoken.

Epilogue

Making this work and writing about it was far more difficult, psychologically and emotionally, than I anticipated. As a survivor of sexual assault, I felt satisfaction in provoking discourse about this subject and bringing it out of the shadows. I had considered involving volunteers to assist in this ritual, as another way of engaging the public. But after a few days, I realized it was important that I carry out the completion of the ritual by myself.

This experience has expanded my ideas of installation and performance art. I now view performance art less as theatrical (playing a part) action and more as an experience of reality, for the artist and the viewer. I was being myself, a survivor of sexual assault, as I transformed the image of the cords.

Retracing the Trace was first presented in 2012, and the ritual/performance was made over ten days, during which I was in the gallery all day moving the cords by myself. Visitors seeing the work at the beginning of the process saw a different image from that seen by visitors coming in at the end.

In May 2015, the Eiteljorg Museum in Indianapolis documented my installation of the work in the Harvey Gallery in order to videotape the process. That video then became an important part of this work. When the work has been shown subsequently (three times, most recently in 2020) with either some or none of the cords still on the floor, visitors see the process via the video.

After I had re-created this installation—*well after* going through the process of making the body print, looking at the print, and removing that image one cord at a time—I realized that something else had informed the creation of this work.

In 2009, I made an installation called . . . *the body and blood*. The subject was violence against women from a global perspective and human rights. This work was exhibited in a gallery in the student center at the University of North Carolina at Asheville. It comprised 24,480 dried rose petals. For thirty-four days, a portion of the petals was poured over a honeysuckle basket placed on a table made to resemble an altar. This work can be seen on my website, along with my statement.[2] Midway through the thirty-four days, I went to the gallery on a Sunday morning to place that day's allotment of petals on the basket. When I walked into the gallery, I was stunned to find the work had been vandalized. During the night, someone had gone into the gallery and pushed/scattered the petals around the floor. I was devastated.

I realized later that I had felt angry my work had been touched, let alone willfully disturbed. More importantly, I felt personally violated—again. My instinct was to close the exhibit and post a statement on the door. But I realized that my power was to carefully collect the scattered and broken petals and redo the pouring of them over the basket, and to continue the daily ritual to completion. It was a way of not being silenced—asserting the work and my voice.

Three years after that incident, I made *Retracing the Trace*.

I now know that in addition to Mendieta's *Siluetas* series bringing to mind the mud and leaves at the site of my rape, the scattered rose petals that I cleaned up and made whole again also informed the final version of *Retracing the Trace*.

Notes

1. Luzene Hill, "Luzene Hill—'Retracing the Trace,'" YouTube video, 5:50, accessed May 28, 2023, www.youtube.com/watch?v=T_Rn6grvXno.

2. Luzene Hill, . . . *the body and blood*, accessed May 28, 2023, www.luzenehill.com/installations.

9
Women Who Can't Be Knocked Down

Clarity Haynes

We never laughed about the attack. I wanted to laugh, but everyone was so serious. As soon as I told them he used the word *rape* and pulled down my pants, they were convinced it was not a mugging but an attempted rape.

It might sound crazy to say that I didn't think it was that. I still don't, sometimes. It's easier to think that I was mugged. It's one way I protect myself, I guess.

When I went to the district attorney's office to be prepped for my testimony, I was given a sticker to wear on my sweater that said "Special Victims." There were signs on walls and on doors that said "Special Victims." I was a *special victim*, just like on *Law and Order: SVU*.

Patricia Lockwood wrote a poem called "Rape Joke."[1] I read it again recently, and it is my favorite poem about rape, I think. Because it touches on the taboo of humor. I can't help laughing when someone falls down. There is something hilarious about falling down. Why is it not hilarious when someone has been pushed down violently and has to run for her life while pulling up her pants?

There is a 1992 Sue Williams painting called *A Funny Thing Happened*. She painted cartoonish women being raped by cartoonish men on sidewalks, next to scrawled text reading: "A funny thing happened on the way to the . . . STORE, HOUSE, BUS, DUMPSTER, PROTEST, SUBWAY."

For me, a funny thing happened on the way to the . . . GYM. Later, I had planned to go to the ART SUPPLIES STORE and then to my STUDIO, but instead I ended up at the POLICE STATION.

I felt so undignified and raw when I ran away pulling up my pants, yelling *help, help, help*, trying to be loud like when I'd practiced yelling *No!* in front of the TV during an *Oprah* self-defense episode in the early 1990s. But I couldn't run fast enough or yell loud enough, because it was like a nightmare in which I was too slow, as if underwater. Too quiet, as if mute.

When I was fifteen, my boyfriend Gus jerked my pants down in the middle of the street on the Calvert bridge. We'd snuck out to meet each other late one night, it was dark, and there was no one around to see, but it surprised me. And it felt dumpy and unsexy to have to jerk my pants back up again. Rape is not about sex but about violence, something I only understood when I encountered Alex Faiola. Alex had never met me but was enraged by me, wanted to kill me. He hated me for no reason, except that I know the reason. The reason is that I was a woman.

There were other, subtler times, and they stand out in my memory like popcorn on a string. All connected by that one thing. Hate. None of them personal. But I took them in as if they were. How can you know why you are a target when you are five, nine, fourteen, fifteen, sixteen, seventeen, eighteen, nineteen, twenty, thirty-five?

I tell myself that now, at almost fifty, I know when I am a target. Except now it feels more like indifference. The things that don't happen. My work being overlooked, undervalued. It's a different kind of joke.

There is being raped, and there is getting raped. *Getting* raped means you did something to get raped. You went out too early or too late, or you had the wrong energy. You didn't look confident enough. You weren't aware of your surroundings.

Being raped sounds like you were already lying on the ground. Like you had no agency. Like a field being ploughed.

I wasn't raped. I was lucky. My mother said, "One man attacked you, but another man saved you." This should go down in some kind of book of proverbs, I think. *Chicken Soup for the Soul*, in a chapter called "Don't Hate Men, Hate Patriarchy."

There were lumps on my skull from where my head smashed into the pavement. I was sore all over my body. Muscles ached that I didn't know I had. The stress of the attack had made me tense up everywhere. Fight or flight. I fought first, pushed against his chest, shouted "GET OFF ME!"

But he said, "SHUT UP BEFORE I FUCK YOU UP," and I understood that I needed to be compliant in order to stay alive.

He said, "HURRY UP BEFORE I RAPE YOU," and pulled down my pants with a practiced hand.

But someone came along. His name was Rick, and he had been in his kitchen making pancakes for his daughters when he heard the commotion.

I don't remember screaming, but apparently I did, and garbage cans were knocked over. Rick was from Philly and wasn't afraid of a fight. I imagine that the other neighbors cowered inside, called 911 maybe, but didn't dare to intervene.

Rick came to the grand jury to testify right after I did. He had a black eye from Alex Faiola. His black eye was the reason I got away. The reason I know Alex's name is because they announced it in court when they introduced my testimony. I recited the story in front of a courtroom of people. I couldn't see them even though my eyes were open. They were all a blur, but my story was clear.

Alex held me captive for a few minutes, horizontally, on the sidewalk, on Park Place in Park Slope, Brooklyn, on October 22, 2006, according to the police report, on a sunny morning, at 8:22 a.m. I only knew Alex for that short time. But there is an intimacy in the fact that my life was in his hands. I tried not to infuriate him further, suggested giving him my iPod, or some money, said, "Okay . . . Okay . . ." breathlessly, like I was on his side.

When I had the chance I ran away, but I felt almost sorry, like I'd tricked him, was breaking some kind of promise. Alex chased me but didn't catch me. The police caught him instead. I said, "Yes, that's him," from inside the police car, and our eyes met. He was standing on the corner, his arms held back by two police officers, and I recognized him because his face was full of rage.

I wasn't raped then, but I was raped another time, years before, when I didn't know it was rape. I was in the bedroom of a house that a guy named Frank was squatting in. His friend Hector, whom I was sort of seeing, wouldn't let me out of the room until I had sex with him. I couldn't figure out why I was so pissed off afterward, taking the subway home alone, looking for more trouble, which I found. I'd been drinking since 11:00 a.m. and was still drinking that night at 2:00 a.m.

I don't like being a special victim, stripped of my dignity, but I know that it is nothing personal.

I want to slough it all off and see through the untruths. To know who I am: vulnerabilities, tenderness, ugliness, failures, as well as brilliance, joy, love, and success. As long as they are all true, they are mine.

The bullshit that accumulates, the misogyny that lands on me, is not mine and never was.

And if I want to laugh, I laugh. It's just laughter, after all. It feels good.

And I paint. I create monumental bodies, protectors. Gargantuan icons. Women who can't be knocked down.

It took me years to find the language to tell this story.

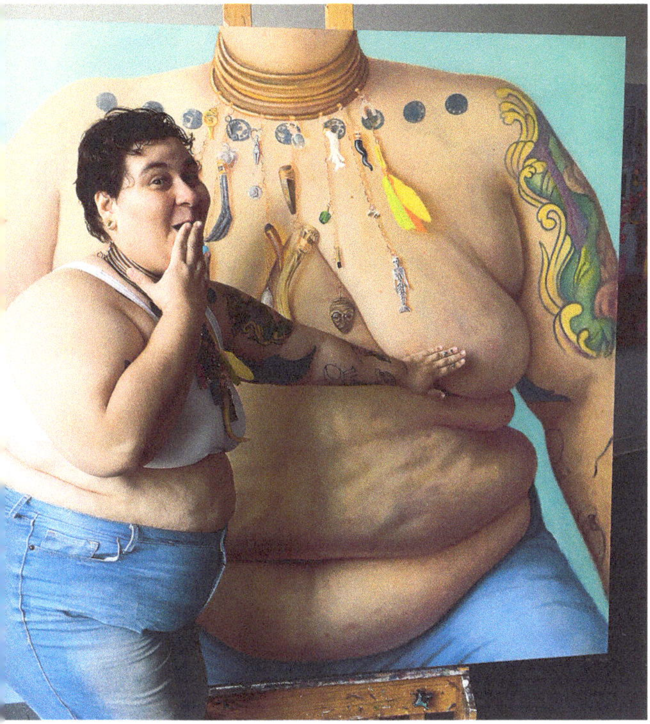

Portrait subject Aullar Mateo with their portrait, *Grace* (2019), by Clarity Haynes. Oil on linen, 62 × 62 in. Courtesy of *Hyperallergic*. Photo by Clarity Haynes.

I recently read Nancy Princenthal's book *Unspeakable Acts: Women, Art, and Sexual Violence in the 1970s*, and she says that finding language for violence is the first step in mitigating its effects.[2] The book explores the story of feminist artists who began to address rape in their work in the 1970s, a time when it was being discussed for the first time out in the open. Artists such as Yoko Ono, Suzanne Lacy, Ana Mendieta, Valie Export.

My work does not address sexual violence directly, but recently, when asked why my paintings of torsos are monumental in scale, I realized that the answer—at least in part—is tied to what happened on October 22, 2006.

In the days after the attack, I was terrified to go outside of my apartment. I weighed the risks: Was it too early? Too late? I took cabs instead of walking, as often as I could. But I was halfway through the MFA program at Brooklyn College, and I was determined not to let the assault interrupt my groove.

At home, I tacked up the most enormous sheet of paper I could find, from the largest roll I could get at New York Central Art Supply. Using photographs of a woman named Janet who had modeled for me years before in Philadelphia, I drew the largest figure I had ever made. From the floor to the

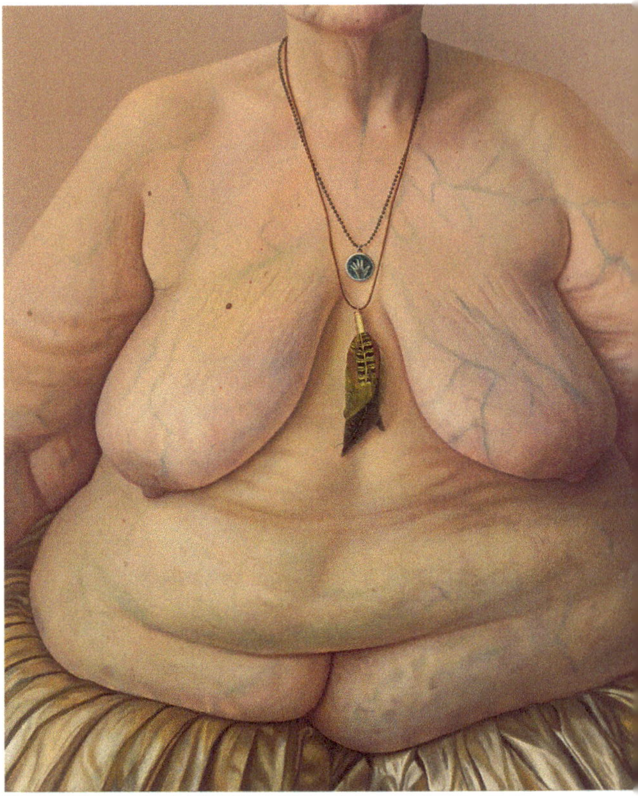

Clarity Haynes, *Goddess Nancy*, 2018. Oil on linen, 58 × 54.5 in. Photo courtesy of the artist and New Discretions.

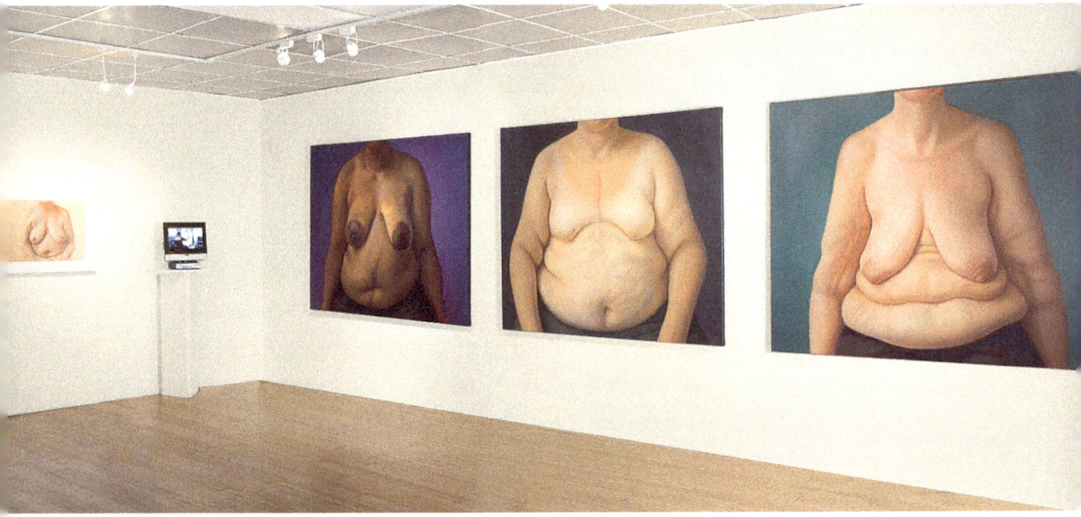

Clarity Haynes exhibit, *Taking Space: Contemporary Women Artists and the Politics of Scale*, Pennsylvania Academy of Fine Arts, November 19, 2020–September 19, 2021. Photo courtesy of the Academy.

ceiling, Janet's torso took up the entire wall. She wore black stretchy pants and no shirt, and she was gorgeously fat. As I drew, she took voluminous form and became more and more solid. Over the days and weeks, she became a protective goddess, and as I worked, I felt rage. Rage that I had been so vulnerable to the assault, even though as a lesbian I had fought against that kind of subjugation all my life. I wanted Janet to make men looking at her feel small and powerless. No one could knock her down. No one. She was as sacred and impenetrable as a Buddha statue.

I never showed anyone that drawing, and I never documented it. But it was a turning point, because in the years that followed, I began to make torso portraits—which until then had been life-size—into larger-than-life paintings. I worked on the paintings sometimes for years, and I worked with models, so I wasn't alone. My sitters became friends, and the figures in the paintings became more and more detailed, irrefutable, like mountains I could imagine climbing. They were straight, gay, bisexual; cisgender, nonbinary, and trans. Gwen, Emily, AnnMarie, Ellen, Roxanne, Lyz, Leonora, Jaece, Robin, Janie, Goddess Nancy, Dilma, Mariam, Brenda, Genesis, Grace. Each painting represents a relationship that will always be a part of me.

It might be a cliché, but it's true: art heals.

It's not easy to talk about trauma, especially sexual violence. But as a queer feminist artist, it's important to me to not hide the truth about my life, about women's lives, about LGBTQ lives. As a cisgender, white, middle-class woman, I've been protected by my privilege. And yet violence has still affected me. It impacts so many of us. But we survive, and, more and more, we are finding language, in words and art, to tell the truth.

Notes

Reprinted with permission from the online journal *Hyperallergic*. Original title: "Art Heals: After a Sexual Assault, an Artist Paints Women Who Can't Be Knocked Down." Published February 4, 2021, https://hyperallergic.com/618731/art-heals-after-sexual-assault-artist-paints-women-who-cant-be-knocked-down.

1. Patricia Lockwood, "Rape Joke," *The Awl* (blog), July 25, 2013, www.theawl.com/2013/07/patricia-lockwood-rape-joke.

2. Thomas Micchelli, "When Trauma Becomes Art," review of *Unspeakable Acts: Women, Art, and Sexual Violence in the 1970s*, by Nancy Princenthal, *Hyperallergic*, November 16, 2019, https://hyperallergic.com/528629/nancy-princenthal-unspeakable-acts-women-art-and-sexual-violence-in-the-1970s.

10
Repressed

Sean Shannon

The flashbacks to the day I was raped started happening shortly after I left home for the first time, for the few months I was able to escape from my father's brutality to attend a small liberal arts college in southern Ohio. Between nine years of constant bullying, from my father and many of the people at the private school I attended for nine years, and being socialized as a male during the worst of the AIDS crisis in the 1980s, it took me months to finally understand the freedom I had at that new college. As my mind was finally able to explore that fundamental question of "who am I"—and I was finally in an environment where I felt safe, both physically and emotionally, to engage in that exploration—maybe my mind was finally able to deal with what happened on that summer day in 1987.

I barely had time to seek help from the counselors at that college before my father cut my financial support out from under me, forcing me to return home and work for him. Six years later, when old age finally dulled my father's abuse, I was able to go back to a bigger university in my hometown and to attend as a transgender woman. I don't know if my gender realization experience was any different from anyone else's in the late 1990s, but I do know that if my father had still felt like he could control me, probably none of it would have happened.

My father died in 2008, and in the eight years that followed, my mother slowly opened up about not only what my father had told her about trying to turn me "into a man" but the physical and emotional abuse he inflicted on her as well, dating back to when she "decided" to get pregnant for the first time, in 1965. I was also an unwanted child, and my father was dead set on molding me in his image because of the "investment" of his time and money that he'd had to make on me. The violence of forced cisheteronormativity was only one of the ways he tried to control me, but it was one of the most detrimental to my early years, and I still deal with the psychological and emotional damage of that violence every day of my life.

In the eight years between my father's death and my mother's passing in 2016—ten days before the US presidential election that year—I saw some signs that things were getting slightly easier for transgender youth. But with the rise of far-right movements across the world near the end of that period, especially the open violence against queer people in Russia captured on smartphone video and shared across the world online, I knew that whatever gains were made by nonheterosexual and non-cisgender people in the United States could easily be ephemeral, reversed even more quickly than they came, if the same winds started blowing across the United States. As anti-trans rhetoric became more common and more normalized, first by celebrities spewing hate speech and then by conservative politicians ramming through openly discriminatory anti-trans legislation, it was too easy to see where it would all lead. With the ongoing COVID-19 pandemic taking up so much of people's attention, too many who formerly claimed to be "allies" were turning a deaf ear to those of us still stuck in the pot as the water came to a boil these past few years.

My only memories of transgender people from before I first went to college are from the television shows I grew up watching during the 1980s, exploitative daytime talk shows and the like. I wouldn't even think about saying whether things are worse for transgender people now than they were then, simply because I lack that lived experience of consciously realizing I was transgender back then. What I can say is that now, more than ever, trying to talk about my experiences as a rape survivor feels like I'm risking my own life, when so many people are going into public arenas to claim that my mere existence as a transgender woman makes me a "rapist in waiting" and that I'm a threat to "normal society" that must be stopped.

Some would say that the pieces in this volume are their own revolutionary acts, that we artists are engaging in our own forms of heroism by raising our voices on these issues during these difficult times. All I know is what I've known nearly all my life, long before that summer day in 1987: I write because I have to.

1995

Seven years.

Seven years of not remembering
the woodpile in front of me,
the lazy humidity of a Michigan summer,
shorts and lemonade and tricolor bunting
all over the island.

Seven years of not remembering
his fourteen years pinning my eleven down,
what he said about "something funny"
he was going to show me
as I felt like I needed to poop
and I said that I needed to poop
and he shushed me and said not to tell anyone
and I didn't know what I'd tell anyone
because all I knew was I was lying on my stomach
and this son of my father's friends
led me to this woodpile behind his house
and I really needed to poop
and I didn't know why.

Seven years of no memory of that afternoon,
while I fought to survive an abattoir of a school
and a father who tried to mold me into the son he always wanted
with his fists and his words but mostly his fists
until he realized he could just cut the cords
on everything that kept me from trying
to kill myself again.

Nineteen years,
nearly nineteen years
of being called a liar so much that
I almost started believing it myself,
even after the counseling,
even after the therapy,
even after the support from the few friends

I'd made after I finally escaped
to college for a few months,
only to have my father cut that off from me as well,
forced to work for him or starve on the street,
yanked away from nearly everyone who might believe me.

2022

Being told I'm not a "real woman" because I wasn't born with a vagina.

Being told I'm a mockery of "real womanhood."

Being told I'm a pedophile in disguise
and no one will believe me if I try to dispute it.

Being told I'm a threat to anyone who becomes
even tangentially aware of my existence
because I'm just a man in makeup and women's clothing
looking to trick people into something I can't even
stand to think about after all the memories of that afternoon
and never being able to enjoy anything like that
unless I'm doing something to myself because after
forty-six years it can still feel
like I'm the only person who really believes me.

Being told I deserve constant ridicule,
a never-ending torrent of abuse from passersby
and stand-up comedians and everyone in between,
my existence a punch line to their jokes.

Being told I deserve to be murdered
if I ever try to have sex with someone else again,
if I ever pee outside my apartment again,
if I ever look the wrong way at someone else again,
if I ever say another word,
if I ever ask what is going on.

If I'll never stop being told those things,
maybe there's no use in counting the years any longer.

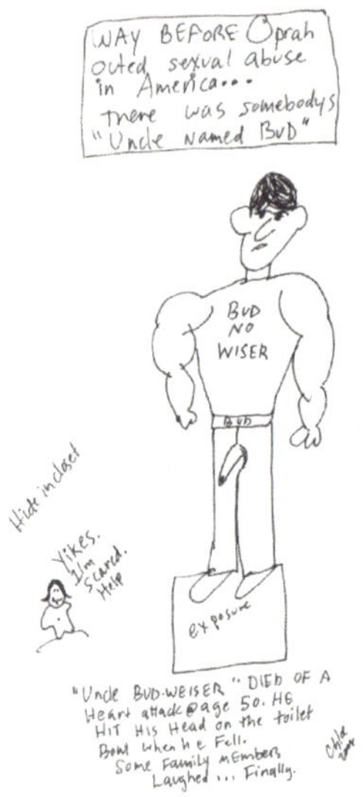

Chloe Dzubilo (d. 2011), *Bud-No-Wiser*, 2008. Ink on paper, 11 × 14 in. Courtesy of the Estate of Chloe Dzubilo, Fales Library and Special Collections, and Visual AIDS. Photo by Christopher Burke Studios.

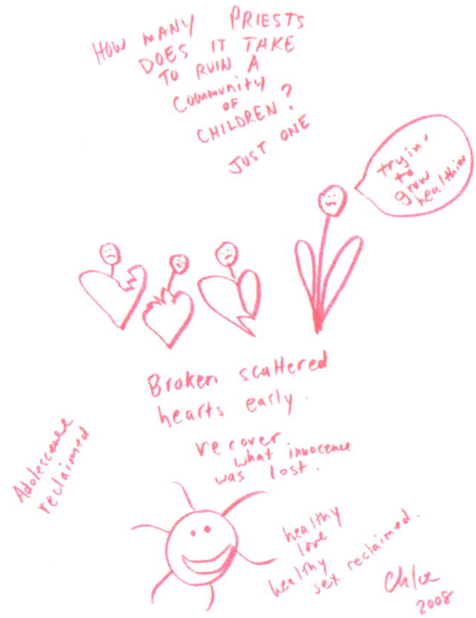

Chloe Dzubilo (d. 2011), *How Many Priests?*, 2008. Marker on paper, 11 × 14 in. Courtesy of the Estate of Chloe Dzubilo, Fales Library and Special Collections, and Visual AIDS. Photo by Christopher Burke Studios.

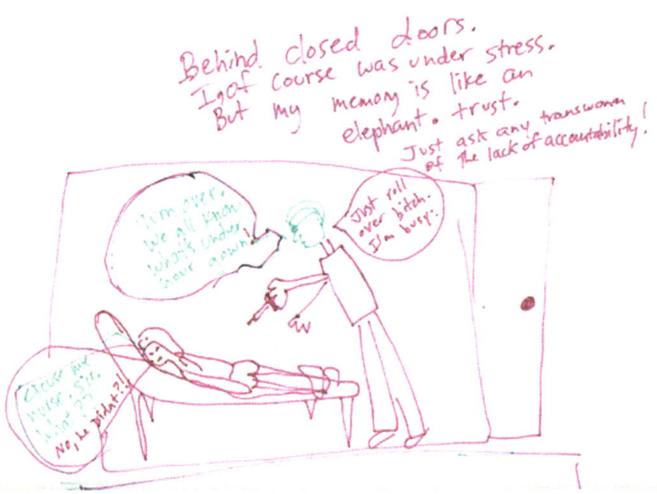

Chloe Dzubilo (d. 2011), *Behind Closed Doors*, 2010. Marker on paper, 14 × 11 in. Courtesy of the Estate of Chloe Dzubilo, Fales Library and Special Collections, and Visual AIDS. Photo by Christopher Burke Studios.

11

The Education of Mz. Chloe

T De Long

Chloe Dzubilo's bio as a list: "activist, sex abuse survivor, mentor, poet, singer, songwriter, counselor, systems buster, sexologist, gender observer, feminist, transgender, advocate for trans people, patriarchal busting smart ass fox bitch, entrapper of white 'straight id'd' medical provider, writer, animal lover, wild horse lover, equestrian teacher, student of addiction, queer activist, maternal mentor for other women's abuses."

As a partner, artistic collaborator, and executor of the Estate of Chloe Dzubilo, I appear in some of the work as a subject matter—us navigating the world as a trans couple, yet to the world we could be perceived and sexualized many different ways. The constant needing to settle our "gendered" relationship before interacting with us on a serious level became all too predictable. The work that appears in this book was made in the span of three years at the end of Chloe's life.

I encouraged and witnessed the creation of these drawings, made with a keen sense of urgency, so intense that some were finished in a matter of seconds, pouring out and filling a pad in a few hours. I can see her right now, sitting at her desk scattered with pens and markers, completely in the moment, head down, clenched lip, laughing or crying. "I needed a good cry," she would say. These are stories of stigma, prejudice, discrimination, and abuse—giving a life and voice to a collective, cascading trauma. An unfiltered, graphically unfettered illustration of uncomfortable truths from a hand with a willed intention of reaching those who would become a future audience. Struggling to connect with material that resonates. Too often the art and academia fields alienate those whom the work was intended to serve.

It was Chloe's mission to be of service to others and to share, at times, from

Chloe Dzubilo (d. 2011), *Kickboxing*, 2008. Ink on paper, 11 × 14 in. Courtesy of the Estate of Chloe Dzubilo, Fales Library and Special Collections, and Visual AIDS. Photo by Christopher Burke Studios.

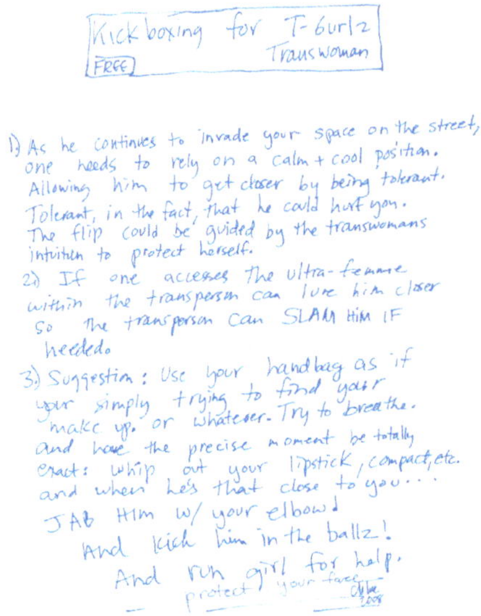

Chloe Dzubilo (d. 2011), *Two Young T-Girls*, 2008. Ink and marker on paper, 11 × 14 in. Courtesy of the Estate of Chloe Dzubilo, Fales Library and Special Collections, and Visual AIDS. Photo by Christopher Burke Studios.

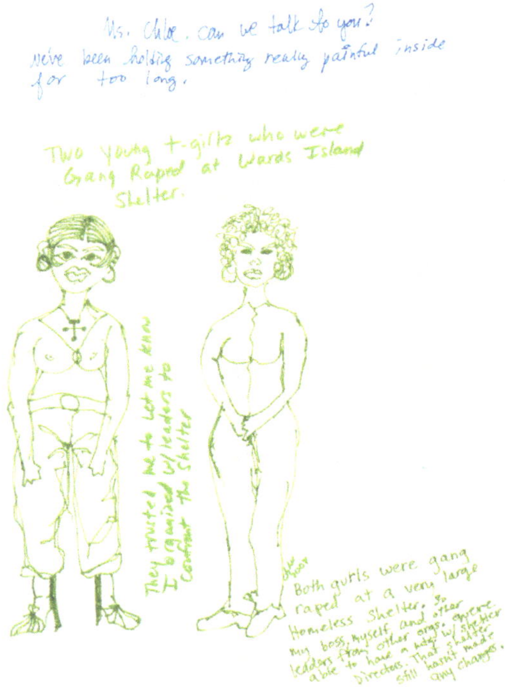

an unpopular place. It was not popular to criticize the medical establishment, to identify the harmful side effects of drugs. It was, however, common to pathologize transgendered people. Her ideas were ahead of her time, and only now, years or decades later, that work is still unfolding and starting to make sense, as research has evolved to prove that what she experienced and documented was true. I couldn't foresee at the time the impact that her documenting these realities would have. The truth hurts sometimes, and there is no need for a protective frame. Chloe's work was and becomes ever more consequential and reaffirming to those open enough to see it, or who need to see it. Chloe began working with Visual AIDS in 2010 as a living artist with HIV, and the organization continues to share her voice and work. Her papers, archives, and artwork are placed with New York University's Fales Library and Special Collections and with Participant Inc. in New York City.

In Chloe's own words:

> My spirit is a trooper in the fight as long as I continue to be honest and real and to sacrifice for others' rights if I must. Then that is my purpose.
>
> To inspire others to be strong. To stand up against all types of oppression.
>
> I want to be useful.
>
> I feel for anyone who has been oppressed;
> there is no greater struggle that was faced with defeat.

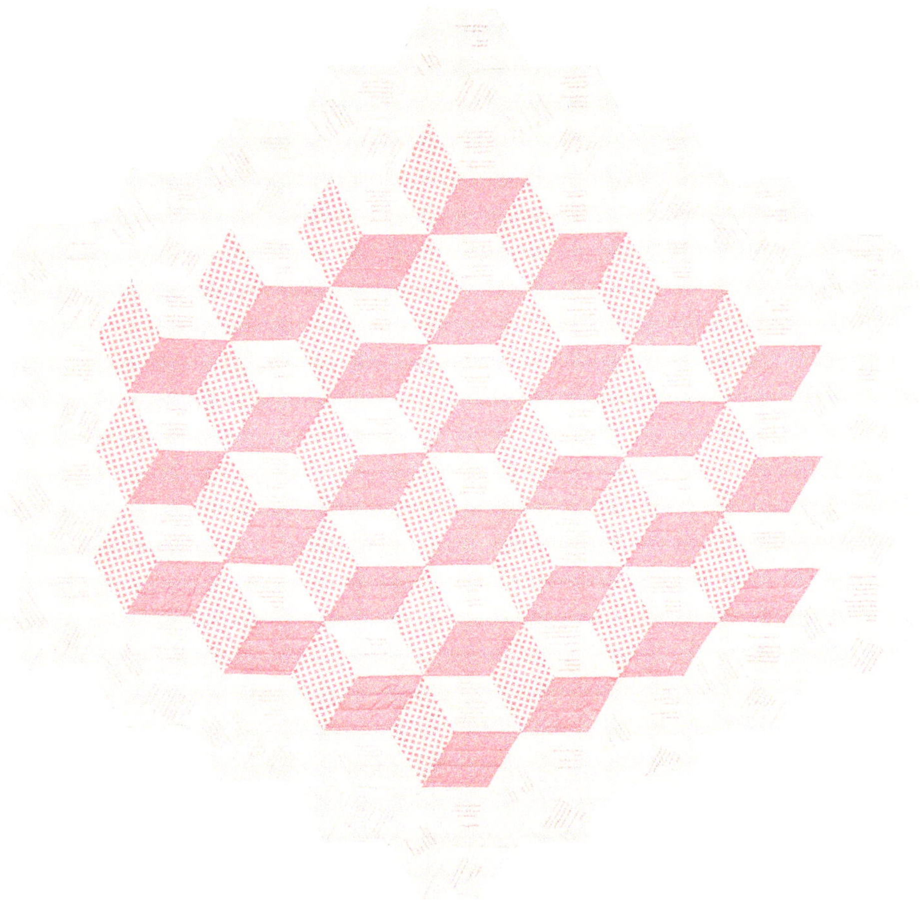

Ruta Butkus Marino, *Hush-a-Bye, Baby I*, 2016. Cotton, digital printing, machine piecing, and hand quilting, 77 × 76 in. Tumbling block quilts have traditionally been made to welcome babies into the world. The words are quotations of female survivors of childhood sexual assault. Photo by John Seyfried.

12

Discomforters
Stories of Sexual Abuse through the Medium of Quilts

Ruta Butkus Marino
and Jennifer Karash-Eastman

In 2015, the artist Ruta Butkus Marino became aware of Project Unbreakable, a web-based sexual assault campaign, as she was organizing an exhibition of photographs for an It's On Us program to combat campus sexual assault at John Carroll University, in Cleveland, Ohio. Consumed by thoughts about the survivors of Project Unbreakable—and their stories—Marino created a large (63 × 90 in.) quilt that incorporated the actual words of survivors whose assaults happened at home. She sewed thirty-five traditional house-blocks, each seven-by-nine inches in size, in nontraditional colors. Instead of cheerful houses with yellow fabric squares representing lights in windows, the walls of these pieced houses are constructed of dark red fabric. The windows, doors, and roofs are black, as a contradiction to the assumed safety of the home. Each house is bordered by digitally printed statements from Project Unbreakable survivors of sexual assault, as well as by pieced Xs and Os, the traditional way to sign hearts and kisses when signing off handwritten letters. A symbol indicates a female or male survivor, and the speaker's relationship to the survivor is included, either attacker (father, brother, uncle, aunt, cousin, friend of the family, boyfriend, husband) or witness (grandmother, mother, friend, police officer). The words are small, compelling the viewer to come close to the quilt to read the statements. The quilt's title, *Home Is Where It Happens*, is stitched into the borders on two sides, with mirror images on the opposite sides (see p. 122).

The eighty-two statements on the two-inch borders around the houses include

Ruta Butkus Marino, *Hush-a-Bye, Baby I* (detail), 2016. Photo by John Seyfried.

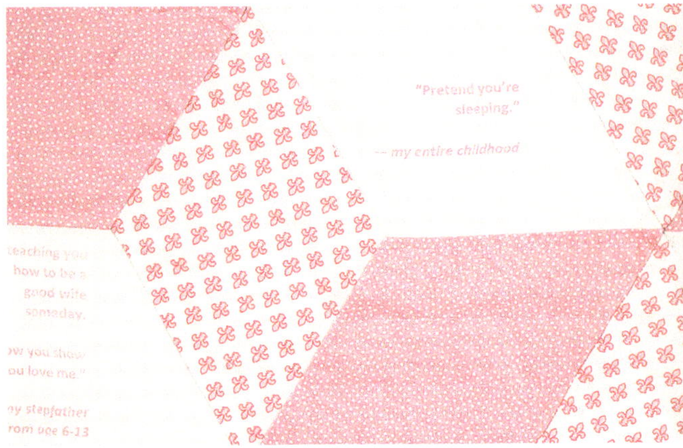

"You are only here for men's pleasure!" —My father, giving me to family members and his friends.

"Daddy wants to play a special game." "It's our special time." "You can tell how much I love you." "You don't MATTER to anyone else." —7 years of his tricks.

He said it was my duty, as "a good, Christian wife"—whether I liked it or not.

"This is what me and your aunt do. Doesn't it feel good to be a grown-up?"

"You are going to drive men crazy. I'll teach you how to be a woman." —my grandmother. I was 4. The "education" continued until I was 10.

"Do you have *ANY* IDEA what YOU'VE DONE to this 'family'?" —my grandpa, after I told him my stepdad had been raping me for YEARS.

"Tell them you lied about it because he wouldn't let you play his video games." —my mother. I was 13 & just tried to report the abuse my brother put me through. Nothing came of me trying to report my brother.

"Our family is blessed. You could be pregnant and I could be in jail. God had mercy." —my ex-step-father after the court downgraded 7 years of childhood sexual abuse [to] battery . . . even though I testified and he confessed.

"I'm sorry I'm a bad Daddy." —the morning after my father sexually molested me. I was 12.

"Now we must pray and you must ask GOD for FORGIVENESS for the things you've done." —said my step-father after he'd sexually assaulted me . . .

Home Is Where It Happens became an annual art exhibition at a local community college, garnering much attention from visitors, who were drawn in by the "traditional-looking" quilt but gasped audibly when they read the texts. The gallery director organized a discussion session with the artist and a local women's center. The session was well received. Based on this response, Marino knew she had to continue making quilts, as there were more Project Unbreakable stories to share with this wider audience. Making the horror of this epidemic visible with quilts resonated with viewers who had never before been exposed to the range and violence of rape culture. She carefully researched traditional quilt blocks whose names reflected the themes of specific stories. Every part of her quilt-making process was intentional. The quilts she made are hand quilted but machine pieced, with words digitally printed on white cotton fabric.

Titled *Discomforters*, the quilt series she created engages communities in trauma-informed/trauma-sensitive dialogue. The goal of *Discomforters* is both to address abuse, victim blaming, and misogynist cultural norms and to prevent further sexual assaults.

From the Internet to the Art Gallery

Discomforters began as an idea designed to share Project Unbreakable with a non-internet audience. But Grace Brown, a nineteen-year-old college student and friend of a sexual assault survivor, developed it as an online project. Brown compiled and published thousands of photographs of survivors of sexual assault, each holding a sign describing their experiences through statements made by perpetrators. Following the guidelines of Project Unbreakable, most of the words did not reflect the survivors' feelings or reactions, but rather were what the perpetrator, family member, friend, or police officer said in response to their disclosure. The effect of using these words along with a photograph of the survivor was both shocking and disturbing, giving details and context that challenged societal norms about sexual assault survivors. Those details were consistent with the fact that sexual assault, child abuse, and domestic violence survivors are frequently blamed for what has happened to them, both by society at large and by the very individuals who perpetuate these crimes. By using the words of the perpetrators, the survivors were able to expose this logical fallacy. Through various manifestations, the project's mission was "to increase awareness of the issues surrounding sexual assault, child abuse, and domestic violence, and encourage the act of healing through art."[1]

Brown collected more than four thousand submissions from all over the world, before discontinuing the site in 2015. While she received a great deal of media attention and support from project participants, some criticized her work as inauthentic because she was not a survivor herself.[2] Others implied she was exploiting the stories for her own ends.[3] According to Brown, the intent of the project was to expose the world to the brutal experiences of sexual assault survivors. Brown allowed participants to disclose the words and actions of perpetrators, as well as the words and reactions of the people they told, to illuminate the horrific levels of victim or survivor blaming in our society.[4] The photographs of the survivors bear testimony to the fact that sexual assault is gender-neutral, race-neutral, age-neutral, and socioeconomic status–neutral.

Quilting Inspiration

The *Discomforters* series quilts continue a rich tradition of quilts that speak to issues important to their makers. Generations of women have made and continue to make quilts simply to comfort, protect, and celebrate their loved ones.[5] As evidenced by the Smithsonian National Museum of American History's National Quilt Collection, quilting is an integral tradition in the United States. The collection consists of over five hundred quilts and quilting-related items, incorporating "quilts from various ethnic groups and social classes, for quilts are not the domain of a specific race or class, but can be a part of anyone's heritage and treasured as such. Whether of rich or humble fabrics, large in size or small, expertly crafted or not, well-worn or pristine, quilts in the National Quilt Collection provide a textile narrative that contributes to America's complex and diverse history."[6]

For many, quilts are simply a practical item used as a blanket, but often they are much more, including visual documentation of historical and cultural events as well as representations of popular mythology. The Underground Railroad Quilt Code was thought to communicate information to slaves via symbols and pictures on how to escape to freedom but has no actual basis in fact. The myth has survived through oral history, and although no actual quilts from the time period are currently known to exist, many children's books about the Underground Railroad continue to use the Quilt Code as their story line.[7] Quilting is a therapeutic art for some artists to manage mental illness.[8] In addition, as part of spiritual communities, women's church groups have made quilts for charitable causes for over two centuries, chronicled by quilt historians, such as those who documented the work of nineteenth-century Ohio Ladies' Aid Societies.[9]

Collective projects such as the Boise Peace Quilt Project, conceived by two quilters from Boise, Idaho, in the 1980s, quietly raised awareness of the nuclear arms race between the United States and the Soviet Union with an offer of friendship to the people of the Union of Soviet Socialist Republics. The project inspired others to use quilts as the means to advocate for peace or to protest other issues.[10] The largest community arts project in the world, the AIDS Memorial Quilt Project (1987), garnered international attention and has forever linked quilting with the goals of the United States' human rights and social justice movements.[11] Betsy Greer coined the term *craftivism* in 2003 to describe this "practice of engaged creativity, especially regarding political or social causes."[12]

Quilts have become a powerful medium to raise awareness for human rights and social justice issues. The quilts in Marino's *Discomforters* series offer support and empathy to survivors of sexual assaults while calling out their perpetrators. They serve as a revelation to those who have yet to realize the extent and circumstances of these crimes. Statistically, the Rape, Abuse and Incest National Network (RAINN) reports that every ninety-two seconds, a sexual crime occurs in the United States. While the number of rapes has fallen by more than half since 1993, only five out of every thousand perpetrators of rape face jail time.[13] Awareness, education, and prevention, along with survivor services and advocacy, are the tools that Marino ties to the *Discomforters* quilt series in her effort to end sexual violence.

The Creation of *Discomforters*

Over more than three decades, Marino has created quilts for her family and friends and also many original art quilts that have been showcased in invitational and juried exhibitions. *Discomforters* became Marino's first set of activist quilts. She researched traditional quilt blocks whose names reflected the themes of the specific stories and selected fabric colors to match the themes. Every part of the quilt-making process was intentional.

Like generations of quilters who create "tumbling block" quilts to celebrate the birth of a child, Marino sewed one in 1986 to welcome the birth of her son and another in 2017 to welcome the birth of her first granddaughter. This traditional block made an ideal platform to spotlight the appalling abuse that happens to young children, girls and boys alike. She used it for her next two quilts in this series.

Hush-a-Bye, Baby I uses a baby pink fleur-de-lis pattern printed on white fabric as the medium value and a pink fabric with white polka dots as the dark

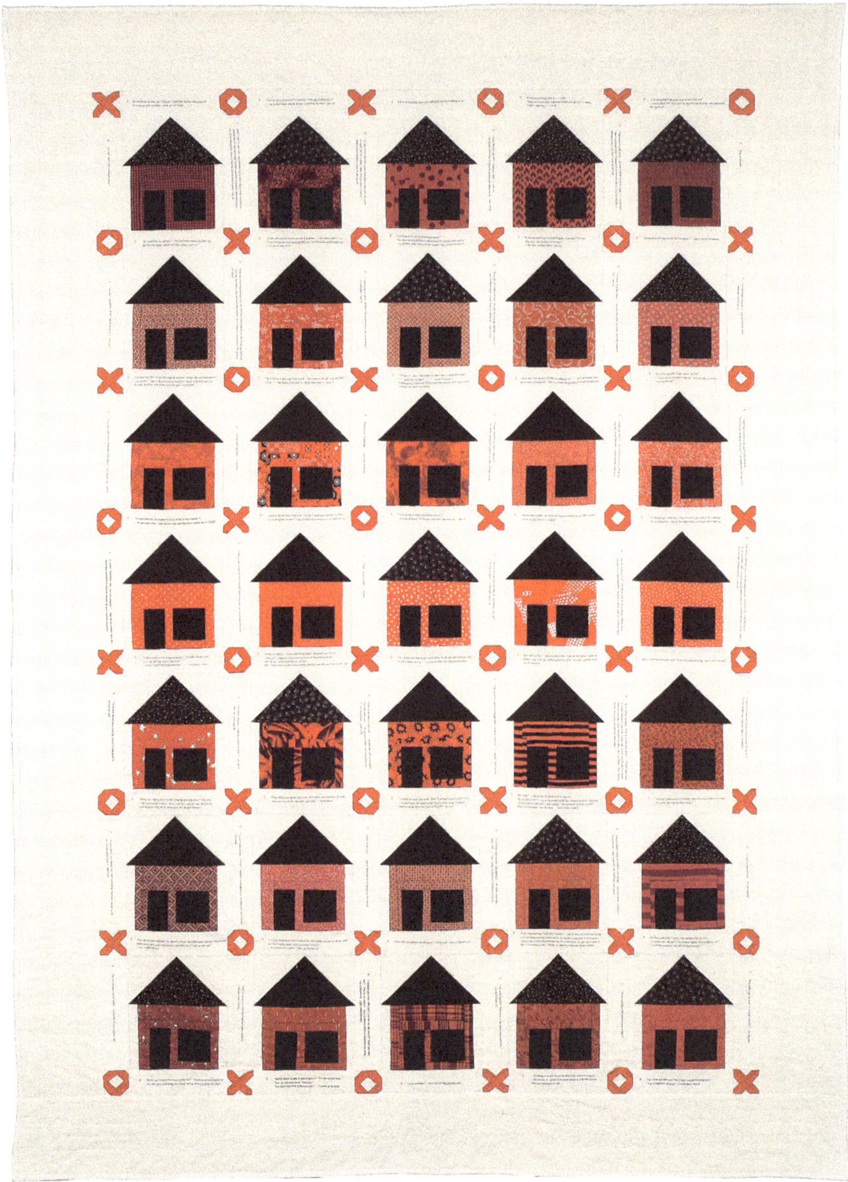

Ruta Butkus Marino, *Home Is Where It Happens*, 2016. Cotton, digital printing, machine piecing, and hand quilting, 63 × 90 in. This traditional house quilt block undermines the assumed safety of the home. The words are direct quotations from survivors of sexual assaults committed at home or perpetrated by family members or acquaintances. Photo by John Seyfried.

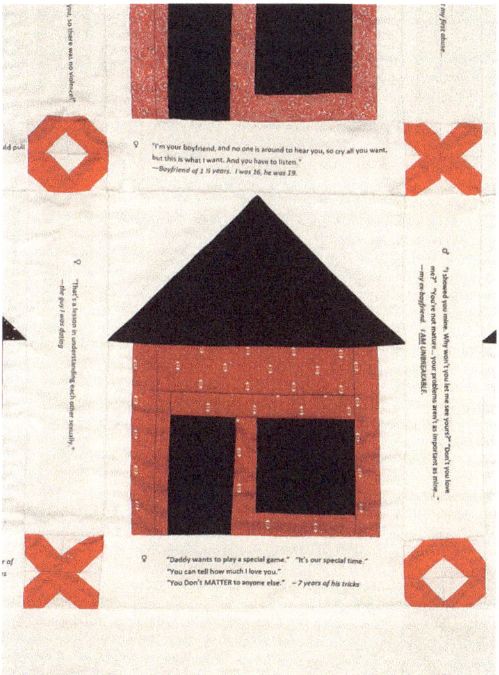

Ruta Butkus Marino, *Home Is Where It Happens* (detail), 2016. Photo by John Seyfried.

side of each ten-inch, three-dimensional-looking block, in this quilt about abuse suffered by girls. The edges of the girl's quilt form an irregular shape, with a border around the thirty three-dimensional pink blocks of twenty-two white tumbling blocks, printed with statements on all three sides of each block. On the white fabric top side of each block, Marino added digitally printed words in pink (see p. 116, at beginning of chapter).

Hush-a-Bye, Baby II is a quilt about the abuse of boys. The narrow, vertical shape of the boy's quilt, with its twenty-two tumbling blocks, is deliberately evocative of a penis. Baby blue flowers on white fabric and blue fabric with white polka dots form two sides, with blue printed words on the white side.

A description of the speaker, who may be the perpetrator of abuse or the seemingly trustworthy confidant, is integrated directly into each block on both quilts. The disparate sizes of the pink (76 × 77 in.) and the blue (27 × 75.25 in.) quilts may not reflect disparate rates of male and female abuse, but instead merely indicate that fewer men than women were brave enough to post about their childhood experiences on the Project Unbreakable website.

A sampling of the ninety-six statements on *Hush-a-Bye, Baby I*, the girls' quilt, includes the following:

“Pretend you’re sleeping” —my entire childhood.

“I’m teaching you to be a good wife someday.”

“You’re going to make me a lot of money.” —Director & “Daddy” of the porn business I was sold to . . . I was 7.

“Just kiss it.” —my nana’s best friend’s son. I was around 6–8. He was aged 14–16.

“Open your legs.”—(I was 5 yrs old) —said my babysitter so her brother could insert.

“Honey, what makes you think you have the RIGHT to say ‘NO’ to me? I am an ADULT, you are a CHILD.”

He said he would give me twinkies.

“Let’s play a game. Just a game. You don’t have to nap right now.” —my abuser when I was 4 in my great-grandmother’s bed.

My mom died when I was 9. (My dad gave her an STD.) 2 months later: My dad: “This is what daddys and daughters do.”

The first time I was molested, I was about 5. By 2 of my older cousins. Then by my grandfather. I was about 12.

A sampling of the twenty-two statements on *Hush-a-Bye, Baby II*, the boys’ quilt, includes the following:

“I’ll kill your sisters” —my stepfather on my 13th B-Day. Little did I know they were told almost the same thing.

“I’m just trying to teach you how to wank, like my brother taught me.” —Teacher and family friend.

“Why do you let the cat in your bed but not me?”

“This is what my friends and I did at your age.”

“That doesn’t make sense—you were never out of our sight!” —my parents.

“No one will ever love you like I do, you know that right? This is all you get.” —I was eight years old.

There was only silence as he stuck his tongue down my throat and then other things. I was 4.

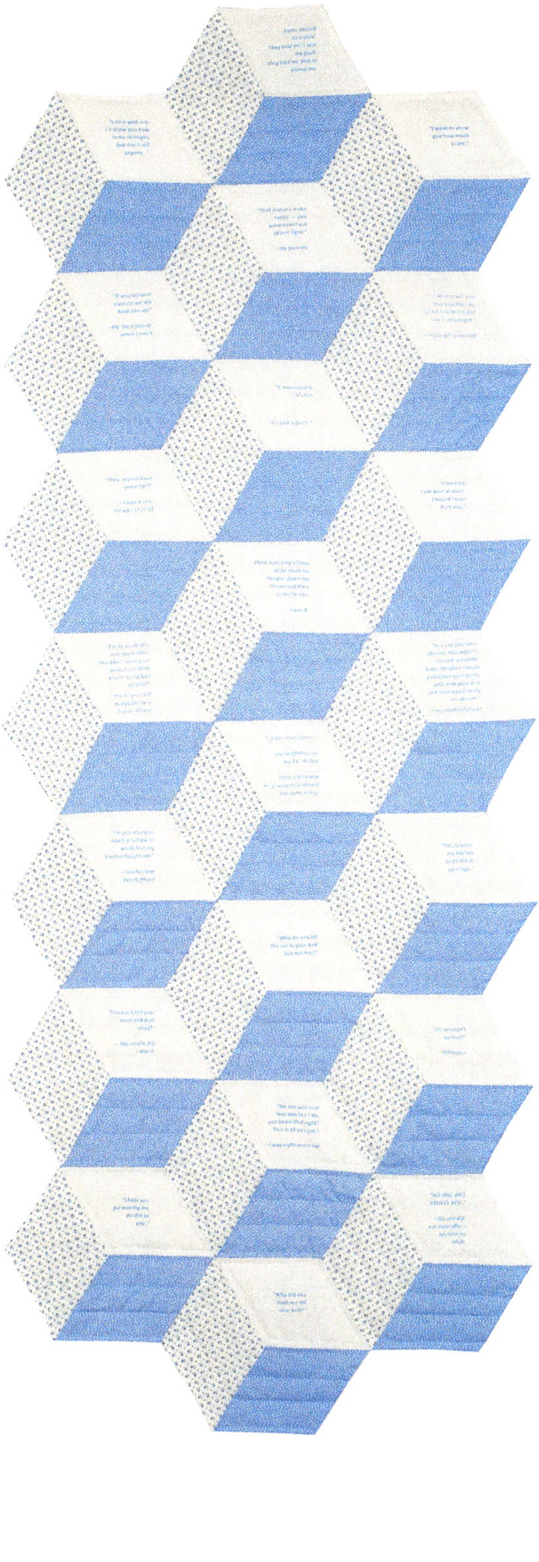

Ruta Butkus Marino, *Hush-a-Bye, Baby II*, 2016. Tumbling block quilt, cotton, digital printing, machine piecing, and hand quilting, 27 × 75.25 in. The words are direct quotations from male survivors of childhood sexual assault. Photo by John Seyfried.

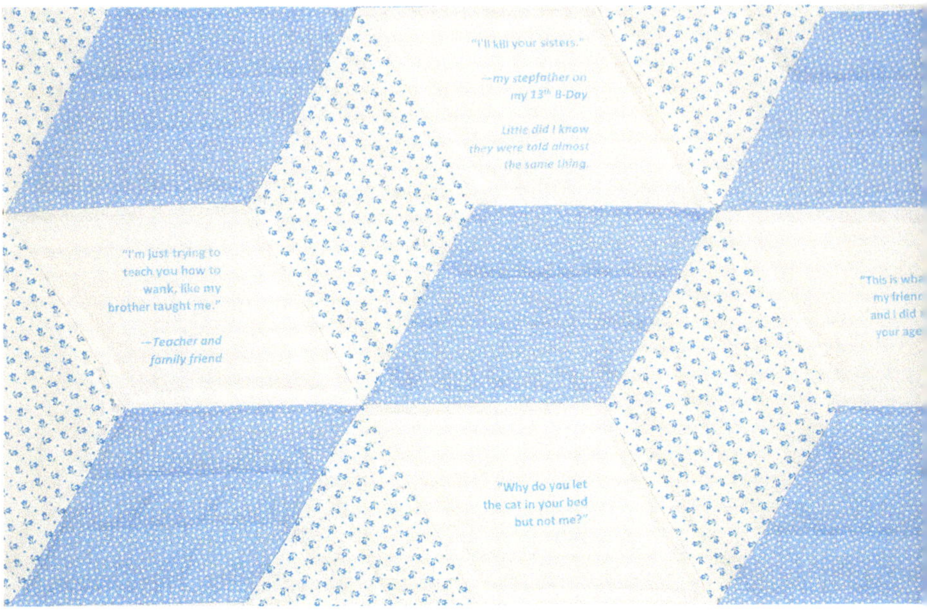

Ruta Butkus Marino, *Hush-a-Bye, Baby II* (detail), 2016.
Photo by John Seyfried.

> "Come on do this one more time. You don't want your parents to think you're being bad do you?" —my 17 year old babysitter to a 5 year old me.
>
> "He wouldn't do that!" —Grandma.
>
> "I hate you for making me do this to you."

Quilters have used countless variations of star blocks, giving their interpretations many different names. Marino's *Silence Is Golden* (72 × 52 in.) uses six eighteen-inch "silent star" blocks, done in tone-on-tone gold and yellow fabrics, with words in gold font on white fabric incorporated into six sections of each block. The words were intended to silence the survivors, as spoken either by the perpetrators or by people to whom the survivors turned for help and support. The speakers' identities are deliberately omitted, but all represent close family members and friends and, in one case, a parent's boss.

A sampling of the thirty-six statements on *Silence Is Golden* includes

> "We have to keep this between us. My kids won't have a father & you will ruin a marriage."

"Can I write you a check to keep you quiet?"

"IF YOU TELL ANYONE . . . I'LL KILL YOU."

"If you tell anyone, I'll fire your dad."

"Call the cops. Do it. Do it. Do it. You'll be dead before they get there."

"If you tell I'll kill mommy, nannie & grandpa."

"If you tell your parents we will beat you up!"

"I'll slit your fucking throat."

"Now we can't make it known that you're more special than your sisters."

"If you say anything, I'll kill your mother."

"If you say anything to my girlfriend, I'll seriously hurt you. She won't let me put it in her butt."

Blame Game (42 × 60 in.) has six eighteen-inch blocks sewn in pink and maroon batik printed fabric, with dark red words printed on white fabric in four sections of the pinwheel shape within each block, underscoring the violence of the statements. *Blame Game* reflects the skepticism that abounds

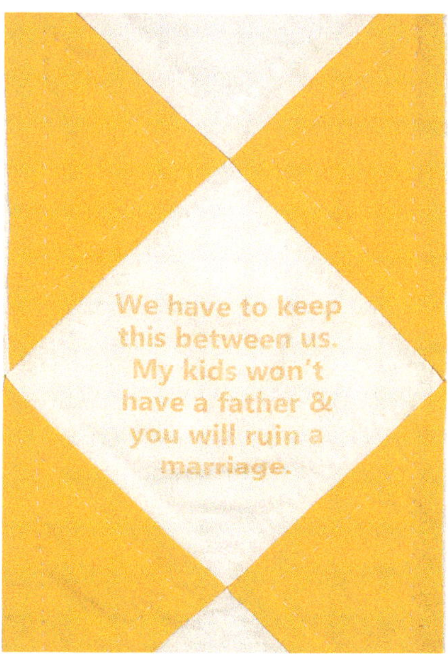

Ruta Butkus Marino, *Silence Is Golden* (detail), 2016. Cotton, digital printing, machine piecing, and hand quilting, 72 × 52 in. Quilt block: silent star. The words, intended to silence victims, were spoken by the perpetrators of the sexual assault or by the people to whom the victims turned for help and support. Photo by John Seyfried.

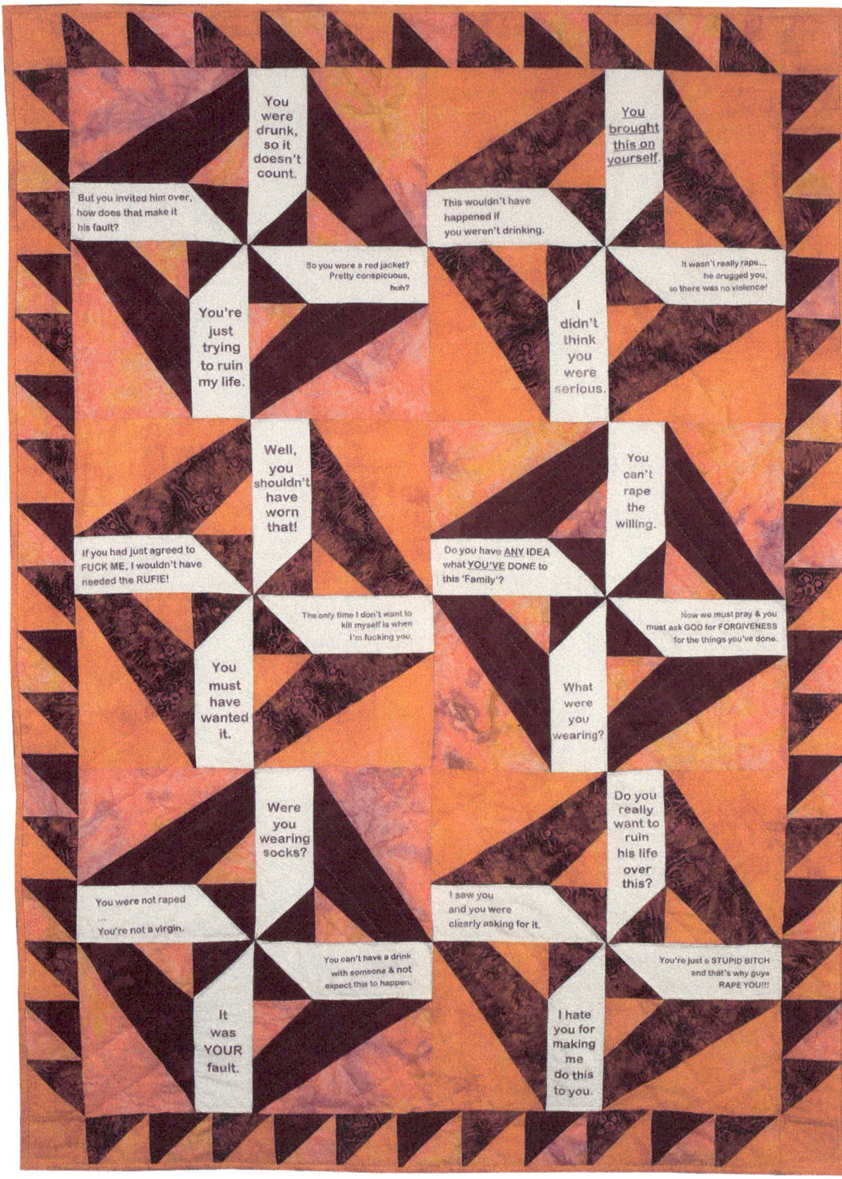

Ruta Butkus Marino, *Blame Game*, 2017. Cotton, digital printing, machine piecing, and hand quilting, 42 × 60 in. These words, spoken by the perpetrators of the assault or by the people to whom the victims turned for help or support, were intended to blame or shame the victims. Photo by John Seyfried.

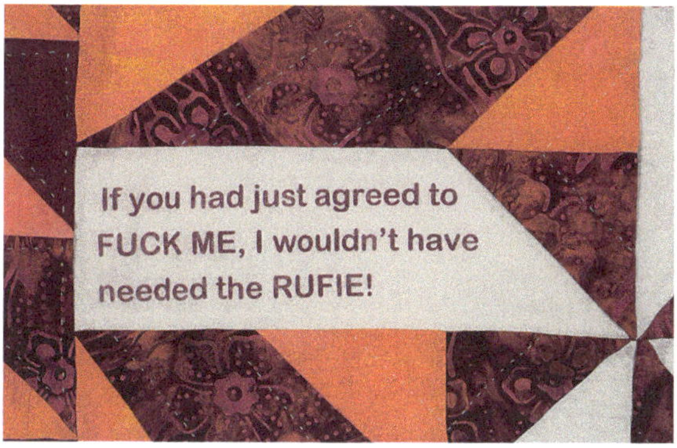

Ruta Butkus Marino, *Blame Game* (detail), 2017. Photo by John Seyfried.

in the United States regarding what qualifies as sexual assault, as well as the tendency to blame the survivor instead of the abuser. It also reflects the reality that a child in the United States becomes a survivor of sexual violence every nine minutes. A trauma-sensitive approach to any survivor is, "Listen. Be there. Communicate without judgment."[14] But that approach rarely occurs. In *Blame Game*, a traditional quilt block titled "my mistake" represents the words intended to blame or shame the survivors by both perpetrators and confidants.

A sampling of the twenty-four statements on *Blame Game* includes

> "If you had just agreed to FUCK ME, I wouldn't have needed the RUFIE!"
>
> "You were drunk, so it doesn't count."
>
> "So you wore a red jacket? Pretty conspicuous, huh?"
>
> "But you invited him over, how does that make it his fault?"
>
> "It wasn't really rape . . . he drugged you, so there was no violence!"
>
> "What were you wearing?"
>
> "This wouldn't have happened if you weren't drinking."
>
> "You're just trying to ruin my life."
>
> "You were not raped . . . You're not a virgin."
>
> "Do you have *ANY* IDEA what *YOU'VE* DONE to this 'Family'?"

In Marino's *Love Doesn't Shove* quilt (46.5 × 61.5 in.), hearts created by the words themselves, rather than traditionally pieced or appliquéd heart blocks, express the words of intimate partner violence. Black and blue words were the natural color choice. Noelle Ivec created thirty-three hearts in Photoshop and digitally printed them in several sizes on white fabric. The quilt binding was made from the same printed fabric. The hand quilting creates large interlocking ring pairings of the "no" symbol in red thread. The quilt shares a name with an organization dedicated to raising awareness about teen dating violence, of which Gabriella Kreuz, a John Carroll University alumna, was the founder. As the survivor of intimate partner violence while in college, Kreuz learned how to leave an abusive relationship through a group sponsored by the university's Violence Prevention and Action Center. She continues to pay the lesson forward with this organization.[15]

A sampling of the many statements on *Love Doesn't Shove* includes

> "I'm about to kill myself and make you listen to me pull the trigger . . . You deserve that after putting me through this." *He did not kill himself. My emotionally abusive ex-boyfriend of 9 years after I started dating again after HE dumped me.
>
> "IT'S MY BIRTHDAY, YOU HAVE TO GIVE ME SEX." —MY BOYFRIEND.
>
> "This is my world bitch, you just live in it." —It took me 7 years of abuse to leave.
>
> "What, am I raping you? I'm just showing you how much I love you." —My husband of 10 years . . . after I told him I wanted out. He told me nobody would love me as much as he did. He was wrong!
>
> "WHAT? I'VE NEVER BEEN REJECTED BEFORE! YOU SHOULD WANT TO GET WITH ME!"
>
> "YOU'RE MY WIFE."
>
> "This is something I want to do at least once in my life, if you won't do it, I'll find someone else who will."
>
> "The only way you'll ever leave me is in a body bag." Oh yeah?
>
> "IT'S NOT 'RAPE' IF WE LOVE EACH OTHER."
>
> "Look at me please. I need you to look at me. You scared me . . . I thought I did something wrong." You did.
>
> "That's a lesson in understanding each other sexually" (the guy I was dating).

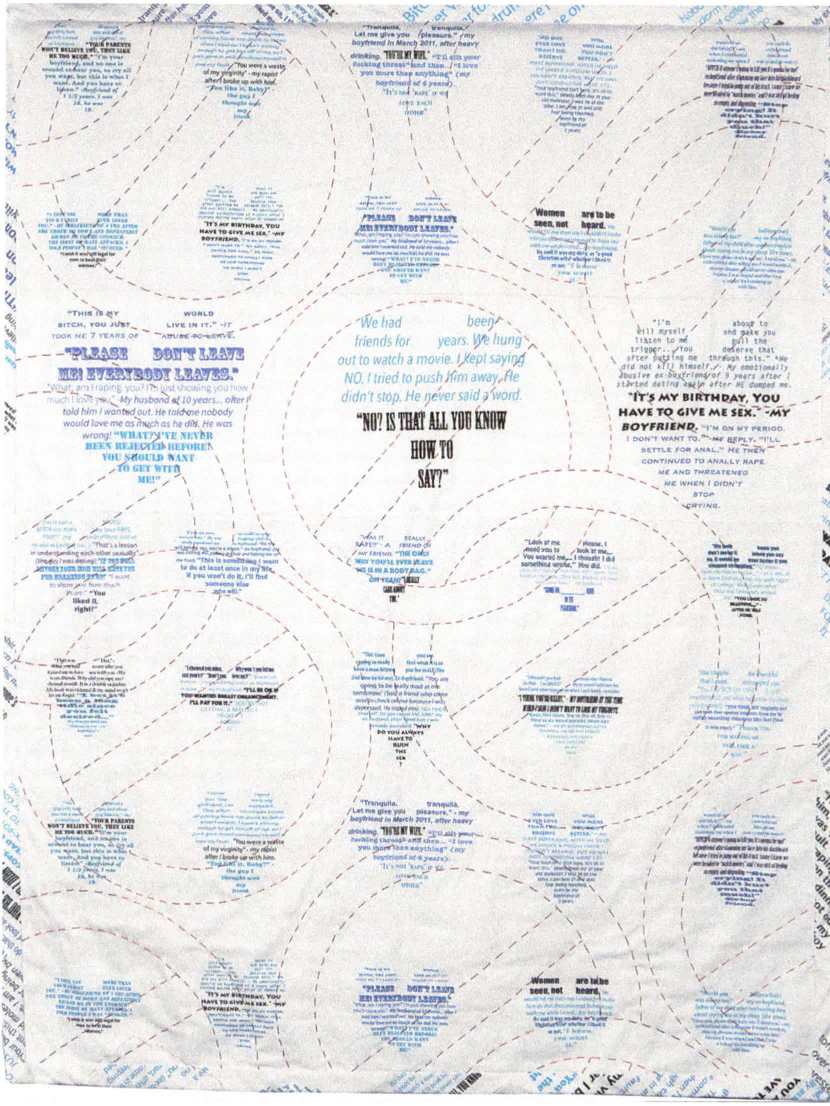

Ruta Butkus Marino, *Love Doesn't Shove*, 2017. Cotton, machine piecing, and hand quilting, 46.5 × 61.5 in. The words forming the hearts are direct quotations by perpetrators (responding parties) to their victims (reporting parties), who were in intimate relationships with one another. Digital manipulation by Noelle Ivec. Digital printing by Spoonflower. Photo by Rick Zack.

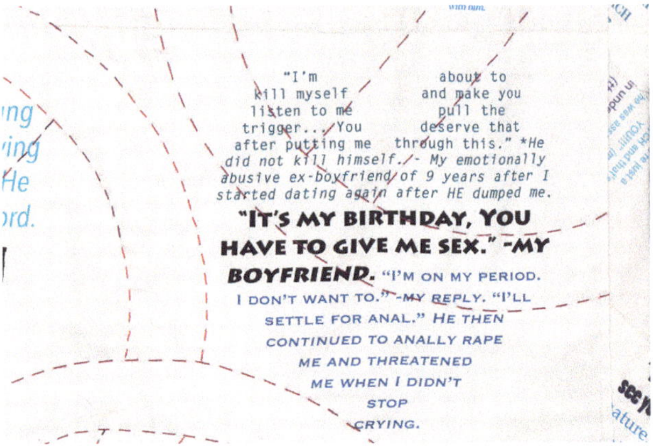

Ruta Butkus Marino, *Love Doesn't Shove* (detail), 2017. Photo by Rick Zack.

The Project Unbreakable website featured posts of survivors' own words about healing and moving forward. The repetition of "I believe you," the empowerment quilt's one simple yet compelling sentence, may be the most direct and powerful expression of support that can be given to all survivors, although few submissions actually featured such supportive words spoken by others.

Believing survivors is the theme of *Empowering* (23 × 68 in.), which repeats a traditional quilting block called "David and Goliath" five times. The name of the block underscores survivors' ability to overcome those who sought to overpower them. The blocks are eleven-inch squares, and the white outer borders repeat the title in quilting stitches, with green stitching between some of the letters to both emphasize and hide the word. The quilt's green fabrics and words convey a sense of growth and rejuvenation. One viewer wrote: "The simplicity of the repetition of 'I believe you' in the Empowerment quilt is a relief after the terrible stories told in all the others. It allows the viewer to feel a fraction of the relief that survivors must have felt when someone believed them."

Marino's *One in Five* (48 × 61 in.) dispenses with words entirely, featuring the shocking and now inadequate statistic that one in five women will experience sexual assault of some kind in her lifetime. (It is now closer to one in three.) Marino used a very old, battered quilt, giving it new life as the backdrop for the embroidered tally marks counting off by fives on the emoji Everywoman. No words are necessary—the power of the tally marks confront the viewer. One visitor to an exhibition at the Ginko Gallery and Studio in Oberlin, Ohio, wrote on seeing the quilt: "*'One in Five' is the best example of conceptual art I've ever seen! It is very moving as are all the pieces, but this one is special."* Another viewer at a different venue commented: *"The quilt with no words really stood out to me because there are so many people who have not shared their story."*

Another repurposed vintage quilt, *If, Then* (82 × 82 in.), repeats a sentence coined by the career prosecutor Anne Munch, an attorney with twenty-seven years' experience as an advocate for victims of domestic violence, sexual assault, and stalking. Marino heard the phrase at a trauma-informed interviewing workshop led by Dave Markel in January 2019 and knew it belonged on a quilt.[16] Using teachers' bulletin board letters as templates, the three-and-a-half-inch block letters were machine appliquéd in red and beige fabrics that blend with the red and beige fabrics of the "feathered star" blocks, making the words fade in and out deliberately as the sentence is repeated across the quilt.

Combining the traditionally comforting medium of a handmade quilt with the explicit words of sexual violence creates a shocking contrast, as does sexual violence within the supposedly safe context of a friendship or family. The hope is that these quilts can offer comfort to survivors of sexual assault and acknowledge the painful experiences they suffered. Perhaps the heartbreaking comment left in the guestbook by one visitor will not be repeated by anyone else: *"My mother still doesn't believe me 30 yrs later."*

Community Response and Discussion

Marino included a trigger warning at the entrance of her *Discomforters* exhibition. Frequent triggering often manifests in post-traumatic stress disorder and evokes feelings of anxiety, panic, fear, disgust, and extreme sadness, along with detachment or emotional numbness. Thus, Marino's warning was meant not as self-censure, but rather as an alert to those who might have difficulty viewing her art. The warning read: "The quilts contain references to sexual violence and assault, which may be triggering to some people." This kind of warning prepares audiences for an experience that might evoke discomfort or, in this case, could take a sexual violence or assault survivor back to a traumatic experience. The *Discomforters* trigger warning also informed viewers about the purpose of Marino's work, especially for those who might not understand why artwork, and, more specifically, survivor statements, could trigger an emotional reaction. It was an example of shock and awe, or art for art's sake. It was a call to collaborative action against sexual violence by artists, educators, and community partners.

While there is a need to better understand the impact and implications of trigger warnings, especially on college campuses, the trigger warnings can also indicate that discomfort with certain triggers should not keep educational content hidden away.[17] To the contrary, they can suggest that education about sensitive topics such as sexual violence must continue in order to change systems of oppression and further inspire mechanisms for prevention, response, and advocacy. This is especially the case with sexual violence on college campuses, where 24 percent of women and roughly 5.5 percent of men experience rape or sexual assault through physical force, violence, or incapacitation.[18]

Thus, even with its trigger warning, *Discomforters* was designed to start or continue a community dialogue using a trauma-informed/trauma-sensitive approach to engage, address, and change sexist, abusive, and misogynistic behaviors to prevent further sexual assaults. The topic of sexual assault at home, in school, in the workplace, in the military, and in the church is timely, with new allegations surfacing and receiving much attention almost daily. Marino hoped that these quilts honored the voices of too many and by being exhibited as widely as possible could help reduce, if not eliminate, the necessity for others to tell similar stories.

Discomforters reflects Marino's belief in the importance of education for sexual violence prevention. Evidence suggests that education is an effective means of preventing sexual violence.[19] Many college campuses across the United States have started requiring sexual violence education for all students. Due to logistical challenges of scheduling training classes in person, many online training platforms are now available, and there is promising research on their effectiveness.[20] However, this education should begin well before college.

Comments by viewers of the *Discomforters* exhibition reinforce these observations:

Ruta: powerful! Amazing!

Wow! Should be seen by everyone. Thank you.

This needs to be seen on every college campus in America.

Disturbing. I'm glad I saw it.

Wow! Incredibly powerful . . . using the medium of a "homey" quilt provides an extra punch to the messages.

They also express the importance of the exhibition to younger audiences:

I now have an open mind on the subject of sexual abuse. (Male high school student)

Shocking, I knew a little about this topic but this gave me more details about sexual abuse and what women have to go through. (Younger male high school student, brother of the first)

Thank you, thank you. Thank you! (Mother of the two male high school students)

After *Discomforters* was launched, Marino soon understood that the exhibition alone was not sufficient to handle the quilts' impact on viewers. When she spoke to a university psychology class about her quilts, one young woman suddenly understood that an experience in her life was, in fact, an assault. Marino then realized the need to have local counseling services, as well as other survivor services such as hotline numbers, available to those attending lectures, panel discussions, and other events focusing on sexual violence.[21]

From then on, Marino's art-based approach of initiating discussions around sexual violence prevention included panel programs with the artist and community members to discuss how to assist those in need and offer information about licensed therapists and psychologists, legal counsel, survivors' advocates, hotline volunteers, and educators with expertise in sexual violence. Those who viewed the exhibition and attended discussions found trauma-informed ways to help protect their communities against violence and abuse, as well as how to help survivors find the appropriate services for their needs.

Conclusion

The *Discomforters* series offers viewers a way to consider and discuss the experiences of those who have suffered sexual abuse and how society in general, as well as family members, friends, and colleagues of survivors, can support survivors and prevent further sexual assault. Viewers of all ages were drawn in to see the "pretty, traditional" quilts, only to be shocked and disquieted when they started reading the words. Some needed to walk away. Many wrote #MeToo comments in the guestbook. Many thanked the artist or shared their own experience in person.

Marino's *Discomforters* series fosters real change through awareness, dialogue, and access to information. After finishing a quilt about human trafficking in 2020, Marino shifted her quilt making to create cheerful quilts of comfort, which she donated to survivors of abuse in 2021. She continued making more in 2022.

Marino began making these quilts in 2015, before the #MeToo and #TimesUp movements empowered thousands and gave hope that their voices were finally being heard. Thanks to the silence breakers of 2017, more women and men are being empowered to speak up. The time has come to stop the cultural norms that perpetuate sexual abuse and to create safer environments for all people—at home, in the workplace, in schools and universities, in the military, and in society overall.

Notes

1. Grace Brown, "About Project Unbreakable," Project Unbreakable, 2015, https://web.archive.org/web/20150821090721/http://project-unbreakable.org/about.

2. Grace Brown, Project Unbreakable, Tumblr, 2011–15, https://projectunbreakable.tumblr.com.

3. Maren Westra, "Photographer Grace Brown Gives Victims a Voice with Project Unbreakable," *Daily Nebraskan*, October 9, 2012, www.dailynebraskan.com/news/photographer-grace-brown-gives-victims-a-voice-with-project-unbreakable/article_1e3cfea8-11c7-11e2-9197-001a4bcf6878.html.

4. Grace Brown, Project Unbreakable, Instagram, 2017, www.instagram.com/projectunbreakable.

5. Roderick Kiracofe and Mary Elizabeth Johnson, *The American Quilt: A History of Cloth and Comfort, 1750–1950* (New York: Clarkson Potter, 2004).

6. Smithsonian, National Museum of American History, Behring Center, "About the National Quilt Collection," accessed August 13, 2019, https://americanhistory.si.edu/collections/object-groups/national-quilt-collection/about.

7. Leigh Fellner, "Betsy Ross Redux: The Underground Railroad 'Quilt Code,'" 2003–6, https://web.archive.org/web/20130120160626/http://ugrrquilt.hartcottagequilts.com/betsy%20ross%20redux.pdf; Frances Dowdell, "Quilts in Children's Books, Part Two: The Underground Railroad Quilt Code," *Quilt Fiction* (blog), accessed August 23, 2019, https://quiltfiction.com/blog/underground-railroad-quilt-code.

8. Janet Catherine Berlo, "Quilting to Save My Life," *Chronicle of Higher Education*, March 30, 2001, B11–B13.

9. Ricky Clark, George W. Knepper, and Ellice Ronsheim, *Quilts in Community: Ohio's Traditions* (Nashville: Rutledge Hill Press, 1991).

10. World Quilts: The American Story, "Peace and Protest," International Quilt Museum, University of Nebraska–Lincoln, accessed May 30, 2023, https://worldquilts.quiltstudy.org/americanstory/engagement/peaceprotest.

11. Robert McRuer, "Disability and the NAMES Project," *Public Historian* 27, no. 2 (2005): 53–61.

12. Betsy Greer, ed., *Craftivism: The Art of Craft and Activism* (Vancouver, BC: Arsenal Pulp Press, 2014).

13. RAINN, "Scope of the Problem: Statistics—How Often Does Sexual Assault Occur in the United States?," accessed May 30, 2023, www.rainn.org/statistics/scope-problem.

14. RAINN, "Perpetrators of Sexual Violence: Statistics," accessed May 30, 2023, www.rainn.org/statistics/perpetrators-sexual-violence.

15. Gabriella Kreuz, "Love Doesn't Shove," accessed August 23, 2019, www.lovedoesntshove.org.

16. Anne Munch and Patti Powers, "Consent and the Court of Public Opinion," *Resource* (Newsletter of the National Sexual Assault Resource Center), Fall/Winter 2005, www.nsvrc.org/sites/default/files/2012-03/Publications_NSVRC_The-Resource_Fall-Winter-2005.pdf.

17. Marshall Alcorn and Sue Grand, "Guest Editors' Introduction to Special Section on Cultural Shifts in Pedagogy: Controversy, Safe Spaces, and Trigger Warnings," *Psychoanalysis, Culture and Society* 23, no. 2 (2018): 180–84; American Association of University Professors, "On Trigger Warnings," accessed August 13, 2019, www.aaup.org/report/trigger-warnings; Sarah McMahon and G. Lawrence Farmer, "An Updated Measure for Assessing Subtle Rape Myths," *Social Work Research* 35, no. 2 (2011): 71–81.

18. David Cantor, Bonnie Fisher, Susan Chibnall, Reanne Townsend, Hyunshik Lee, Carol Bruce, and Gail Thomas, *Report on the AAU Campus Climate Survey on Sexual Assault and Sexual Misconduct* (Washington, DC: Association of American Universities, 2015).

19. Victoria L. Banyard, Robert P. Eckstein, and Mary M. Moynihan, "Sexual Violence Prevention: The Role of Stages of Change," *Journal of Interpersonal Violence* 25, no. 1 (2009): 111–35.

20. Daniel Zapp, Robert Buelo, Lauren Soutiea, Alan Berkowitz, and William DeJong, "Exploring the Potential Campus-Level Impact of Online Universal Sexual Assault Prevention Education," *Journal of Interpersonal Violence* 36, no. 5–6 (2018): NP2324–NP2345, https://doi.org/10.1177/0886260518762449.

21. American College Health Association, *Addressing Sexual and Relationship Violence: A Trauma-Informed Approach* (Silver Spring, MD: American College Health Association, 2016), www.acha.org/ACHA/Resources/Addressing_Sexual_and_Relationship_Violence_A_Trauma_Informed_Approach.aspx.

13
Resetting Sights

Susanne Slavick

Violence is . . .
structural and amorphous,
physical and psychological,
local and global,
political, economic, and social—
inflicted by states, institutions, and individuals . . . on bodies.
All too pervasive, violence *persists.*

As an artist and curator, I have created projects that address the causes and consequences of violence. My work recognizes that there are many ways to propel and express the violent impulses that course through a culture's veins. I organized the exhibitions *No Glory*, *Out of Rubble*, and *Cutting Losses* (2011–15) to address the violence of war and the rubble it leaves behind, both literally and figuratively.[1] Moving from international conflicts to those on the domestic front, I developed *Unloaded* and *Up in Arms* (2015–19) to address a common instrument of violence—the gun—and its impact on US society.[2]

Violence is one expression of power, whether between persons or nations. Air strikes, chemical warfare, minefields, and internment are just a few of the military measures that continue to wound and annihilate people and places. Sexual violence is another weapon in war's arsenal and legacy. But rape and sexual violence can occur under myriad circumstances. According to the Rape, Abuse and Incest National Network (RAINN), 80 percent of rapes are committed by someone known to the victim, and 33 percent are committed by a current or former spouse or partner. But rapes are also committed outside of intimate relationships—by strangers, gangs, or someone unremembered.[3]

The links among these acts of violence are clear in books on the subject by Ann Jones. In 1999, she published *Next Time, She'll Be Dead: Battering and How to Stop It*; eleven years later, she released *War Is Not Over When It's Over*.[4] The former explores the history, legality, and personal politics of men's violence against their intimate partners. The latter is a searing inquiry into the domestic and sexual violence that militias and civilians inflict on wives, widows, and teenage girls, both during and after war. Through women's stories and images, Jones identifies gender inequality as fueling such violence—a condition that threatens or even precludes peace—within our most intimate communities and across the globe. From the bedroom to the battlefield, the scales of violence expand and contract, but the pain is always immeasurable.

For many, the word *domestic* evokes home, a place where we expect comfort. Home may be the planet that sustains us. It may be a homeland that fosters a subjective sense of belonging or a nation that grants or demands official citizenship. Functionally, it may be the bricks and mortar that shelter us; emotionally, it may be the locus of the family that raises us. Typically, it is the place we want to feel most secure. How tragic when this alleged bastion of comfort and safety turns lethal.

For too long, domestic violence was ignored and tolerated as a private, personal affair, with little public redress, largely at women's and children's expense. The US Congress waited until 1994 to pass the Violence Against Women Act. This act and ensuing additions in 1996 recognized domestic violence for what it is, was, and remains—a crime. Federal law stepped in to assist state and local criminal justice systems that were inadequate, overburdened, or disinclined to pursue prosecution of domestic violence offenses.

It also took until 1994 and 1996 for Congress to amend the Gun Control Act, making it a federal crime in certain situations for domestic violence abusers to possess guns. Up for reauthorization every five years, the Violence Against Women Act lapsed in 2018 due to the US federal government shutdown. At that time, the law only prohibited the purchase of firearms by individuals who were married to, living with, or co-parent of a child with the victim and who had been convicted of a partner abuse felony or had a protection order against them. In early 2019, reauthorization of the act failed to pass. Under strong pressure from the National Rifle Association, the Senate rejected the House of Representative's new provision to close the "boyfriend loophole," which restricts convicted spousal abusers from accessing firearms but does not always impose the same restrictions on dating partners who have been charged with abuse.[5] In February 2022, reauthorization was finally negotiated, but without closing the boyfriend loophole. It is a distressing concession when over half of all intimate partner homicides are committed with guns, compounded by the fact that women are five times more likely to be murdered when their abusers have access to a gun.[6] Easy access to firearms amplifies misogyny, racism, and hate crimes, with lethal consequences in and outside of intimate partner relationships.[7]

One of my motivations as an artist is to reveal and remember our past and current behavior, in all its beauty . . . and cruelty. I have hand painted scenes of rebirth, reconstruction, and restoration over manipulated media images of places decimated by war, incorporating scenes and motifs from artistic traditions of the very cultures under attack. Doing so emphasized and honored the vibrant history and specific creative achievements of cultures older than ours. Facing images and artifacts of a designated enemy's civilization makes it more difficult to consider its people anonymous and to dehumanize or eradicate them. For example, the US invasion of and protracted war in Iraq prompted *Regenerate*, in which I inserted a gardener from a twelfth-century illumination in the Mesopotamian *Book of Antidotes* by the Pseudo-Galen (an unknown author invoking the authority of a second-century Greek doctor named Galen). Maintaining the style of the first school of Baghdad, I painted this gardener over a manipulated documentary photograph of a raided archaeological site in Iraq. During war, security for cultural treasures is lax, impossible, or even deliberately abandoned. The gardener transposed from the past to the present starts to shovel in the "surface scatter" of the broken remains of disturbed and stolen artifacts from even more distant times. He is breaking ground to grow again, preparing for the future. I make such images with the crossed eyes of the romantic and the realist, a form of double vision that hopes for persistence, resilience, and survival while also grappling with the damage we have done and still do to each other.

Five years after the passage of the Violence Against Women Act, I painted a series of works that examined another kind of site that is both functional and sentimental—the bed. Mattresses, pillows, or cushions stand upright, confronting the viewer frontally and mirroring the violent response to softness so prevalent in US culture. I interrupted the respite they normally provide through bifurcation, punctures, or amputations, visual metaphors for premeditated assaults or "crimes of passion"—a vile euphemism for vengeful rage and the capricious or calculated exercise of unchecked power. The cushions in smaller paintings assume simple geometric shapes—square, circle, and triangle. Larger paintings such as *Point of Entry* and *Contrary Comfort* present pastel-colored rectangles that signify mattresses.[8] Their upholstery buttons create diagonal grids that are suspended in the atmospheric hazes

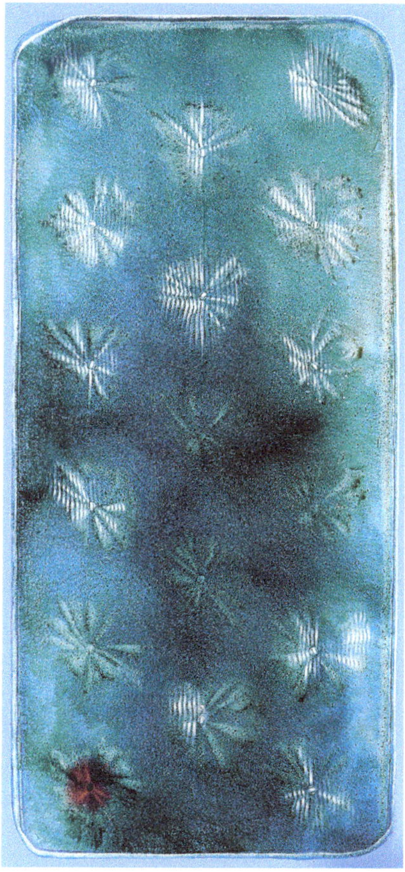

Susanne Slavick, *Point of Entry*, 1999. Oil and acrylic on panel, 80 × 36 in. Courtesy of the artist.

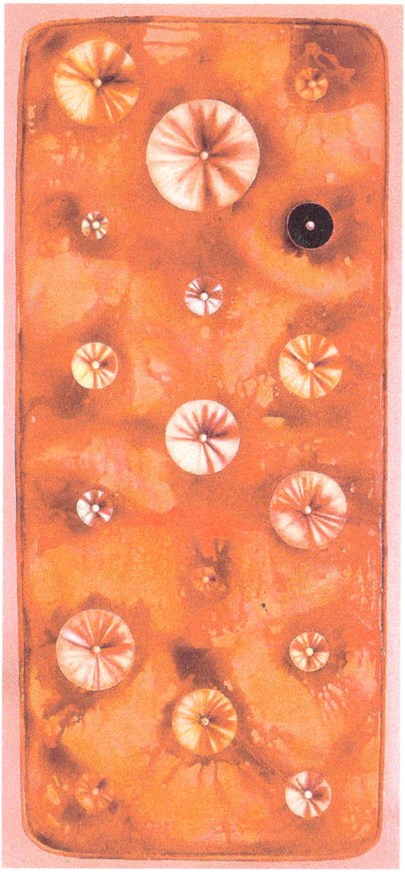

Susanne Slavick, *Contrary Comfort*, 1999. Oil and acrylic on panel, 80 × 36 in. Courtesy of the artist.

floating within the bedding's perimeters. Grids are abstract structures that can represent rationality, predictability, stability, and order. My grids depart from these qualities and their more austere counterparts in modernist painting, where they establish the impenetrable flatness of the picture plane. My grids are stuffed, bulging and undulating; they are penetrated and pierced. They are grids with body and thus vulnerable. The buttons anchoring their stuffing are pressure points spotlit in a sea of bloody fluid or ghostly stars floating in a blue nocturne. They are sitting targets with no cover. And then there are the holes.

Presumably, the bed is a site of rest and refuge. There we sleep, unaware, but trusting that our lives will continue upon awakening. Domestic abuse and

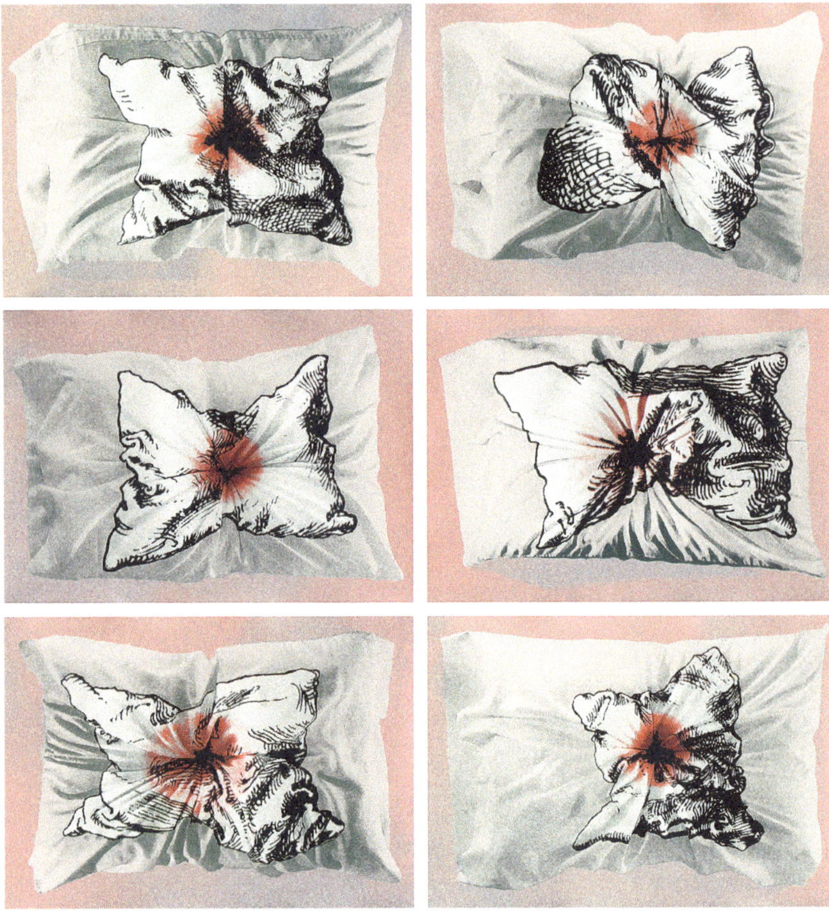

Susanne Slavick, *(Re)Setting Sights I–VI*, 2002. Screen prints on Stonehenge paper, each 22 × 30 in. Courtesy of the artist.

sexual violence puncture that trust, violating innocence and the innocent. In *Point of Entry*, a forensic term for where a weapon (or its projectile) enters a body, a deep penetration opens to blackness, rimmed in red. In *Contrary Comfort*, a pearl is suspended in another hole. Unlike a bullet, it is a lustrous thing born of defense against intrusion and irritation. The pearl, like the pea in the fairy tale *The Princess and the Pea*, also tests our sensitivity, for the princess's sleep is ruined by the bruising pea buried under a mountain of mattresses. In real life, these buttons, peas, pearls, and holes are not benign or buried. They ruin our sleep and ruin our lives.

(Re)Setting Sights, a series of six serigraphs, features pillows that typically

cradle our heads in slumber. But they allude to whole bodies as targets, for predators armed or unarmed.[9] The series layers several modes of representation, injecting doubt about our own perceptions. Artifice lies upon artifice. My delineated pillows are derived from studies of six pillows observed, hand drawn, and etched in a 1493 image by Albrecht Dürer. These pillows are as they should be—relaxed and ready to be aired and plumped, untainted by any hint of violence. Mourning that innocence, I divided his single composition into six separate images, creating single pillows that I then photographed, enlarged, and silk-screened onto real pillowcases. These linens then encased actual pillows that were "punched" in their centers to suggest violent impacts. The reconstructed pillows were photographed again, and the resulting images were digitally manipulated, silk-screened, and combined with hovering reticles from gunsights that were printed over some of the pillows' violated centers. In one print, an actual bullet pierces the glass surface of the frame, frozen in suspension just above the wound it (or any violent act) will cause.

In literature and art, ruses, conceits, and contradictions can sometimes convey truths more powerfully than simple declarations of fact. In that sense, these multiple and contradictory layers of documentation and invention can function like double negatives that convert to a positive, to something true, even if painful. *(Re)Setting Sights* urges us to consider who and what is targeted in a culture of violence, and how that culture might shift. Could our aims be truer in affirming rather than negating life, becoming less vicious and less lethal, especially to those with less power? Might they inspire rather than inflict, nurture rather than injure, and question their own direction?

Notes

1. *R&R (. . . &R)*, *No Glory*, *Out of Rubble*, and *Cutting Losses* were curatorial projects that grew out of *R&R (. . . &R)*, a studio project concerned with the aftermath of war. Curatorial projects are documented at Susanne Slavick, accessed May 29, 2023, www.susanneslavick.com/curatorial-1. *R&R (. . . &R)* is documented at Susanne Slavick, "R&R (. . . &R), 2006–2011," accessed May 29, 2023, www.susanneslavick.com/#/rrr; and Susanne Slavick, "R&R (. . . &R): Stations, 2008," accessed May 29, 2023, www.susanneslavick.com/#/rrr-stations.

2. *Unloaded* and *Up in Arms* were traveling curatorial projects and are documented at Susanne Slavick, "Unloaded, Touring 2015–2019," accessed May 29, 2023, www.susanneslavick.com/curatorial-1#/unloaded.

3. RAINN, "Perpetrators of Sexual Violence: Statistics," accessed May 29, 2023, www.rainn.org/statistics/perpetrators-sexual-violence, citing US Department of

Justice, Office of Justice Programs, Bureau of Justice Statistics, National Crime Victimization Survey, 2010–16 (2017).

4. Ann Jones, *Next Time, She'll Be Dead: Battering and How to Stop It*, rev. ed. (1994; Boston: Beacon Press, 2000); Ann Jones, *War Is Not Over When It's Over: Women Speak Out from the Ruins of War* (New York: Henry Holt, 2010).

5. Alana Wise, "Senators Announce a Deal to Reauthorize the Violence Against Women Act," NPR, February 9, 2022, www.npr.org/2022/02/09/1079717258/senators-announce-a-deal-to-reauthorize-the-violence-against-women-act.

6. Educational Fund to Stop Gun Violence, "Domestic Violence and Firearms," accessed May 29, 2023, https://efsgv.org/learn/type-of-gun-violence/domestic-violence-and-firearms.

7. Marissa Edmund, "Guns and Violence against Women: Key Challenges and Solutions," Center for American Progress, January 5, 2022, www.americanprogress.org/article/guns-and-violence-against-women.

8. These and related works are documented at Susanne Slavick, "Contrary Comforts 1999," accessed May 29, 2023, www.susanneslavick.com/#/contrary-comforts; and Susanne Slavick, "Pillow Talk," accessed May 29, 2023, www.susanneslavick.com/#/pillow-talk.

9. *(Re)Setting Sights* and related works are documented at Susanne Slavick, "Targets 2000," accessed May 29, 2023, www.susanneslavick.com/#/targets.

14
Stitch. Write. Repeat.

Jennifer Patterson

A split stitch—

Make one stitch. Double back and poke the needle through that stich, right in the middle. Move forward, after the split, make another stitch the same length as the first. Then make another, back from that middle and out. Same length again. And on and on.

Sometimes it can feel a whole lot like backtracking, retracing, but sometimes, it's splitting the middle wide open, using the break to shape the new.

Embroidery as a way of marking: the fabric (a body), the thread (the wounding). Threads going through holes, stitching, splitting, breaking open. Breaking into the wound, splitting it open, over and over. Each stitch new. Breaking to shape anew.

+ + +

What is the center what is the center what is the center of this?
Ah.
The body.
I am very good at starting everywhere besides the body, all that Libra
stellium vata air air air spinning around in my head.

We're gonna talk about

THE BODY

The body that knows failure, that knows rupture.
The body that is a huge scar.
The body that is a huge beating bloody wound.
The body as the ultimate witness to trauma.

The marked body.
The traumatized body.
The queer body.
The freak body.
The forgotten body.[1]

The body as primary material, the primary source.
The body as an archive.

The architecture of a body.
The architecture of trauma.

How the body is always reaching for homeostasis, for medicine. How sometimes the medicine is poison, sometimes the poison medicine. How sometimes it's as simple and as complex as finding the right dose.

The body as in between. As a bridge between "before" and "after"—the third space, the third land, the ecotone (remembering of course that there are endless befores and afters). The two ends of that long winding spectrum.
Always on and pushing at the edges.

"The body" as never singular, always multiples. Multitudes.

My body as a *sharp edge*.[2]
My body as a *wandering question*.[3]
My body as a graveyard.
My body as a site of wreckage, roots deep.
My body as a battleground.
My body as a bundle of live-wire nerve endings.
My body as rows and lines of thread.
My body as a pile of rubble.

My body as a holder of names and secrets.
My body as dearly departed.

"My body is essaying. It is working through."[4]
My body is searching, often weary and worn.

My body is a pile of rotten bones.
My body is a state with no nation.
My body is a land(mass) with no borders. Seeping.

My body could never live in *Philadelphia* again, never in *Happy Valley*.
My body that has suffered the blows, the breaks.
My body cowers at the prick of an acupuncture needle.
My body as the site turned back on itself.
My body as the *feeling I just can't shake*.[5]
My body, survivor body, as the ultimate failure,
as the ultimate blessing.

+ + +

I, the big mess, want to be a healer. I, the big mess, want to be healed.

+ + +

I am forever wanting a way to map the trauma that lives in my body: mark it, follow the trail, carve it and remove it, return to before or settle into after. I am forever searching for adequate translation of the trauma in my body, of speaking from inside the wounds, transferring them from skin to something else. "Skin as text and textile."[6]

Sometimes I turn to trauma theory. About the body but not in it. Not of it. I'm enticed by how it is presented as fact. Theory with a capital *T*, also, sometimes brings me down, makes me doubt my orientation, doubt the rooting of my knowledge in my body. Kazim Ali helps me to navigate the theoretical, both critical and the creative (and the in-between space): "The text is a body because it is made of the flesh and breath and blood of a writer. The 'mind' which declares intention is a collection of senses, sense-responses, and memories. Chemically it is invented in the brain. Thought is matter. Work resists binaries between thought (theory) and action (creative work)."[7]

The body as a sharp edge. The body as a wandering question. The body as understood through words. The body as a vessel: it holds the experiences, the pleasure, losses, the failures, the pain; the memories are stored in skin and bone and muscle, sinewy, weaving throughout, settled into shapes. By "failure," I mean it by definition: the inability to perform, a fracture or giving away under stress.[8] I also don't imagine it is a onetime failure but something that can and does happen over and over. I can use this body, this knowledge, this physical, emotional and spiritual understanding. The body can be radicalized, it can be that ever-referenced phoenix rising from the ashes. I'm reminded: the body(ies) can be the work. But first they have to burn.

+ + +

In *Spontaneous Particulars: The Telepathy of Archives*, Susan Howe weaves together text and images, disparate parts to make a whole. She writes of the roots of the word *text*, noting that "the English word 'text' comes from Medieval Latin *textus* 'style or texture of a work,' literally 'thing woven,' from the past participle stem of *textere*: 'to weave, to join, to fit together, construct.'"[9] She harks back to Gertrude Stein, who says, "What is the difference between a sentence and a sewn? What is the difference between a sentence and a picture? They will sew which will make it tapestry. . . . Think in stitches."[10]

As a ritual of transference, as an attempt to weave my own tapestry, I work to translate skin into words into threads. After writing (and sometimes during) I map the words with embroidery thread. Sometimes (many times) I need another way of entering the body(ies).

I am a tiny embroidered circle. I am using my hands and then yours to ride round and round myself. Make homes around myself. Make homes in myself.

An active meditation.

I imagine stitching as making and remaking and sometimes unmaking the wound; maybe the thread as violator, the textile as violated, but the stitch, the stich, it is forever linking and joining the two, inverting them too.

Stitches as healing, as meditation.

Break the thread, break the linkage.

I see my stitched intentions reflected in the work of the Healing Sutras on vintage textiles by the embroidery artist and painter Erin Endicott. She writes:

> To stitch; a thread or line that holds things together—this is the literal translation of the ancient Sanskrit word "sutra." The "Healing Sutras" grew out of years of work examining psychological wounds (mainly my own), their origins and how they insinuate themselves into our lives. . . . By bringing these dark areas into the light, by making them visible, I think we can

> heal these wounds. Some people talk through their issues to bring healing, some write them out to shed light on them, I choose to make them into visible, visceral objects. . . . One stitch at a time, hour after hour . . . this is where the healing lies.[11]

A roundtable discussion at Naropa University's Jack Kerouac School of Disembodied Poetics, called "Sewing Is Writing Is Body Is Sewing," expands further with Rachel May's piece titled "Sewing the Body Whole." In it she writes: "What makes the process so intimate is the mind-body connection that's evident in sewing and writing. New media theory and cognitive science offer inroads into this exploration of sewing and the body, sewing and writing. N. Katherine Hayles describes the repetitive process by which we remember, creating new pathways in our brains; if we lose a part of our memory, that memory can be jogged, so to speak, by developing new pathways nearby: 'New circuits take over where the old fail'; this is called neural plasticity."[12]

The stitch, over and over, makes new.

There has also been a fair amount of research about the meditative and transformative aspects of knitting, a similar creative, repetitive process that, for me, mirrors embroidery. This research suggests that the repetition in knitting activates the parasympathetic nervous system in a part of the brain called the amygdala, which helps quiet the often highly activated "fight or flight" response that many people with trauma histories and post-traumatic stress disorder (PTSD) have to manage daily. Not only is the amygdala where the "fight or flight" response lives, it's also where obsessive compulsive disorder lives, and, interestingly, it's also where our sense of touch originates.[13]

But if repetition heals, can it also harm? Trichotillomania (compulsive hair pulling) is often described as a compulsive disorder, an anxiety disorder, or self-harm. It is finding the imperfection, pulling strand after strand. Losing minutes, hours, days, years. As a child, trichotillomania was a way I was able to disconnect, to dissociate from the abusive reality of my home, and, as an adult, I still find myself reaching with regularity. I looked to psychology for help with this, looked to plants too. Sometimes there is relief, but often I find myself still searching for the imperfection, still searching for dissociation. I've struggled with it for the better part of thirty years, but when I am embroidering my hands are occupied, fingers entangled in thread; it allows me to focus on being present and to find comfort in another kind of repetition.

"One stitch at a time, hour after hour . . . this is where the healing lies."[14]

A wound as a word as a picture, giving shape to the energy rippling in a body after experiencing trauma(s).

+ + +

The first time I read the line "for text to be like skin" on the back of Melissa Buzzeo's book, *What Began Us*, I knew I had found my orientation to writing and the intention behind my embroidery work.[15] I have been asking myself questions my whole life, but I only recently started answering them:

What is the physicality of a wound?
Can we dive into the wound, the loss: excavate and unearth it
and then move back out of it?
What types of loss feel nearly impossible to come back from?
What kind of life settles into our bones if we don't take the time to grieve?

If not grieved, loss has a way of living in the body. But grieving often means moving into the hard parts of ourselves and making a home in it, settling into the shadows.

I'm realizing that, for me, the phrase "for text to be like skin" is also about absorption—saturation. How much can the text hold? How much can language contain? Does it hold lines and shapes, like skin, do they turn into bruises, like skin, do deepest purples give way to a subtle yellow?

When will I be saturated?

Or as Arianne Zwartjes says in her sweeping epic poem of an essay on the body and trauma and loss: "Trauma is a shear in ordinary blacktop. A fissure in the everyday fabric. Like flannel being ripped. The shredding of each fiber in a mostly straight line. The frayed edges that result. The way the cloth loses its flat plane, becomes irregularly stretched and taut, gaping and baggy. . . . Blooming wound on this terrain of skin."[16]

Giving language to the trauma of sexual violence is not just remembering it or replaying it in one's mind in order to write; it's the feeling, the remembering in the body.

What does it mean to have deep wounds that are almost beyond language? Beyond words? What does it mean to always try to find words anyway? How can we move into this writing the unwritable, this way of knowing that is in the deep well of the body? As a queer survivor of multiple forms of violence, many people have imagined and also diagnosed me as someone with PTSD and other mental health issues—and sentenced me to a disconnected, dissociated life birthed of trauma, very much inescapable.

My body knows better. So I write. I look for words that can hold the shape of skins, traced over and over. I write from inside the wound, inside the places people would rather I heal before reporting from. I reject the ways people believe a survivor *should* be in their body as the only way to heal: the whole and healthy and clean ways. I am committed to affirming that my way of connecting to my body is an inherently embodied practice. So long as I have a body I am embodied.

When words are not enough, then I return to hands, return to the handmade and tangible. Visible. I use my body to interpret my body—the hands that mark, the hips that twist, thighs that bruise; the experiences, the losses, the visceral sensations that singe through the bruises. I am celebrating. I am honoring. I am giving voice to the parts others would rather I silence. When I use my body for pleasure, when I choose to utilize something that I have sole ownership over that has historically been used against me, I can transform. Transgress old limits and borders.

Both my words and other people's words become a hybrid, between creative nonfiction (my lived experience as a queer survivor of multiple forms of violence) and visual representation (embroidery as a metaphor of re-wounding). I'm imaging these pieces as a large weaving or fiber art project, words and threads binding the rough edges together. I'm seeing the thesis as many bodies organizing, overlapping and connecting. They take turns shaping each other; sometimes the words lead or hold space and other times the lines of stitches trace a solid structure into the work, map and give language to my embodied experience as a queer survivor. A return to a body that was lost. Or. Learning there can be no return (the past is gone) but only a creation of a new in the present, in the moment to moment.

+ + +

How do I make this something more than a list, a litany of harms inflicted by others on my body? How do I own the harm I have committed, too? My mouth. Rage. Open and screaming and, at times, desperate.

Be as critical of myself as I am of others, writer, and friend, Seema Reza has said. Allow myself to be unmade.

Hold myself in the line of fire. Don't turn away.

Return to child selves. Acknowledge the wounded selves, when they have led the way. Call in the wise elder future selves. Let them be in conversation. Let all receive care.

Stitch. Write. Repeat.

+ + +

A survivor's body as a failed body—doctors and the DSM (Diagnostic and Statistical Manual of Mental Disorders) claiming we are so often dissociative, disconnected, disembodied—very nearly dismembered. Our heads ripped off our bodies, spirits ripped out of skin.

When I first began writing again, after a few years of not, a lover (who was a poet) introduced me to Bhanu Kapil's *The Vertical Interrogation of Strangers*.[17] In it she interviewed women in India and Indian women in England. She pieced together poems about violence, theirs and hers, the rawness on the page for all to see, she wrote about dismemberment and I learned to as well.

I wanted the definition.

I thought I knew dismemberment—the poetry I wrote often spoke about how I couldn't feel my legs, couldn't find my pelvic bone, couldn't find my feet. Trying to use words to stitch together a dismembered body. I searched the internet and the visuals screamed. Broken, torn bodies bent over medians on roads, jammed into holes. The red a deep brownish crimson. This is not the dismemberment I know. I have never witnessed this. I do know of a splitting, a loss.

Sometimes there aren't words for the way we lose our bodies. Sometimes we don't know they are gone. Sometimes limbs are extracted, a literal, visual dismemberment, but more often they are not.

A lost limb isn't always a loss. Sometimes we remain high functioning in that always oppressive way—full of expectation from ourselves and others—other times we find ourselves deteriorating, then relearning and trying to recover what was ripped away. The phantoms stimulate the imagination, make us feel as if we are whole, but we will never feel whole.

Sometimes I'm in a car and over and over I see it crashing. It's not that I've lost control—I am choosing this wreck—letting go of the wheel in search of whatever's next. For some bodies, ones that are used to trying to maintain so much control, there comes a time where there is comfort in loss of control. Comfort in a ripping out of what's expired—the impatient demand for new.

+ + +

Even if I think I've left my body, in fact I am always in it, always using it, creating with it. In this sense, using my body (fingers and hands) to write *about* my body, and my sometimes feelings of disconnection can bring me back to it. It places me right in it. It allows me to push into something I often pull myself out of; it allows me to settle into "the wandering question that haunts my soul and hacks and saws at my body."[18] It allows my body to be both the question and the answer.

Sometimes writing feels like an unloading, a sharing of what is often seen as damaged and conflicted parts of my self: "turn[ing] [those] sharp edge[s] away from my flesh."[19] Sometimes I find a new understanding of something I've gone over and over in my head, but I don't see it until it's been pulled out and scrawled on a piece of paper. Using writing as a healing tool is messy work, at times counterintuitive; it demands that we explore that which is often unspeakable and beyond language. But if undertaken, the writing can also lead to release. As Louise DeSalvo notes in *Writing as a Way of Healing*: "Writing about traumatic or troubling life experiences initially unleashes difficult, conflicting emotions. In the long run, though, we feel better emotionally and are healthier and achieve a level of understanding of our lives that only writing can provide."[20]

Seema Reza writes:

> According to the research on writing and healing conducted over the last three decades, writing in a way that merges the chronological fact-based account with the subjective emotional experience for 20 minutes a day can have a significant impact on physical health—white blood cell counts go up, sick visits are fewer, blood pressures lower. Also, when you kick up dust inside yourself, when you make connections that you hadn't made before, discover things about yourself that you hadn't previously considered, you can feel like sh*t. . . . In the transition from passively experiencing emotion through actively arranging it into words and finally arriving at witnessing it upon completion, we are changed.[21]

+ + +

I can never quite figure out the appropriate tense when I write. How *then* is always *now* and *now* is some kind of future I can't always find words for.

I write in sentence fragments sometimes. "The bliss of the disorienting text . . ."[22] They feel right to me, they sound right when I read them back to myself. Fractures, stops and starts. Like speaking, like thinking, like lines of a poem collapsed into themselves.

Can form be writing in repetition, writing in fragments, writing without a care for linearity, writing to simply write that which is unwritable (until it's written, that is), writing with no concern for clarity—writing the way memory and traumatic experience live in a body, writing the way memory and traumatic memory get stuck in the throat?

The answer is yes.

Kapil writes "of the fragment as 'rough'—where the edge of it is, like glass or fur or light, so that it adheres to other fragments, not through historical or phatic means: but through the force of attraction. I place the fragments in a chrysalis: to recombine."[23]

To write with a focus on the body, to navigate that terrain, to come up to the edges, cliffs, to settle into the valley of dangerous emotions and feeling. But this writing is also bigger than me, bigger than my body.

+ + +

Survivorhood as an altered state, an ever-expansive state of consciousness.

Survivorhood as another way of deeply knowing.

Notes

This chapter is an excerpt from the in-process manuscript titled "Assaults & Rituals."

1. Inspired, in part, by Thom Donovan's long-form essay "Somatic Poetics," *Jacket2*, October 18, 2011, https://jacket2.org/article/somatic-poetics.

2. Hélène Cixous, *"Coming to Writing" and Other Essays* (Cambridge, MA: Harvard University Press, 1992).

3. Cixous, *"Coming to Writing."*

4. Kate Zambreno, *Apoplexia, Toxic Shock, and Toilet Bowl: Some Notes on Why I Write* (New York: Guillotine, 2013), 14.

5. Nick Cave and the Bad Seeds, *Push the Sky Away*, Bad Seeds Ltd., 2013, music album.

6. Arianne Zwartjes, *Detailing Trauma: A Poetic Anatomy* (Iowa City: University of Iowa Press, 2012), 89.

7. Kazim Ali, "Genre-Queer: Notes against Generic Binaries," in *Bending Genre: Essays on Creative Nonfiction*, ed. Margot Singer and Nicole Walker (London: Bloomsbury, 2013), 28.

8. Dictionary definition of *failure*: *Merriam-Webster.com Dictionary*, Merriam-Webster, accessed January 1, 2016, www.merriam-webster.com/dictionary/failure.

9. Susan Howe, *Spontaneous Particulars: The Telepathy of Archives* (New York: New Directions, 2014), 19.

10. Howe, *Spontaneous Particulars*, 19.

11. “Erin Endicott Interview: Contemporary Embroidery,” TextileArtist.org, accessed January 1, 2016, www.textileartist.org/erin-endicott-interview-contemporary-embroidery.

12. Rachel May, “Sewing the Body Whole,” *Something on Paper*, no. 3 (2016), www.somethingonpaper.org/issue-3/round-table-may; N. Katherine Hayles, *How We Think: Digital Media and Contemporary Technogenesis* (Chicago: University of Chicago Press, 2012), 64.

13. May, “Sewing the Body Whole,” citing Hayles, *How We Think*, 64–65.

14. “Erin Endicott Interview.”

15. Melissa Buzzeo, *What Began Us* (Providence, RI: Leon Works, 2007).

16. Zwartjes, *Detailing Trauma*, 36, 37.

17. Bhanu Kapil, *The Vertical Interrogation of Strangers* (Berkeley, CA: Kelsey Street Press, 2001).

18. Cixous, *“Coming to Writing,”* 7.

19. Cixous, *“Coming to Writing,”* 7.

20. Louise DeSalvo, *Writing as a Way of Healing: How Telling Our Stories Transforms Our Lives* (Boston: Beacon Press, 2000), 93.

21. Seema Reza, “Becoming Ourselves through Writing—Even When It’s Uncomfortable,” *Elephant Journal*, May 16, 2017, www.elephantjournal.com/2016/05/becoming-ourselves-through-writing-even-when-its-uncomfortable.

22. Ali, “Genre-Queer,” 32.

23. Bhanu Kapil, *Ban en Banlieue* (Brooklyn, NY: Nightboat Books, 2015), 103.

15

The Clothesline Project
A Tool for Addressing Domestic Violence

Emily Bonistall Postel, Elaina Behounek, and Alesha Durfee

Education and increased awareness of societal issues are fundamental components to creating social transformation. We have found that art and creative expression can play a key role in this process for issues related to sexual violence (SV) and domestic violence (DV). Art and creative expression can be used to open dialogues, challenge stereotypes about survivors, think critically about societal reactions toward victimization, and investigate the role of socialization, power, patriarchy, racism, sexism, and heteronormativity within these reactions. Combined with social action, art can be a powerful tool for SV and DV prevention, education, interruption, empowerment, and, ultimately, healing individuals, communities, and society.

We integrated the Clothesline Project as artistic activism into college courses and community engagement projects at three different universities. The Clothesline Project is an international, grassroots, arts-based, trauma-informed movement where groups of people create art installations consisting of T-shirts hung on a clothesline that contain messages about SV and DV. The project is intended to increase awareness about SV and DV, destabilize stereotypes about "survivors" and "violence," celebrate a person's strength to survive, and provide another avenue to break the silence that often surrounds these experiences. Elevating the voices of victim/survivors through art creates a heartfelt story of hurt, hope, and healing. The opportunity to create a T-shirt expressing their complex emotions, documenting their abuse, sharing their experiences, and conveying the impacts of all three can be transformative for victim/survivors and "participant/artists."[1] This transformation is both internal and external. Artists see themselves as active "changemakers" whose experiences can be used to help others, and the project, by displaying the shirts, provides counternarratives to societal stereotypes about violence and victimization.

Furthermore, by engaging community members as both participants and audience, the project forces the community to confront the often-invisible victimization that occurs regularly in our own backyards but is ignored. These art installations allow the audience to develop understanding and empathy as the installations bring statistics to life, show the diversity of victim/survivors, challenge stereotypes and myths, and redefine victim/survivors as agentic, brave, and resilient. Finally, planning and executing the project has a profound effect on event organizers. It deepens their understanding of these issues and empowers them as changemakers. In doing so, the project has a powerful impact on people's perceptions and attitudes about SV and DV, ultimately motivating them to continue working toward social change long after the project ends. As one of our participants said, "I will continue to spread awareness about the different types of abuse and will be forever grateful for getting to participate in such a life-changing event."

While our projects share common elements, their design and implementation varied; as Rachel Anderson Droogsma points out, "No rules govern individual Clothesline Projects."[2] When we discussed our projects with one another, comparing different techniques and strategies, we found ourselves learning from each other and thinking even more expansively about future projects. Our hope for this chapter is to share our collective knowledge to help others use the Clothesline Project to engage in activist art for social change.

The Clothesline Project

The Clothesline Project was initially conceptualized by the artist Rachel Carey-Harper in 1990 as a grassroots effort to give voice to victim/survivors by creating a visual representation of the violence faced by women in the United States.[3] The first project was hosted later that year in Massachusetts. Using color-coded shirts that represent different types of violence, participants artistically express their experiences of abuse, give statements of support of survivors, and call for societal action against abuse. The shirts are then hung and displayed on a clothesline, which represents the way "neighboring women shared stories with one another while hanging clothes to dry."[4] Like other arts installations, such as the AIDS Memorial Quilt (which directly inspired Carey-Harper), the Vietnam Veteran's Memorial, and the Monument Quilt, much of the impact of the project comes from the sheer

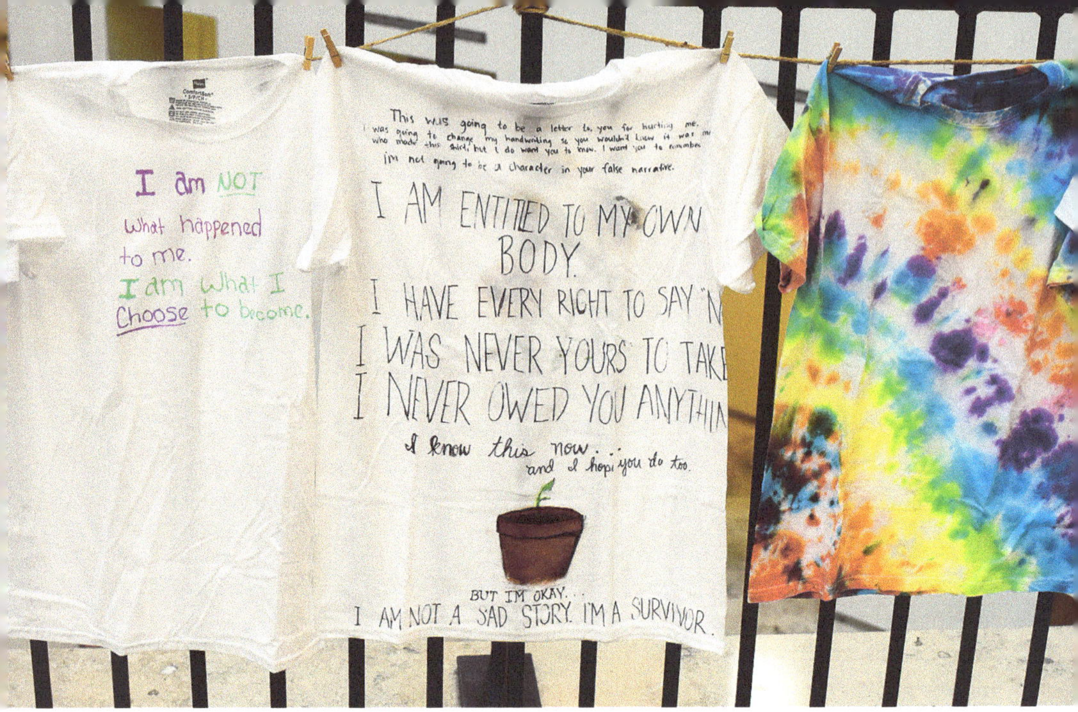

Artistic expressions of polyvictimization via tie-dye and through victim/survivor experiences written on T-shirts for the Clothesline Project at the University of Kentucky, 2018. Courtesy of Emily Bonistall Postel.

number of those represented in the installation. As one participant told the sociologist Patricia C. Hipple, "It's palpable. It's like walking into an enormous cathedral. It's profound."[5] Additionally, the diversity of the messages and experiences written on the shirts works to convey the complexity of SV and DV. The project visually presents expressions of support, grief, anger, and community solidarity. The visual appeal of the installation easily draws in community members, who are often awed by and frequently identify with the messages displayed.

From the very beginning, the project has had the ability to facilitate social change through the transformational power of art.[6] Since 1990, researchers from diverse disciplines have explored the project as both a healing and an empowering experience for victim/survivors and a powerful instrument for social change.[7] Hipple analyzed five projects from 1990 (the first project) through 1996. She argued that these early displays of shirts served "to literally record and document the discourse of resistance and provide a vehicle for its elaboration and public declaration" and provided "a way for the voices of women to be heard, to challenge female subordination and male domination, and to resist gendered violence."[8] At the same time, these projects were acts of "disguised resistance." By displaying "disembodied" (and therefore anonymous) shirts, participants could "embolden their speech" while remaining physically safe.[9] Finally, the anonymity of T-shirts worked to create solidarity among survivors. Stripped of markers of social marginalization, viewers instead focused on commonalities. As one survivor told Hipple, "I went up and down the rows reading the shirts and I just started crying. I just cried and cried and cried. It was a crying of joy and freedom—that I wasn't alone. . . . My shirt wasn't alone. I wasn't alone. Here was a community of women!"[10]

By 1993, the feminist sociologist Lora Bex Lempert began incorporating the Clothesline Project into her family violence college course.[11] Although the project was discussed on the first day and in the syllabus, it was not until the second half of the course (after the students had spent weeks studying SV and DV) that they created shirts "in honor" of a survivor of their choosing and hosted an event. One primary outcome of these projects was "personal empowerment and advocacy."[12] Subsequent projects were even more expansive in scope. In an analysis of a 2004 campus Clothesline Project, Brian K. Payne and Rebecca Fogerty noted that even students who "apparently did not have histories of victimization" participated, demonstrating that "everyone is involved in the response to violence." "This is not just an issue that affects victims; rather, it is an issue that inevitably affects everyone."[13] They analyzed the messages on the shirts in their project and found that they represented primarily five types: (1) messages to victim/survivors, especially about the importance of speaking out; (2) messages to potential offenders that emphasized offenders', not victim/survivors', responsibility for SV and DV; (3) ideas about love and how love does not include violence; (4) ideas about prevention directed at everyone, not just victim/survivors and offenders; and (5) "awareness themes," including victim/survivor experiences, statistics, and other information.[14] In a feminist standpoint analysis of the messages in the survivors' art, Droogsma describes the project as a collective critique of society's role in violence against women.[15] She argues that it "constitutes an activist art because it emerges out of collaboration, encourages marginalized persons to creatively express themselves, and invites all members of the community to become involved."[16] The efficacy, poignancy, impact, and flexibility of the project encouraged each of us to try it.

Project Scope

This chapter is based on our experiences of conducting the Clothesline Project at three campus communities that vary in size and structure, demographics, and geographic location.[17] The design and implementation of the Clothesline Project can vary based on the organizing community, but projects typically share the same main components and the similar goal of generating an arts-based, trauma-informed experience that allows for healing, resource provision, and fostering activism. The projects at all three universities were organized by students enrolled in a course related to victimization. Though the impact of our projects in the larger community is not quantifiable, our affiliation with the classroom did give us a unique opportunity to capture the impact of the community on our participants. The participants spoke about the transformation the project had on their understandings about SV, DV, and survivors: "Seeing all of the college students stop by and make tee shirts made me happy to know that others are willing to help support our community as well as let their voices be heard. Throughout the course this semester I have learned a lot of new information and statistics dealing with sexual assault and domestic violence that I will carry on with me throughout the rest of my college semesters and career."

The power of working with community partners to provide an artistic outlet for victim/survivors and their loved ones allowed participants to understand that, through community, support and social change are possible. The quotations included in this chapter are directly from students' reflection papers, in which they illustrated the profound impact the opportunity to participate in the Clothesline Project had on them.

Praxis: Linking Campus and Community

The Clothesline Project allowed students to engage in the feminist project of "praxis"—putting the theory and knowledge they learned about SV and DV in our classes into practice.[18] Instead of doing a final exam or assignment and then moving on to the next class, students had to use their knowledge to work with community partners; plan community events; create for those events educational materials that were relevant, relatable, and accessible; and respond to attendees when the installation was open to the public. This included explaining the purpose of the project, helping attendees create their own shirts or note cards (site 3), discussing and answering questions about SV and DV during the installation, and connecting attendees and participants with support services when requested.

Community engagement was a critical component of each project. We opted to partner with community organizations to remove the traditional divide between campus/academia and the broader community, and we found that to be extremely effective. Students collaborated with on-campus organizations as well as community agencies (e.g., a halfway house, the boys and girls club, a DV shelter, a Girl Scout troop, or the police department) to create and host smaller events that led up to the larger Clothesline Project installation. For example, connecting with local DV shelters allowed students to engage in healing work with victim/survivors while gaining deeper understandings about the effects of domestic abuse. The projects changed event organizers' understandings of SV and DV, as well as of their responsibilities as socially engaged community members. By sharing three specific examples, we illustrate the importance of engaging in praxis and collaborating with community partners (rather than just doing a campus event) to create a truly transformative experience.

At sites 1 and 2, instructors and students hosted events at local DV shelters that allowed staff and residents to create shirts. (DV shelters were chosen for October projects to honor National Domestic Violence Awareness Month.)[19] Students were deeply affected by this experience in myriad ways. Shelter-based projects dispelled many of their stereotypes about shelters, survivors, and survivors' purpose for being at the shelter. Instead of imparting knowledge to survivors, the power dynamics were flipped, and students learned from the survivors.

Some students had never thought about how many children were living in shelters. They learned that those children needed just to play and not be defined by their direct or indirect victimization. When the kids asked to create shirts "for Halloween" instead of focusing on DV, the students had to think through their assumptions about the goal of the event. Should they restrict the painting to the effects of SV and DV for the purposes of the project, or should they facilitate the kids' pleasure in an upcoming holiday? They decided that helping the children make Halloween shirts allowed the kids to recapture some of their childhood, which was effective in combating the impacts of DV, if only for a short time—just not in the way that the students had expected it to. It also freed up the children's mothers to create their own T-shirts for the event. A follow-up classroom discussion allowed the students to continue exploring power dynamics, stereotypes, and the ethics of asking victim/survivors and their families to create shirts.

Guiding Principles: Intersectionality and Polyvictimization

Our projects utilized an intersectional approach to victimization, emphasizing the role of a survivor's unique position in the "matrix of domination."[20] The

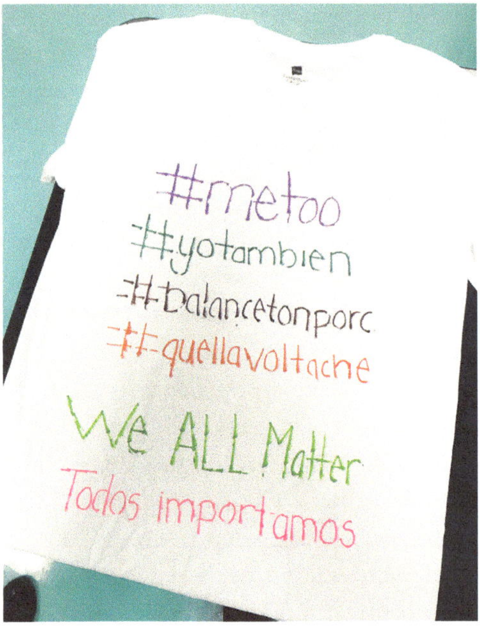

"We ALL Matter." Artistic expression on T-shirt for the Clothesline Project at the University of Kentucky, 2018. Courtesy of Emily Bonistall Postel.

Clothesline Projects reflected firsthand experiences and revealed the ways that lives are shaped and constrained by intersecting identities, such as race, class, and gender. They also demonstrated how white privilege determines the many services available to DV victim/survivors and how sexism, racism, economic inequality, and other factors constrain victim/survivor life choices.[21] Recognizing such complex factors shaping victim/survivor lives helped to ensure that all victim/survivors felt included and validated by the project.

It was important to convey these principles in the images and language used in event advertising. Students at site 2 realized that all the T-shirts had been designed in English, so they created shirts in multiple languages and used photos of these on all advertising materials (at site 1, students made shirts in multiple languages unprompted). Additionally, although the "traditional" project explains that the goal is to "let each woman tell her story in her own unique way, using words and/or artwork to decorate her shirt," our event organizers opted to use gender-neutral language to be inclusive of 2SLGBTQIA+ survivors.[22] This information guided the creation of materials for the event, such as handouts and flyers with statistics, red flag warnings, diagrams of the power and control wheel, and other resources helpful to survivors and their support networks. At the site 1 art installation, many of these handouts were provided in both English and Spanish, and several handouts were designed for marginalized populations, including immigrant and 2SLGBTQIA+ survivors.

In a "traditional" project, the shirts are color coded to represent the type of abuse the participant experienced. Because social stigma related to types of abuse and victim/survivor identity (e.g., sexual victimization of male victim/survivors), students at site 1 were concerned that making participants decorate a shirt with a particular color would put undue pressure on the victim/survivor, possibly forcing a disclosure they may not be ready to make. Additionally, students felt that the type of abuse should not define a person and thus should not define the color of their shirt. They opted not to place color restrictions on the shirt making.

There was also concern at site 3 that the traditional color-coding of the T-shirts did not acknowledge the possibility of polyvictimization, or exposure to multiple types of victimization.[23] How could someone who experienced both child abuse and SV, or SV and DV, choose a T-shirt color? Choosing a color might make victim/survivors feel the need to "rank" which victimization was worse and thereby minimize the impact of other forms. The decision was to use only white T-shirts for all of the designs and to offer a tie-dyeing station. Victim/survivors who had experienced multiple types of violence could make a tie-dyed shirt with the corresponding number of colors (e.g., a person who experienced child abuse, SV, and DV would have a tie-dyed shirt with three colors). At the art installation, these tie-dyed shirts were placed sporadically among the other shirts to provide visual representation of the overlapping nature of victimization and the concept of polyvictimization.

Transformational Power of the Clothesline Project

Increased visibility, education, and calls to action around victimization can be uniquely successful when using an arts-based approach. The Clothesline Project accomplishes this in two independent but interrelated ways: the individual T-shirts and the art installation. Each T-shirt represents an artistic expression of a victim/survivor's voice, experience, and truth: "Because making a tee shirt is another form of expression, sometimes these stories were not elicited verbally, or through words, but [rather by] symbols." Another participant reflected, "As someone who wants to become an art therapist, seeing and feeling the healing that comes from designing that tee shirt puts everything in perspective." This healing extends beyond the victim/survivors, as their art also has a profound impact on the event organizers and the art installation's audience.

The project provided an opportunity for participants to see the intersections that characterize people's lives in real time: "The shared experiences of so many survivors put on display taught me that survivors come in all shapes, sizes, genders, ethnicities, sexualities, and ages. This is something that I had always known in the back of my head, but never fully understood and thought critically about. It taught me to have a broader point of view of the world and understand that the most unlikely person could have gone through a trauma I cannot wrap my mind around. I learned a new way to use empathy."

For some participants, taking in all the shirts together at the art installation "was [the] first time seeing so many perspectives on domestic violence, as written, drawn, and painted displays . . . to see and empathize with." Others felt "the [profound] impact [of] walking through aisles of shirts containing illustrations of different perceptions of domestic/sexual violence." Seeing the representations of victim/survivors all together so clearly showed that each victim/survivor's truth is unique to his or her experience: "I thought it was interesting and humbling to just look at all of the shirts hanging up and know that there was a person's life and a person's story of abuse behind each one. This project made these things less of an abstract statistic and more of something that happens to real people in real life and with real consequences for victims. You can see how this stays with people over time and has lasting effects."

In addition to presenting individual experiences and resilience, the art installation provided connection: "Seeing the words of hundreds of survivors hung up for all to see is dumbfounding, but it brings with it a feeling of togetherness." This sense of togetherness could also become a support system: "The Clothesline Project was more than a powerful visual display. It was an eye-opener and a big support system. Through the project, I learned that when you feel like you're the only person that [has] been through [abuse] or [the] only [one] going through something you're not. There are people and resources out there waiting to help and listen whenever you need it. I can express myself by designing a T-shirt and don't have to look over my shoulder to see or hear someone judging me. I learned when you've experienced pain, strength and trust can be rebuilt along the way."

It was both the individual T-shirts *and* the art installation that created an experience where participants could feel seen and validated. One event organizer disclosed that she, too, was a victim/survivor: "This project showed me that I am not alone. I have never been alone, and I had an amazing support system waiting for me when I was ready to share my story." One participant credited her involvement in the project with her recovery:

> I too am a survivor of domestic violence and was completely captivated by the display of t-shirts. I still have a picture of the shirt [that] resonated the most with me that year—it stated: "You stole months, you stole my innocence, you made me hate myself, but now I am okay, now I love myself, now I have a purpose—to stop those like you. I am dedicated and strong." Walking through the Clothesline Project and reading all the statements of hope, such as the one above, really inspired me [to] embrace my story and utilize it to help and support others around me.

The project creates an opportunity for participants to transform their own understandings into a broader narrative of victimization: "Seeing the way people walked around and admired the shirts and applauded the strong and brave survivors who made them is an image I will forever hold in my heart because it was so great to see that the voices of the survivors through these shirts were heard and honored." In a society rife with victim blaming and victim shaming, the art installation sends a collective community message in support of victim/survivors, serving as a mechanism to construct counternarratives to societal messages of violence that are then "heard" (seen) by attendees and viewers (some projects are displayed online).

Clothesline Project as Counternarrative

Narratives are successful in their ability to evoke emotions in the listener through the narrator's presentation of emotions and symbolic codes. "Symbolic codes surround cultural narratives of identities because they contain images of the rights, responsibilities, and normative expectations of people in the world, and of the expected affective responses to these people."[24] Narratives surrounding SV and DV often blame the victim/survivor, fail to capture the many variations in victim/survivor experiences, and do not consider that the destructive effects may take an invisible toll on the community. In contrast, the art installation emphasizes victim/survivors' diverse and varied perspectives, communicates victim/survivor support, and sheds light on the community impact of SV and DV.

In centering victim/survivors as the narrators of their own stories, one student noted: "The creative potential allowed by the clothesline project empowers survivors to capture their thoughts in experience in any way that feels acceptable for them, rather than enforcing a narrative structure." This gives voice to victim/survivors and reenforces the notion that their voices matter. Despite the prevalence of SV and DV, victim/survivors are often silenced.[25] Participating in the project teaches students to recognize silences, absences, and the destructive power of both. As one student wrote, "Among other things, I have learned that silence is a tool abusers take advantage of, and that part of the pursuit to end domestic violence must involve sharing stories of abuse and using our voices to ignite change and spread awareness." Participants were proud that the projects "helped break the silence, and the stigmatization of 'victims,' by giving them a voice with a blank T-shirt and some markers." This illustrates the power of the T-shirts in creating a counternarrative to violence, one that empowers and supports victim/survivors rather than silences and shames them.

After studying societal reactions to disclosures and the negative effects it can have on a victim/survivor to be silenced, shamed, or blamed, students at site 3 decided to collect the types of supportive messages that victim/survivors deserve to hear. They engaged the campus community in this process by soliciting messages of support written on three-by-five-inch unlined index cards. Community members wrote more than one thousand index cards with messages such as "I believe you," "I'm sorry this happened to you," "You matter," "This was not your fault," "You are not alone," "Your strength is inspiring," "You deserve to feel safe," "Healing is not linear," "Believe survivors," "You deserve a love that doesn't hurt," "Your story is powerful," "We are here for you," "You are courageous," "#metoo," "I'm sorry that people did not treat you the way you deserve to be treated," and "You are worthy of love and respect."

When hanging the T-shirts at the art installation, event organizers reflected on the victim/survivors' messages and then intentionally searched for note cards with supportive messaging appropriate to each victim/survivor. The juxtaposition of the note cards with the T-shirts constituted a powerful visual representation of community support for victim/survivors. It had a tremendous effect on participants: "When I walked up to the courtyard and saw all of the support cards hung up on the walls I was floored. Seeing the kind and supportive words from people in our community, all in one place, was one of the best things I have ever seen."

Art with an Impact

Experiential opportunities can have a long-term influence on individuals' understandings and behaviors.[26] The Clothesline Project allowed students and community members to engage in collaborative artistic activism. For some, it shaped future activism: "I think the most important takeaway for me is educating and promoting leadership in victims and survivors. . . . Though

I am an undocumented, queer, woman of color, there are certain traumatic experiences I have not been through that other women have. [Now] I want to make sure that . . . I always provide a safe space that accommodates to the needs of folks instead of assuming their needs."

For others, the project changed the way they thought of their role in their communities: "It showed that even though I am a man without any personal experience in domestic or sexual violence, I can still be a proponent of positive change through informing others (specifically young men) about how to process and combat abuse." Beyond a deeper personal understanding of the issue, the experience of working with others to change societal discussions about abuse helped to combat misinformation: "This project . . . taught me that everything that I knew about domestic violence before was wrong, and I am a much better activist and community member, armed with the knowledge to spread awareness about it to everyone around me. [Armed] with the knowledge I have gained . . . I know that I am able to make a change, even a small one, [in] the world."

The Clothesline Project empowered participants to believe that they can make social change happen by using their voices not only to make progress in their knowledge and in themselves but to educate those around them who need it most. It also shaped participants' ideas about the kind of activist and community organizer they wanted to be: "one who is inclusive, sensitive, and encourages survivor activists to cultivate their own kind of power, rather than one who decides what 'empowerment' should look like." Through implementing the project in three different spaces, and in slightly different ways, we experienced the power of community to offer a transformational event with the power to enact social change. We hope that others will consider creating their own Clothesline Projects.

Notes

1. A "participant/artist" is a person who does not identify as a "victim/survivor" but chooses to make a shirt, a note card, or another piece of art about SV or DV that is included in the installation.

2. Rachel Anderson Droogsma, "'I Am the Woman Next Door': The Clothesline Project as Woman Abuse Survivors' Societal Critique," *Communication, Culture and Critique* 2, no. 4 (2009): 483.

3. Rachel Anderson Droogsma, "Clothesline Project," Clothesline Project, accessed January 28, 2022, www.theclotheslineproject.org.

4. Teresa Cheek, Kristen Rector, and Cindy Davis, "The Clothesline Project:

An Experiential Learning Project with MSW Students," *Journal of Teaching in Social Work* 27, no. 1–2 (2007): 144.

5. Patricia C. Hipple, "Clothing Their Resistance in Hegemonic Dress: The Clothesline Project's Response to Violence against Women," *Clothing and Textiles Research Journal* 18, no. 3 (2000): 173.

6. Jill Gregory, April Lewton, Stephanie Schmidt, Diane Smith, and Mark Mattern, "Body Politics with Feeling: The Power of the Clothesline Project," *New Political Science* 24, no. 3 (2002): 433–48.

7. Gregory et al., "Body Politics with Feeling"; Hipple, "Clothing Their Resistance"; Laura Julier, "Private Texts and Social Activism: Reading the Clothesline Project," *English Education* 26, no. 4 (1993): 249–59; Barbara Kaelin Mercer, *Personal Significance of Ongoing Participation in the Clothesline Project for Survivors of Childhood Sexual Abuse* (Bloomington: Indiana University Press, 2003); Constance J. Ostrowski, "The Clothesline Project: Women's Stories of Gender-Related Violence," *Women and Language* 19, no. 1 (1996): 37–42; Susan Willis, "Airing Dirty Laundry Transforms Survivors," *Herizons* 9, no. 3 (1995): 11.

8. Hipple, "Clothing Their Resistance," 174; see also Lora Bex Lempert and Synnov Skorge, "Silent No More, We're Hanging Out Our Dirty Laundry: The South Africa Clothesline Project," *Women in Action—Rome then Manila*, 2002, 19–22; Jennie Ruby, "Airing Society's Dirty Laundry: The Clothesline Project," *Off Our Backs* 28, no. 11 (1998): 4.

9. Hipple, "Clothing Their Resistance," 174.

10. Hipple, "Clothing Their Resistance," 173.

11. Lora Bex Lempert, "The Clothesline Project as Student Production: Creativity, Voice, and Action," *Teaching Sociology* 31, no. 4 (2003): 478–84.

12. Lempert, "The Clothesline Project as Student Production," 481.

13. Brian K. Payne and Rebecca Fogerty, "Narratives about Violence: The Words of College Students," *Social Science Journal* 44, no. 2 (2007): 372.

14. Payne and Fogerty, "Narratives about Violence," 371.

15. Droogsma, "Clothesline Project."

16. Droogsma, "'I Am the Woman Next Door,'" 484.

17. Site 1: Arizona State University; site 2: Middle Georgia State University; site 3: University of Kentucky (presented in chronological order).

18. Ricky S. Gutierrez, Debra Reeves-Gutierrez, and Ronald Helms, "Service Learning and Criminal Justice Students: An Assessment of the Effects of Co-curricular Pedagogy on Graduation Rates," *Journal of Criminal Justice Education* 23, no. 3 (2012): 356–80; Molly George, Helen Lim, Schannae Lucas, and Robert Meadows, "Learning by Doing: Experiential Learning in Criminal Justice," *Journal of Criminal Justice Education* 26, no. 4 (2015): 471–92; Julie A. Hatcher and Robert G. Bringle, eds., *Understanding Service-Learning and Community Engagement: Crossing Boundaries through Research* (Charlotte, NC: Information Age Publishing, 2012).

19. National Coalition Against Domestic Violence, "2021 Domestic Violence Awareness Month," accessed January 28, 2022, www.ncadv.org/2021DVAM.

20. Patricia Hill Collins, "Black Feminist Thought in the Matrix of Domination," in *Black Feminist Thought: Knowledge, Consciousness, and the Politics of Empowerment* (Boston: Unwin Hyman, 1990), 221–38. On the intersectional approach, see Kimberlé Crenshaw, "Mapping the Margins: Identity Politics, Intersectionality, and Violence against Women," *Stanford Law Review* 43, no. 6 (1991): 1241–99; Patricia Hill Collins and Sirma Bilge, *Intersectionality*, 2nd ed. (Medford, MA: Polity Press, 2020); Combahee River Collective, "A Black Feminist Statement," *Women's Studies Quarterly* 42, no. 3–4 (2014): 271–80; Deborah K. King, "Multiple Jeopardy, Multiple Consciousness: The Context of a Black Feminist Ideology," *Signs: Journal of Women in Culture and Society* 14, no. 1 (1988): 42–72; Vivian M. May, *Pursuing Intersectionality, Unsettling Dominant Imaginaries* (New York: Routledge, 2015).

21. Denise A. Donnelly, Kimberly J. Cook, Debra Van Ausdale, and Lara Foley, "White Privilege, Color Blindness, and Services to Battered Women," *Violence against Women* 11, no. 1 (2005): 6–37; Brianna C. Delker, Rowan Salton, and Kate C. McLean, "Giving Voice to Silence: Empowerment and Disempowerment in the Developmental Shift from Trauma 'Victim' to 'Survivor-Advocate,'" *Journal of Trauma and Dissociation* 21, no. 2 (2020): 242–63.

22. Droogsma, "Clothesline Project." 2SLGBTQIA+ stands for Two-Spirit, lesbian, gay, bisexual, transgender, queer/questioning, intersex, asexual + pansexual + agender + gender queer + bigender + gender variant + pangender.

23. David Finkelhor, Richard K. Ormrod, and Heather A. Turner, "Poly-victimization: A Neglected Component in Child Victimization," *Child Abuse and Neglect* 31, no. 1 (2007): 7–26.

24. Donileen R. Loseke, "The Study of Identity as Cultural, Institutional, Organizational, and Personal Narratives: Theoretical and Empirical Integrations," *Sociological Quarterly* 48, no. 4 (2007): 666.

25. Courtney E. Ahrens, "Being Silenced: The Impact of Negative Social Reactions on the Disclosure of Rape," *American Journal of Community Psychology* 38, no. 3–4 (2006): 263–74; Elizabeth A. Armstrong, Miriam Gleckman-Krut, and Lanora Johnson, "Silence, Power, and Inequality: An Intersectional Approach to Sexual Violence," *Annual Review of Sociology* 44 (2018): 99–122; Anna Gjika and Alison J. Marganski, "Silent Voices, Hidden Stories: A Review of Sexual Assault (Non)Disclosure Literature, Emerging Issues, and Call to Action," *International Journal for Crime, Justice and Social Democracy* 9, no. 4 (2020): 163–76; Philip N. S. Rumney, "Gay Male Rape Victims: Law Enforcement, Social Attitudes and Barriers to Recognition," *International Journal of Human Rights* 13, no. 2–3 (2009): 233–50.

26. Jay Caulfield and Treesa Woods, "Experiential Learning: Exploring Its Long-Term Impact on Socially Responsible Behavior," *Journal of the Scholarship of Teaching and Learning* 13, no. 2 (2013): 31–48.

16

#WhatWereYouWearing

Jasmin Goodman and Wei Sun

. . . if only we could
end rape
by simply changing clothes

i remember also
what he was wearing
that night
even though
it's true
that no one
has ever asked.

"What were you wearing?" is a question sexual assault survivors around the world have painstakingly had to answer. Victim blaming in sexual assaults is commonly displayed in courts and public forums, and the victims are usually questioned about their own behaviors in causing the incidents.[1] Mary Simmerling's chilling lines above speak to the moment when, after reporting an assault, survivors are asked to recall the length, color, and type of clothing worn during their attack. The implication behind the question is that their attire could, in some way, have prevented the assault. In an effort to end the culture of victim blaming, and to leverage the benefits of art as counteractivism, the University of Arkansas's Sexual Assault and Prevention Education Center debuted the "What I Was Wearing" Survivor Art Installation in 2013.[2]

The installation featured eighteen outfits inspired by the clothing worn by student assault survivors. The items ranged from a child's sundress to a college student's bikini worn after a day of canoeing with friends. In addition to the re-created outfits, brief descriptions of what each survivor experienced were posted to give viewers a better understanding of the traumatic aftermath of sexual assault. Since its inception, similar exhibits have been presented at Ohio University, Baylor University, and other US universities.

In the midst of the global #MeToo movement, there is increased international awareness of sexual assault and harassment. In 2018, Brussels debuted its version of the US survivor art installation. This time, the outfits included a police uniform, a men's shirt and jeans, and a child's My Little Pony T-shirt.[3] In solidarity with survivors around the world, the social media hashtag #WhatWereYouWearing has been shared and translated into many languages on Twitter. Users have started to tell their stories and post pictures. #WhatWereYouWearing, along with #MeToo, has become the newest way for victims to give voice to their experiences and for others to show support so that victims do not have to bear the effects of sexual aggression alone and can survive the sexual harassment and violence. Our study investigates how social media users respond to text and images associated with the #WhatWereYouWearing hashtag. The goal is to offer a deeper understanding of arts-based action as an effective tool for counteractivism.

Social Activism on Social Media

User-driven social media movements are essential to today's digital public sphere.[4] Unlike traditional social justice initiatives that require organizing large groups and coordinating sit-ins, social media activism often begins with an impassioned tweet and a catchy hashtag. By leveraging the autonomy of social media platforms, movements such as #BlackLivesMatter and #Occupy have shaped the public discourse, contributed to digital culture, and allowed users to create and negotiate the meanings of each movement—all the while remaining independent of controlling institutional powers.[5] Through the vehicle of hashtag activism, social media users produce counternarratives that later infiltrate mainstream media and influence policy.[6] Referred to in the literature as the "networked subaltern" and the "feminist counterpublic," they use social media as an effective tool for political activism.[7]

Melissa Brown, Rashawn Ray, Ed Summers, and Neil Fraistat examined social media use as a means for developing and sustaining collective identities through political activism. Using quantitative content analysis, they analyzed 463,957 tweets, including the #SayHerName hashtag. Initially used to amplify the death of Sandra Bland, an African American woman who died in police custody, the hashtag has since expanded to bring attention to the deaths of Black cisgender and transgender women across the United States. Brown et al.'s study found that the #SayHerName hashtag emerged as a new type of feminist activism within the digital public sphere. Hyper-marginalized groups leveraged the hashtag to call attention to the disproportionate amount of violence faced by members of their communities.[8]

Global Impact of the #MeToo Movement

Since its inception in 2006, the #MeToo movement, founded by Tarana Burke, has expanded beyond its initial emphasis on African American women and girls. Sexual harassment and assault survivors from Japan, India, and France have used the hashtag to share their own stories of abuse at the hands of wealthy and powerful men.[9] Wei Sun specifically analyzed the global impact of the #MeToo movement among Chinese women. In a critical discourse analysis of posts and user comments on the popular overseas Chinese website Wenxuecity.com, Sun found that while women across the globe have co-opted the hashtag, within the Chinese diaspora victims are doubted more than they are supported. Commenters often question the timing of women coming forward with stories of abuse, as well as the women's intentions. Most relevant to Sun's study are the women in support of #MeToo who use the hashtag to stand in support of the victims. Those women are hailed as heroes for not only reporting their assaults but also gaining victories in court.[10] Sarah Jaffe calls the #MeToo movement a collective power, through which women around the world are empowered to stand up against sexual assaults. The social movement is "a watershed moment in contemporary feminism, one that has made sexual violence into big news."[11] Phumzile Mlambo-Ngcuka, the executive director of UN Women, states that one billion women worldwide currently suffer from sexual violence. The World Health Organization has declared that sexual violence against women is a world health crisis. Mlambo-Ngcuka salutes the global #MeToo movement, which has shown the "strength of solidarity and sisterhood."[12]

Creative Arts for Trauma Therapy and Counteractivism

The benefits of art as a form of trauma therapy are well documented in the academic literature. Scholars have created and implemented various ways to help trauma victims recover, such as establishing sustained warm relationships, infusing neuroscience into counseling, using corrective emotional experiments, integrating mindful awareness, and applying mediation in prolonged grief disorder.[13] In an effort to address art as both therapy and counteractivism, Lisa Kay and Alice Arnold facilitated a working session for artists and educators to create visual images as a response to violence. More than forty participants created colorful collages as a means for identifying counteractive strategies. In addition to counteractive strategies, the creative works served as a form of emotional release for participants impacted by violence. Ultimately, the session provided a safe space for emotional expression, as well as a heightened awareness of how arts educators can use art as a form of counteractivism.[14]

With the increased international awareness of sexual harassment and assault, and the global impact of the #MeToo movement, our study poses the following research questions (RQ 1–3):

RQ1: How do social media users respond to #WhatWereYouWearing and related images? What themes emerged from the discussion?

RQ2: When social media users respond to #WhatWereYouWearing and related images, what gender differences exist?

RQ3: What cultural implications have been reflected in campaigns of #WhatWereYouWearing and the #MeToo movement?

Theoretical Framework

Public sphere theory and feminist theory provide the analytical framework for our study.[15] The traditional public sphere represents a space where private individuals gather to engage in public discourse about topics of general interest.[16] Through these interactions, citizens develop "public opinion," which is the by-product of their ability to assemble in an unrestricted fashion.[17] Historically, the public sphere was accessible only to members of the European high society assembling in an unrestricted fashion to discuss the political and civil affairs of the day. With the widespread availability of social media and digital technology, conversations in the public sphere now include discussants from all class backgrounds, engaging in conversations that range from politics to social justice. While some scholars suggest that social media is not an extension of Jürgen Habermas's public sphere, we contend that historically marginalized communities—in this instance, survivors of gendered-based sexual violence—use these platforms as a mechanism to exercise political and social commentary.[18] More recently, the public sphere has also expanded to include critical feminist discourse.

Feminist theory also frames our study as it centers and critiques the experiences of women in society.[19] Addressing the marginalization and oppression of women across multiple fronts, feminist theory allows us to examine how women use the public sphere to communicate stories of survival and to connect with a vibrant community of supporters.

Methodology

We use critical discourse analysis and visual framing for our study. The Pew Research Center concluded that more than half of the US public engage in some form of civic activism on social media. The same study found that social media platforms help give voice to the marginalized and underrepresented.[20] In our study, we employ critical discourse analysis and visual framing to analyze English-language Twitter posts using the #WhatWereYouWearing hashtag.

Critical discourse analysis is an effective method for examining the interrelationship between language, power, and ideas and studying how abuse, dominance, and inequality are enacted.[21] Our study also maximizes the benefits of critical discourse analysis by examining a social problem, taking a multidisciplinary approach, and focusing on the role of discourse in challenging power and dominance in society.[22]

Visual framing uses recognizable images to create or perpetuate a shared meaning within a cultural group.[23] Unlike textual framing, visual frames are known to invoke strong emotional reactions, much stronger than traditional text frames.[24] Visual frames also allow for easier understanding and faster audience recall.[25] Consistent with Porismita Borah, our study analyzes all associated images included in posts with the #WhatWereYouWearing hashtag.[26]

We searched Twitter and Instagram using the #WhatWereYouWearing hashtag. This search yielded 120 posts on Twitter and 1,104 posts on Instagram. The posts were then filtered to exclude any tweets or images not related to the global sexual assault campaign. Ultimately, a total of 118 tweets and photos were examined. Each post was examined for its text content, as well as any associated images. The coding sheet was developed based on the research questions and themes present in the dataset.

Discussion

After we carefully reviewed the coding sheet, read the tweets, and examined the associated photos, recurring themes emerged. These are arranged by research questions below, along with a brief discussion.

RQ1: *Social Media Users' Responses to #WhatWereYouWearing*

From the research questions and other prominent themes, we identified several themes. These themes included event promotion, participant response to the national and international exhibits, survivor narratives, references to the hashtag creator, and sexist responses. Forty-one of the 118 tweets were related to promoting local and international survivor exhibits. Twenty-three tweets were by participants responding to the images and narratives shared during the exhibit. Fifteen posts were by survivors sharing their own personal stories of abuse and harassment. Sexist responses and references to the hashtag creator had five tweets each. The dates for the Twitter posts ranged from 2017 to 2019.

THEME 1: PARTICIPANT RESPONSE TO THE NATIONAL AND INTERNATIONAL EXHIBITS

The national and international exhibits provoked sympathy and deep emotions from almost all of the users who posted to Twitter using the hashtag. User @TaylWester wrote, "This is heartbreaking." Another user wrote, "This honestly made me cry." Other users expressed emotions ranging from sadness to anger, frustration, and despair. User @OldCrowNest wrote: "If #WhatWereYouWearing, #YesAllWomen, and #YouOkSis, etc etc etc don't make the point, I don't know what the hell will. So tired."

Twitter user @amyfdavisa wrote: "What you wear is not the cause of the sexual assault. The problem is in the mind and body of the perpetrator, not in the mind and body of the victim. #WhatWereYouWearing The report on this amazing exhibit is from last fall." The accompanying thumbnail image is linked to media coverage of the University of Kansas exhibit. Another user, @FCCBastrop, linked to the same article and asked, "How is this question not extinct yet?"

THEME 2: SURVIVOR NARRATIVES

Beyond the participants' responses to the images and narratives shared during the exhibit, others took the opportunity to answer the question the

#WhatWereYouWearing hashtag posed. Twitter user @PapayaTheBee wrote, "I acknowledge my own sexual assault in a very public way when @steenfox initiated #WhatWereYouWearing." Another user wrote, "My name is khulud khamis and i am a survivor of #sexualviolence."

Twitter user @Sister_Serendip wrote: "When it happened to #MeToo I had trepidation about telling Police what I was wearing bc just as I knew I had every right to be naked in my room I knew #survivors were blamed for assaults. #SneekPeak @MetaTheatreCo #whatwereyouwearing show for #Fiveonfriday." The user included a picture of herself standing before a group of people with the words "What I Was Wearing" projected on an audio-visual screen behind her.

User @dellysmelly shared her own personal story of abuse by writing: "#SexualAssaultAwarenessMonth My favorite black and white striped shirt and high-waisted jeans. I was trying to figure out which toothpaste worked with my coupon. #WhatWereYouWearing."

THEME 3: SEXIST AND PATRIARCHAL RESPONSES

In true form, sexist and patriarchal responses emerged as a theme. Most of the tweets related to this theme were users sharing typical sexist responses to sexual assault and harassment. Twitter user @NikkiNikkinow2 tweeted a series of hashtags that included #WhatDidYouDo, #WhatWereYouWearing, #DontBeSoSensitive, #TakeItAsACompliment, #BoysWillBeBoys, and #Insubordinate (if offender = superior) #GetOverIt.

However, one male user, @andrewsduncan1, tweeted: "Why do women go on about equality but wear clothes showing a lot of flesh in the shoulder, leg and bosom department. It's wonderful to see but doesn't this negate their attempts at equality?" The tweet received 16,300 responses, 254 retweets, and 1,100 likes from other Twitter users. @DrDenaGrayson challenged @andrewsduncan1 by tweeting, "Meanwhile, men strut around topless, showing their nipples, and yet no one seems to care." A female user, @eastwood_pat, wrote: "That's good, but I also see young women teetering around on heels, presumably because they have been told they should, or their workplace culture demands it. Depends on the situation, & maybe that's just what they like."

RQ2: *Gender Differences in User Responses*

Gender does not seem to influence a user's perspective on the issue. Both male and female users posted sentiments on both sides of the debate. Two male users questioned the rationale of the #WhatWereYouWearing question, while a female user, @eastwood_pat, questioned the types of clothing and shoes worn by women. Male user @NicholasFosterr posted: "#SexualAssaultAwarenessMonth it sucks this is even a question. If you are ever in a conversation with a survivor of sexual assault, never ask them #WhatWereYouWearing... because it truly does not matter." The accompanying images were from a survivor installation and featured a black-and-purple dress and a military uniform. Another male user, @NotEven_Steven, wrote in response to @NicholasFosterr's post: "The fact that people even ask that question is what floors me. While one person can't fix what's been done, they can certainly make it a lot worse. I wish more people would remember that."

RQ3: *Cultural Implications toward the #MeToo Movement*

Users expressed a variety of opinions about the global and cultural implications of the rape culture and the #MeToo movement. These posts included perspectives about the US rape culture, as well as the shared experiences of survivors around the world.

Twitter user @ErinSC78 wrote: "The backlog of kits & reports is heartbreaking. To be violated twice, the rape & the kit, and then ignored? And ppl wonder why vics don't come forward? Then news slanders them. #WhatWereYouWearing &other bs questions. Trials where perp goes free? #Disgusting #GiveVictimsJustice."

User @DrPoonamMadar wrote: "Was it really my fault? No. No. No. NEVER. #MeToo #Women #Gender #men #MenToo #Feminisim #Equality #Sexism #stop #harassment #whatwereyouwearing #education #inequality #quote #EmpowerWomen #policy #law #politics."

Most notable and relevant to this research question was the associated image that featured white text against a black background. The text read: "'Was it really my fault?,' asked the Short Skirt. 'No, it happened with me too,' replied the Burqa." An Instagram picture shows a written message: "You RAPED her because her clothes provoked you? I should break your face because your stupidity provokes me."

Findings and Future Studies

The responses to the #WhatWereYouWearing Twitter hashtag offer insight into the role of art as counteractivism. The cultural, gender-based, and global perspectives of sexual assault and harassment give scholars a better understanding of how audiences responded to the survivor installation and, ultimately, offer an updated view on the culture of victim shaming and blaming. Many of the tweets included images from the survivor installation, along with emotional reactions to survivor narratives. Some users found the courage to share their own stories of abuse and harassment and even included photos of what they were wearing when it occurred. A majority of the male users who responded to the installation expressed great empathy and support for all victims of abuse.

The New York City cartoonist Hilary Campbell, in explaining her cartoon "Oh Yeah, Me Too," has said: "The cartoon is pretty self-explanatory, but for me it's just about how women who share stories often find out that we all . . . experience the same pain, no matter how different our backgrounds."[27] Marcelo Svirsky asserts that activism is an open-ended process: it intersects with social struggles, ideas, and affections, which ultimately lead to actions.[28]

According to the Tate Museum in Great Britain, the artists who engage in activism are creating art in the form of "political or social currency, actively addressing cultural power structures rather than representing them or simply describing them."[29] The use of art as counteractivism is to "empower individuals and communities and is generally situated in the public arena."[30] The "What I Was Wearing" display is not a traditional art exhibit; however, it is an effort to end the culture of victim blaming and to leverage the benefits of art as counteractivism.

Notes

Epigraph: Mary Simmerling, "What Was I Wearing?," SAFE Alliance, 2005, www.safeaustin.org/what-was-i-wearing.

1. Katherine Curchin, "The Dilemma of Rape Avoidance Advice: Acknowledging Women's Agency without Blaming Victims of Sexual Assault," *Women's Studies International Forum* 75 (2019): 102240, https://doi.org/10.1016/j.wsif.2019.102240; Kathryn R. Klement, Elizabeth A. Bates, Linda K. Kaye, and Charlotte R. Pennington, "The Impact of Gendered Stereotypes on Perceptions of Violence: A Commentary," *Sex Roles* 81 (2019): 34–43; Jessica Williamson and Kelly Serna, "Reconsidering Forced Labels: Outcomes of Sexual Assault Survivors versus Victims (and Those Who Choose Neither)," *Violence against Women* 24, no. 6 (2018): 668–83; Alexandra I. Zelin, Ruth V. Walker, and Dawn M. Johnson, "Cornered at a Bar: How Victim Clothing, Alcohol Intake, and Relationship with Bystander Impact Intention to Help," *Violence against Women* 25, no. 10 (2019): 1163–90.

2. "What Was I Wearing," 2013, University of Arkansas, Fayetteville, Arkansas.

3. Alice Cuddy, "Brussels Exhibition Shows 'No Outfit Prevents Rape,'" *Euronews*, January 17, 2018, www.euronews.com/2018/01/17/brussels-recreates-rape-survivors-outfits-to-tackle-victim-blaming.

4. Adam William Chalmers and Paul Alexander Shotton, "Changing the Face of Advocacy? Explaining Interest Organizations' Use of Social Media Strategies," *Political Communication* 33, no. 3 (2016): 374–91; Kuhika Gupta, Joseph Ripberger, and Wesley Wehde, "Advocacy Group Messaging on Social Media: Using the Narrative Policy Framework to Study Twitter Messages about Nuclear Energy Policy in the United States," *Policy Studies Journal* 46, no. 1 (2018): 119–36; Judith E. Rosenbaum, *Constructing Digital Cultures: Tweets, Trends, Race, and Gender* (Lanham, MD: Lexington Books, 2017); Sarah L. Steele and Tyler Shores, "Real and Unreal Masculinities: The Celebrity Image in Anti-trafficking Campaigns," *Journal of Gender Studies* 24, no. 4 (2015): 419–35; Wei Sun, "A Critical Discourse Analysis of 'Minority Women for Trump' Campaigns on Social Media," in *Reconceptualizing New Media and Intercultural Communication in a Networked Society*, ed. Nurhayat Bilge and María Inés Marino (Hersey, PA: IGI Global, 2028), 303–27; Julie Uldam, "Social Media Visibility: Challenges to Activism," *Media, Culture and Society* 40, no. 1 (2018): 41–58.

5. Kathy Byers, "One of Five Million: A Story of Showing Up and Being Counted," *Reflections: Narratives of Professional Helping* 23, no. 2 (2017): 70–75; Manuel Castells, *Networks of Outrage and Hope: Social Movements in the Internet Age* (Cambridge, UK: Polity Press, 2015); Ruth Milkman, "A New Political Generation: Millennials and the Post-2008 Wave of Protest," *American Sociological Review* 82, no. 1 (2017): 1–31; Rosenbaum, *Constructing Digital Cultures.*

6. Yarimar Bonilla and Jonathan Rosa, "#Ferguson: Digital Protest, Hashtag Ethnography, and the Racial Politics of Social Media in the United States," *Ethnologist* 42, no. 1 (2015): 4–17; Alyssa D. Niccolini, "'The Rape Joke': Censorship, Affective Activisms, and Feeling Subjects," *Journal of Gender Studies* 27, no. 1 (2018): 102–13; Rosenbaum, *Constructing Digital Cultures.*

7. Castells, *Networks of Outrage and Hope*; John B. K. Purcell, Rebecca Oldham, Dana A. Weiser, and Elizabeth A. Sharp, "Lights, Camera, Activism: Using a Film Series to Generate Feminist Dialogue about Campus Sexual Violence," *Family Relations* 66, no. 1 (2017): 139–53; Rosenbaum, *Constructing Digital Cultures.*

8. Melissa Brown, Rashawn Ray, Ed Summers, and Neil Fraistat, "#SayHerName: A Case Study of Intersectional Social Media Activism," *Ethnic and Racial Studies* 40, no. 11 (2017): 1831–46; Tressie McMillan Cottom, "Black Cyberfeminism: Ways Forward for Classification Situations, Intersectionality and Digital Sociology," SocArXiv, December 7, 2016, https://doi.org/10.31235/osf.io/vnvh9; Safiya Umoja Noble, "A Future for Intersectional Black Feminist Studies," *Scholar and Feminist Online* 13, no. 3 (2016): 1–8.

9. Sanjana Pegu, "MeToo in India: Building Revolutions from Solidarities,"

Decision (Indian Institute of Management, Calcutta) 46, no. 2 (2019): 151–68; Sarah Wildman, "#MeToo Goes Global," *Foreign Policy*, no. 231 (Winter 2019): 24, https://foreignpolicy.com/gt-essay/metoo-goes-global-feminism-activism.

10. Wei Sun, "Rice Bunny and #WoYeShi: Online Reactions of Overseas Chinese to the #MeToo Movements in China and the West," *Howard Journal of Communications* 31, no. 3 (2020): 245–63, https://doi.org/10.1080/10646175.2019.1666069.

11. Sarah Jaffe, "The Collective Power of #MeToo," *Dissent* 65, no. 2 (2018), www.dissentmagazine.org/article/collective-power-of-me-too-organizing-justice-patriarchy-class.

12. Phumzile Mlambo-Ngcuka, "The #TimeIsNow for Solidarity and Sisterhood," *UN Chronicle* 55, no. 2 (2018): 9.

13. Bonnie Badenoch, *The Heart of Trauma: Healing the Embodied Brain in the Context of Relationships* (New York: W. W. Norton, 2008); Eric T. Beeson and Thomas A. Field, "Neurocounseling: A New Section of the *Journal of Mental Health Counseling*," *Journal of Mental Health Counseling* 39, no. 1 (2017): 71–83; Kristi Perryman, Paul Blisard, and Rochelle Moss, "Using Creative Arts in Trauma Therapy: The Neuroscience of Healing," *Journal of Mental Health Counseling* 4, no. 1 (2019): 80–94; Daniel J. Siegel, *The Mindful Therapist: A Clinician's Guide to Mindsight and Neural Integration* (New York: W. W. Norton, 2010); Ilanit Hasson-Ohayon, Tuvia Peri, Itai Rotschild, and Rivka Tuval-Mashiach, "The Mediating Role of Integration of Loss in the Relationship between Dissociation and Prolonged Grief Disorder," *Journal of Clinical Psychology* 73, no. 12 (2017): 1717–28; Sandra Capaldi, Anu Asnaani, Laurie J. Zandberg, Joseph K. Carpenter, and Edna B. Foa, "Therapeutic Alliance during Prolonged Exposure versus Client-Centered Therapy for Adolescent Posttraumatic Stress Disorder," *Journal of Clinical Psychology* 72, no. 10 (2016): 1026–36.

14. Lisa Kay and Alice Arnold, "Order from Chaos: An Arts-Based Approach to Counteract Trauma and Violence," *Art Education* 67, no. 3 (2014): 31–37.

15. Jürgen Habermas, Sara Lennox, and Frank Lennox, "The Public Sphere: An Encyclopedia Article," *New German Critique* 3 (1964): 49–55; Joan B. Landes, "The Public and the Private Sphere: A Feminist Reconsideration," in *Feminists Read Habermas: Gendering the Subject of Discourse*, ed. Johanna Meehan (New York: Routledge, 1995), 91–116.

16. Habermas, Lennox, and Lennox, "The Public Sphere."

17. Habermas, Lennox, and Lennox, "The Public Sphere"; Lisa M. Kruse, Dawn R. Norris, and Jonathan R. Flinchum, "Social Media as a Public Sphere? Politics on Social Media," *Sociological Quarterly*, 59, no. 1 (2018): 62–84.

18. Kruse, Norris, and Flinchum, "Social Media as a Public Sphere?"

19. Landes, "The Public and the Private Sphere."

20. Monica Anderson, Skye Toor, Kenneth Olmstead, Lee Rainie, and Aaron Smith, *Activism in the Social Media Age* (Washington, DC: Pew Research Center,

2018), www.pewresearch.org/internet/2018/07/11/activism-in-the-social-media-age.

21. Sun, "A Critical Discourse Analysis"; Teun A. van Dijk, "A Critical Discourse Analysis," in *The Handbook of Critical Discourse Analysis*, ed. Deborah Schiffrin, Deborah Tannen, and Heidi E. Hamilton (Malden, MA: Blackwell Publishers), 352–71.

22. Van Dijk, "A Critical Discourse Analysis."

23. James K. Hertog and Douglas M. McLeod, "A Multiperspectival Approach to Framing Analysis: A Field Guide," in *Framing Public Life: Perspectives on Media and Our Understanding of the Social World*, ed. Stephen E. Reese, Oscar H. Gandy Jr., and August E. Grant (Mahwah, NJ: Lawrence Erlbaum Associates, 2001), 141–62; Lulu Rodriguez and Daniela Dimitrova, "The Levels of Visual Framing," *Journal of Visual Literacy* 30 (2011): 48–65.

24. Rodriguez and Dimitrova, "The Levels of Visual Framing."

25. Robert M. Entman, "Framing U.S. Coverage of International News: Contrasts in Narratives of the KAL and Iran Air Incidents," *Journal of Communication* 41, no. 4 (1991): 6–27.

26. Porismita Borah, "Comparing Visual Framing in Newspapers: Hurricane Katrina versus Tsunami," *Newspaper Research Journal* 30, no. 1 (2009): 50–57.

27. Jessica Bennett, "The #MeToo Moment: Art Inspired by the Reckoning," *New York Times*, January 12, 2018.

28. Marcelo Svirsky, "Defining Activism," *Deleuze Studies* 4 (2010): 163–82, www.jstor.org/stable/45331440.

29. Tate Museum, "Activist Art," 2022, www.tate.org.uk/art/art-terms/a/activist-art.

30. Tate Museum, "Activist Art."

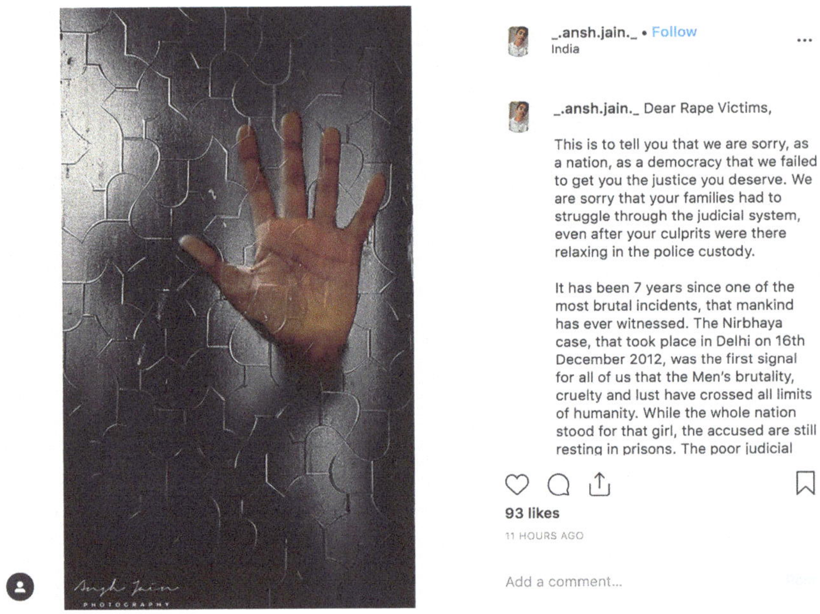

Ansh Jain, photographer. Posted to #metoo on Instagram by @_.ansh.jain._ and archived by the author on 30 November 2019. The account is no longer active.

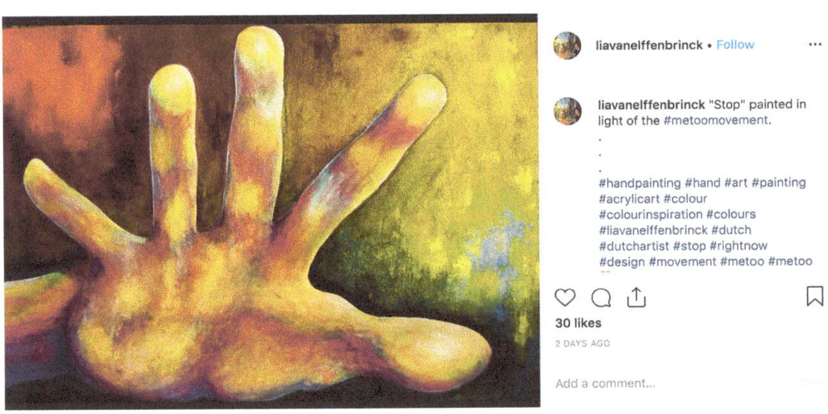

Lia van Elffenbrinck, artist. Posted on Instagram by @liavanelffenbrinck and titled "Stop" in the comments. Archived by author on 9 October 2019.

17

Seeing #MeToo

Shared Images of Sexual Violence

Leslie-Jean Thornton

Picture a hand imprinted on a cave wall some forty thousand years ago, give or take a few centuries. The meaning of that image—and there are many like it around the world—isn't known, but it's incontrovertible such a lasting marker signified that someone was there. It is evidence of human presence and someone's need (or at least their action) to record that fact. Then fast-forward to the recent past and the #MeToo movement. There might be no better way to document the importance of that visual symbol in our present-day lives than to do a Google search on "hand" and "#MeToo."

Instantly, the computer returns a collection of images that resonate deeply with one of humankind's earliest impulses to be known. There is the upraised hand, visually referencing those of the ancient caves, shown as an assertion of identity, strength, and togetherness. There have been many other uses of the hand as a visual symbol through history, but for this point look at how it ties us from that long-ago then to our very close now.

Now look at one of the individual images posted to #MeToo on Instagram.

It, too, features the upraised hand. This one, chosen for its visual connection to my previous example, continues the semiotic thread. This hand is definitely (perhaps defiantly) a statement of presence, but it also signals resistance, meant to deter attack or harm. The effect of this image is deeply personal, seemingly deeply felt and coming from either the experience or the understanding of #MeToo abuse. The face isn't visible, but perhaps the image signals that that complete courage hasn't yet been built. Perhaps all the courage went into raising the hand, the way a bullied child might have to summon the strength to do so in a classroom, or the way people anywhere might have to gather themselves to say yes, me too, in a world that had historically not welcomed their message and for which there would likely be consequences.

The hand in this figure appears to be pressed against glass; a barrier into a pattern has been etched. Is it a cultural reference to an architectural detail, or could it be a reminder of jigsaw puzzles where the meanings become visible the more you piece together? There will be many meanings, depending on viewers' experience and knowledge, but the point is that the image contains evocative elements, such as this pattern. Color, too, affects an image's message. Here, I see rain, tears, fog, and mist, which evoke associations of sadness, pain, separation, and a lack of clarity about something in the past. It is literally gray, as in gray area or area of dispute. And to me, that hand clearly says "stop."

Creating and sharing an image, whether about an important event or a personal realization, carries significance for both the creator and viewers. The acts of doing and sharing have meaning. Those meanings can be held in common with others who share the same perspectives, while at the same time personal context adds relevance specific to each person seeing the post. Others who created or commented on images posted to #MeToo also used or saw hands, positioned in certain ways, as stand-ins for voicing "stop" or setting a limit.

The presence of hands in images posted to the continuously growing #MeToo feed became familiar, almost commonplace, even though their specific meanings varied. The feed itself grew by the hundreds, sometimes thousands, daily during 2019 as I was monitoring it closely; as of mid-June 2022, there were more than 3,140,000 posts to that hashtag on Instagram alone.

In that voluminous feed, hands were shown in ways associated with attack, shame, and defense.

Others suggested suppression, particularly the act of silencing someone who has been or is being abused or violated.

The hands, as symbols, came to represent having or lacking agency and control more broadly. That lack, in turn, became one of several themes evident throughout the feed. Recognizing themes in collections of topical images can be helpful to understanding what the images, taken together, might mean. In this case, the theme reinforces and gives range to one of the strongest assertions of the #MeToo movement: the lack of control and agency is one of the most pervasive characteristics of sexual abuse. Illustrating that fact—through social media and other performative venues—is a way of taking agency and control back, a way of taking matters into one's own hands.

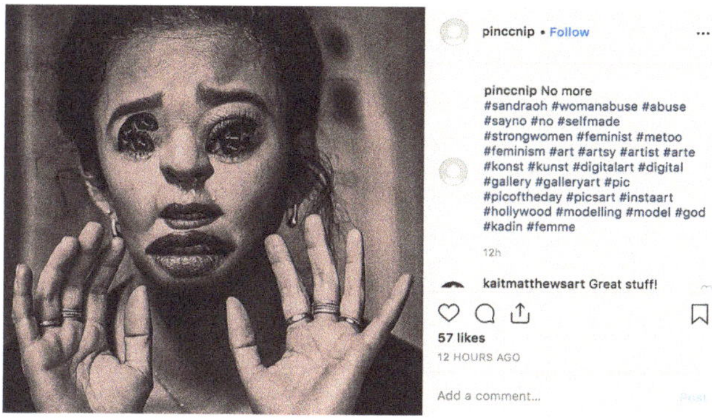

Artist undetermined. Posted by @pinccnip; account no longer exists. The original image appears to be in sepia tones of a slightly reddish brown, an effect that references early photography. Archived by author 15 May 2019.

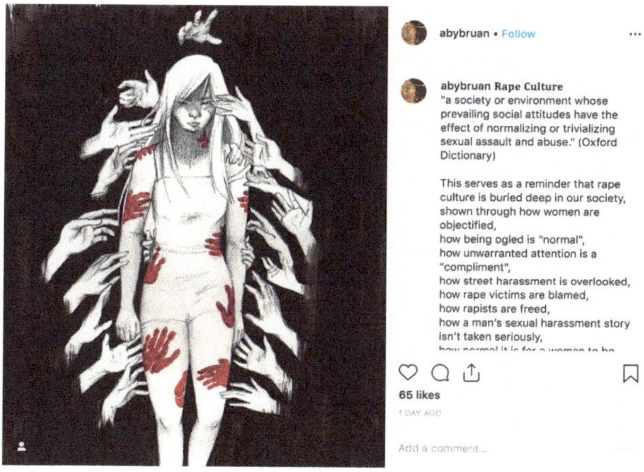

Stephanie Abbey Bruan, artist. Although this image can be deeply interpreted, one intriguing aspect of it is the resonance of the shape defined by the hand-body combination depicted in white with the shape of both a vagina and the mandorla, an almond-shaped depiction of light commonly used to frame paintings of the Virgin Mary in medieval art. The handprints on the woman's body are colored blood red. Posted by @abybruan. Archived by author 7 October 2019.

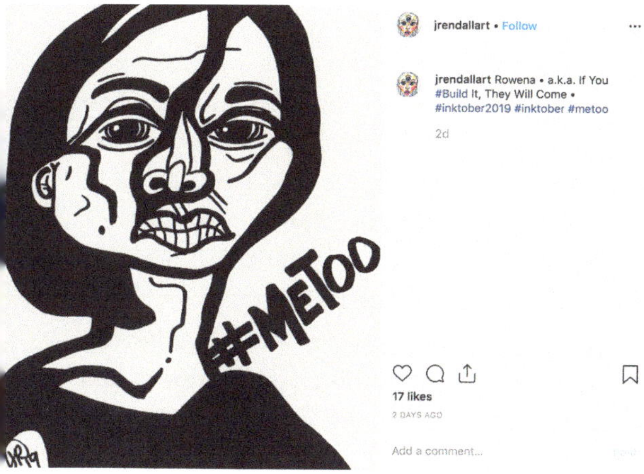

Jessica Lee Rendall, artist. Posted on Instagram by @jrendallart and archived by the author on 9 October 2019.

Marking a Shared Space for Expression

As the #MeToo movement grew into a global talking point, visuals were an important element in at least two major ways. Seeing the words *me* and *too* joined together and hash tagged allowed a kind of brand recognition and identity that, in turn, created a virtual community of like-mindedness. The participants' shared affinity, signaled by their use of what was essentially a hashtag "badge," nurtured something akin to a safe (or at least "safer") zone. With that established, the images posted to that hashtag feed in order to illustrate #MeToo were in a safe enough environment to both demonstrate and evoke reactions across a wide range of cognitive interactions, from simple to complex.

"#MeToo" became a graphical accompaniment on television broadcasts (events, talk shows, news), for example, where viewers were urged to participate in mass outpourings of commentary on Twitter or Facebook or other media, or perhaps at in-person public gatherings, such as protests. The hashtag, in essence, became an artistic device floated on a viewing screen, recognizable not just by its wording (*me* and *too*), but by its shape and context, transcending verbal language. The sight of that symbol—on screens, in print publications, embedded in art forms from graffiti to formal exhibition pieces—became a potential trigger for multiple impulses that included social action and memory. Those two reactions, of course, were not mutually exclusive. Regarding a subject like #MeToo, the cognitive and expressive terrain is almost impossibly complex. "#MeToo" as an element of graphic art was also prominent in social media posts. Its repetition on multiple platforms served to reinforce the validity and scope of the movement, normalizing its presence and amplifying its message.

Concomitantly, and this is the heart of the matter here in this chapter, the images that were shared with that hashtag (both as a symbol/trigger and as an organizing device built into the technology) had an effect and meaning that was both cumulative and participatory. Those images had significance on personal and collective levels. And, one might argue (and I do), they had and have significance as art and artifact. Their ephemerality is part of the point, culturally and historically, and deserves more attention in terms of preservation, as contradictory as that sounds and, in fact, is.

The publications of #MeToo images on Instagram is similarly significant, as the platform itself affords a venue for display unlike other social media platforms. Instagram is visually focused, requiring images in order to work. That requirement results in a gallery of topically targeted images unlike

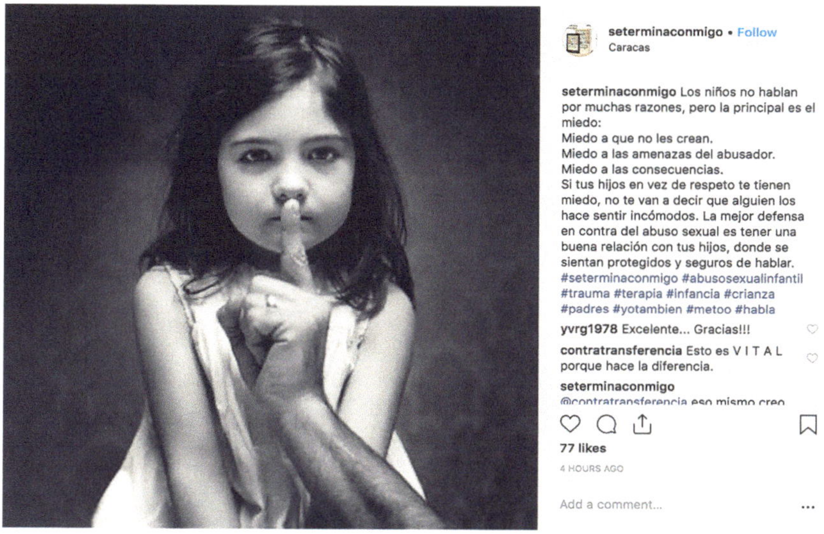

Artist undetermined; the image has been used liberally and uncredited as the background for memes and advocacy posts since at least 2014 according to multiple image searches. The image archived by the author on 15 May 2019 was posted by @seterminaconmigo on Instagram to #metoo.

what one would find on, for example, Twitter or Facebook, which were also popular publication sites for #MeToo.

In the case of #MeToo, and particularly #MeToo on Instagram, there is first a self-reckoning that determines what gets drawn, painted, photographed, digitized, or otherwise placed into a digital image file that can be posted online in a social media environment. Not all of the published images there or elsewhere are original to the poster—many are replications or reposts—but all require decisive action to put them online, and arguably all posts speak for the person or organization putting them forward. That they are so irretrievably public is another factor; once posted, they are there for all to see and even to share, given the technological options available to anyone with a smartphone or computer.

Spoken and Unspoken Voices

The ability (and inability) to speak out, to attest to one's harm or to call for help, is another overarching theme of the #MeToo posts on Instagram. Unsurprisingly for such a complex subject, there are visual elements common within themes but supporting more than one aspect of the discussion. The

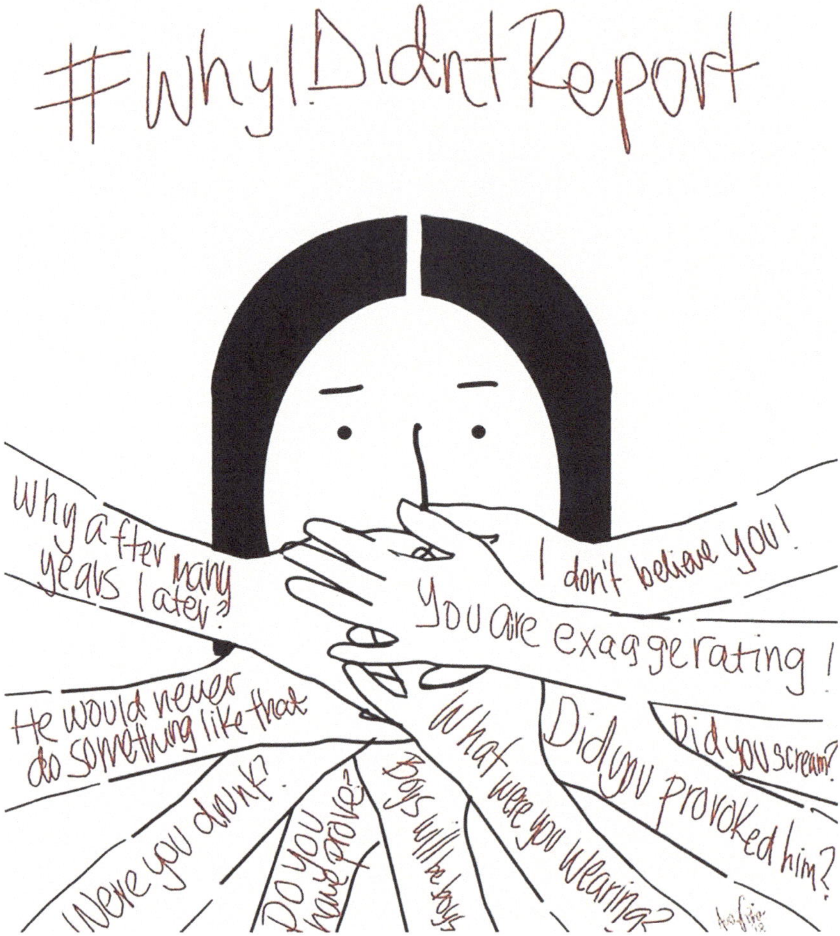

This popular image was originally drawn by Areli Fisher Robles and posted in 2018. Multiple versions exist on social media. This one, in brown, black and white (other versions are colorful, others stark) was archived by the author on 9 October 2019 from an Instagram post by @arelifisher.

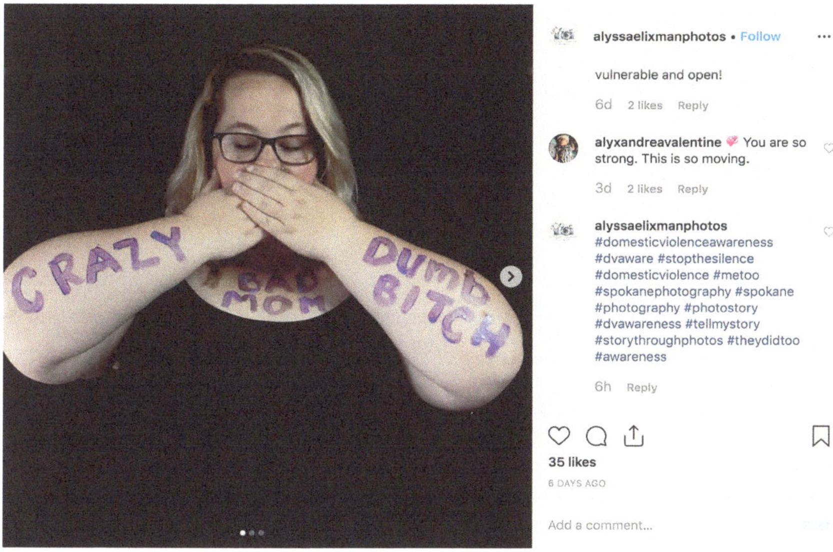

Alyssa Elixman, artist. This photo was the first in a series of self portraits posted to Instagram in October 2019 as part of a month-long awareness campaign for domestic violence. The series is available on the @alyssaelixmanphotos Instagram account. The image shown here was archived by the author on 7 October 2019.

use of the hand symbol, for example, factors into acts of silencing, such as in an image circulated widely within various #MeToo platforms.

Ironically, that photograph of a girl being shushed (signaled to keep quiet) by what appears to be a man's hand was used in various publications and on multiple social platforms according to a Google image search, thereby disobeying what was depicted and signaled in the image.

One might imagine that the many who reposted the image (uncredited to its creator) did so with a sense of rebellion, a message of support for the child and all children who have been harmed and silenced, and an expression of courage on her behalf.

Words called into artistic use in the employment of #MeToo as a visual identity marker and logo of sorts contributed to the theme of vocality, with an emphasis on the mouth as an embodiment of speech. Sometimes the words are incorporated into the fabric of the drawing. At other times, as discussed above, the words are included in artistic devices such as thought bubbles or stand-ins for thought bubbles, intended to identify them as pieces of dialogue.

And yet, other times, the images show how deeply engrained the words have become in the abused person's experience. They become part and parcel of the body, signaling the exercise of control even as the abuser continues to censor expression.

Sometimes, no words are needed.

And sometimes the words are prescriptive, bringing messages from outside sources rather than from internalized hauntings and self-driven shame and regret. Sometime the words come across as a bit too superficial—like a "thoughts and prayers" post seemingly offered up without much sentiment.

That those seem intrusive and irrelevant in the company of the thousands—millions—of other more reflective and substantive #MeToo posts might be a testament to the power of online communities, the goal of the movement itself, and the effectiveness of the art gathered in the #MeToo Instagram virtual gallery.

What Sees and Is Seen

That so many of the eyes are haunting in the art of the #MeToo feed suggests they are an accurate representation of the trauma and unbidden memories suffered by those who have been abused. It's a cliché to call them windows into one's soul, but it's not far-fetched to think of that with these images. Some eyes are drawn wide open in horror.

Some cry, and some are bruised, swollen, and painfully sad.

Some eyes recoil in fear and terror.

Others betray how badly beaten down the abuse victim is by the knowledge that what was done to them was done in secret, unwitnessed by others.

One image of that last kind has had particular staying power with me. It shows the head and shoulders of a person, but the head is a circle of swirling lines, reminding one of perhaps a hornet's nest or a zombie. The eyes are two big round circles, like coals in a snowman. The background is black and a mottled bloodred pattern, like splotches on a wall, and scrawled underneath the shoulders are the words "No one saw what you did."

The comments accompanying the post make clear what that message means. It's not accusing the person in the image of unseen actions. Rather, it refers to people who report abuse but are not believed. "No one saw what you did" therefore become the words of the abused directed at the abuser. The abused person's eyes reflect a slow death from futility, shunning, and being alone with the truth. Two streams of blood trickle from deadened eyes. There is no nose to provide air, no mouth to speak or take in sustenance. Just. Those. Eyes.

If you look at the eyes in all the figures cited here and elsewhere on

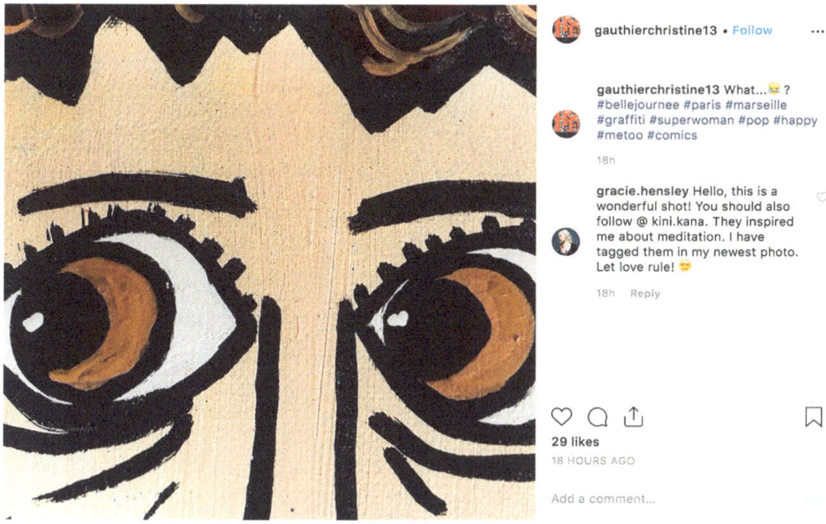

Christine Gauthier, artist. The eyes capture fear, vulnerability, and vigilance. The image was posted by @gauthierchristine13 on Instagram and archived by the author on 15 May 2019.

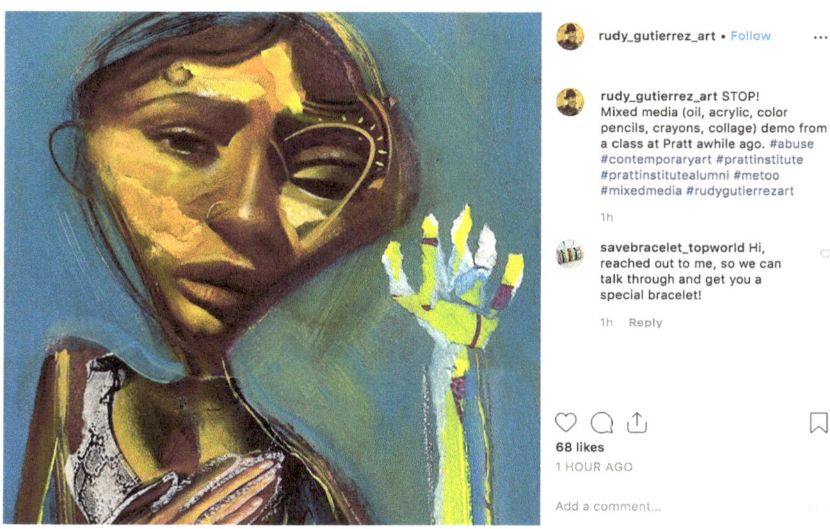

Rudy Gutierrez, artist. This photo of a mixed-media image was a demonstration for a class taught by the artist at Pratt Institute in New York. It was posted by @rudy_gutierrez_art on Instagram and archived by the author on 30 May 2019.

Instagram, you see sadness, pain, weariness, and resignation, as well perhaps as some resentment or some hate burgeoning in the girl being shushed. There may even be some bewilderment in the woman who has society's hands covering her mouth while also questioning her assertions and motives. One woman has her eyes closed, another has them averted, and one looks pointedly at an attacker while defiantly raising her hand to (presumably) fight back. A comment accompanying that image says, in translation from Catalan to English, "We are on the right track." What the women—and sometimes men—in such images have in common—even the ones whose eyes are covered—is that they are guardians and victims of what they have seen, and probably see again and again in their memories. Through these images, those whose eyes have not seen what victims' eyes have seen stand a chance of glimpsing their painful reality. Those who have also seen such things might find validation and solidarity, although society's belief and help might go even further.

Beyond Articulation

The concept of being a witness, and of speaking truth to power, carries with it an assumption of agency—something people under attack or who have been attacked tend to lack. Initial social media support of #MeToo in late 2017, primarily on Twitter, Facebook, and Reddit, resulted in an outpouring of information that included assertions, recollections, defenses, attacks, counterattacks, and swarms of emotion. By comparison, posts on Instagram, which became a popular home for #MeToo discourse later than the other platforms, were more focused, more serious, and (in keeping with its stereotyped reputation among the social media savvy) more from the heart. This, coupled with the platform's need for an image to make it work, most likely translated into attracting people willing to put in more deliberate effort. On Twitter and other platforms, users can easily repost (pass along someone else's post by hosting it in their own feed); on Instagram, that function is not enabled. There are apps that can handle reposting, but they aren't built into the platform's system itself. This lessens dramatically the phenomena of knee-jerk or perfunctory posts and nurtures an environment that is cultivated (in the sense of nourished).

The #MeToo community on Instagram in 2019 and 2020 pre-COVID-19 flourished in expressive art. That visuality offered much that words alone did not. It allowed people to show, not tell, and in so doing attest to some truths that might not have been, for them, something they felt safe enough, or articulate enough, to say out loud. These artifacts—and there are many thousands—are valuable records of a turbulent time that is still not fully understood. They are, alas, ephemeral unless captured, and capturing them is hard to do. Still, even in this brief exploration of one historic feed and a handful of images, it is possible to recognize multiple points of view, experiences, and reactions. While spokespeople have done a thorough job of articulating the purpose of #MeToo as a movement, the art posted to #MeToo social media platforms speaks a language that transcends those definitions. The art asserts presence, as did those hand paintings on caves long ago.

Part 4
Looking Ahead

The two chapters in part 4 bring *Art, Activism, and Sexual Violence* to what the editors hope is an impactful close following readers' engagement with the art the book contains. Writing these chapters provided the editors with an opportunity to share their own moments of discovery and to provide readers with an expanded context and an interpretive process for the compelling art they encountered in part 3. Together the chapters probe more deeply into the international context in which sexual violence in the United States should be understood and suggest that this book, far from being the final word on its novel juxtaposition of art and scholarship with gender-based violence, is really the beginning of a new conversation. The editors hope that the volume has equipped readers with insights that will allow them to innovate in their own attempts to prevent further harm from sexual violence as well to heal the many lingering wounds afflicting survivors.

Chapter 18 begins the book's final journey by recognizing that sexual violence is an ever-escalating global pandemic that has only worsened during the viral pandemic that transformed societies around the globe after 2020. Kitch's chapter also acknowledges the obstacles and challenges that exist to "curing" or even preventing this social pandemic, obstacles that can seem discouraging—even overwhelming. Despite those obstacles, however, chapter

18 discusses effective approaches to sexual violence, which sometimes entail redefining sexual violence from a women's issue to a men's issue. With that in mind, the chapter provides examples of actions and projects initiated by male allies that offer hope for the future. Chapter 18 concludes with an analysis of the creative work featured in *Art, Activism, and Sexual Violence* and its important contributions to rethinking and remaking cultures of sexual violence.

Chapter 19 concludes the book by addressing the gaps that inevitably exist in any effort to tackle an enormous issue like sexual violence. Gilpin's chapter adds additional international information and leaves readers with options for further reflection as well as further investigation of art-related sexual violence projects and performances not included in *Art, Activism, and Sexual Violence* that can nevertheless inspire activism and creativity.

The two chapters in part 4 represent the editors' hope that such new directions, in addition to the art and analysis included in *Art, Activism, and Sexual Violence*, will help to transform public narratives about what sexual violence is and does, as well as policies designed to address the complex issues that may unwittingly contribute to (and sometimes support) sexually violent behavior. Equally important, the editors hope that the emotional impact of the creative work offered in this book can reach the hearts of those who need it most by shining a light on both the suffering and the resilience of violence survivors.

18

Quelling an Epidemic

Tackling Sexual Violence through Allies and Art

Sally L. Kitch

Epidemic took on urgent new meanings as a viral pandemic swept the world in successive waves of infections and deaths starting in 2020. But epidemics—even pandemics—are not limited to physical illnesses. The World Health Organization (WHO) interagency working group on violence against women declared sexual violence against women and girls an epidemic in 2013. Even then the numbers of victims was staggering. They are now worse. WHO found that nearly a third of the world's women (one in three), aged fifteen and older across 161 countries, were subjected to acts of sexual or physical violence by intimate partners and non-partners between 2000 and 2018. Statistics in that range (30–33 percent) applied to all regions of the world except the western Pacific, Europe, and the United States, where the percentages of women subjected to such violence ranged from 20 to 26 percent.[1] The United States was at the highest end of the exceptional group, at 26 percent. Sexual trafficking of women and girls, many of them younger than fifteen, was also a burgeoning business during those years. Female victims represented 72 percent of all human trafficking in the same period.[2]

Those alarming numbers remained steady or grew through 2019, according to the World Bank. By that year, 35 percent of women had experienced sexual violence by intimate partners (28 percent) or non-partners (7 percent), and 38 percent of murdered women around the world had been killed by intimate partners. Then as now, gender-based assault is prevalent across societies, cultural groups, and social classes, and females (or those considered female) of all ages, from infancy to old age, are subject to sexual assault. The price of such violence includes victims' emotional, physical, and mental harm—including death—as well as costs to national economies of US$1.5 trillion per year (2 percent of global domestic product), according to the United Nation's (UN) figures.[3] Those economic expenditures can rise to 3.7 percent of an individual country's annual gross domestic product.[4]

Because *women* is not as transparent a term as it once seemed, these statistics do not cover the full extent of gender-based sexual violence, especially in the United States. Whereas 91 percent of rape and sexual assault victims in the United States are female (9 percent are male), for example, rates of sexual assault other than rape are higher for lesbians (46.4 percent) and bisexual women (75 percent) than for cisgender women (20 percent).[5] As of 2020, 47 percent of transgender people had been sexually assaulted at some point in their lifetimes, a statistic that is probably an undercount because of trans people's reluctance to report abuse. Sexual assault rates for transgender people were at least ten points higher if targets were American Indian, multiracial, Black, Middle Eastern, homeless, or disabled and almost twenty points higher if victims had done sex work, as many transgender people must do to make a living.[6] Because trans people have a nearly fifty-fifty chance of being incarcerated during their lifetimes, as punishment for survival-based crimes such as sex work, petty theft, and drug sales, the violence levels in the US prison system are especially dangerous for them.[7]

Violence rates for transgender men and women are roughly even, but transgender women are more likely to be sexually assaulted or murdered by male domestic partners or dates. Some killers know the sexual identity of the victim before sexual contact, in which case they may feel guilt and remorse about their sexual encounter. Other killers experience "trans panic" when they discover the physiology of the victim during a sexual encounter.[8] Twenty-five percent of transgender women survivors consider the violence against them hate crimes, versus less than 1 percent of cisgender women.[9] The psychoanalytic feminist theorist Jacqueline Rose attributes trans violence to masculine rage. Violence against trans people, Rose writes, is fear of and rage against the obfuscation of acceptable sexual arrangements that allow people to consider themselves normal and, importantly, to maintain stark lines between male and female. In Virginia Woolf's view, such violence against the accepted sexual order represents patriarchal authority "'gone frantic because it is losing its grip.'"[10]

Despite these distressing numbers and exorbitant costs, not to mention the insights sexual violence provides into what Rose calls "disturbing dimensions of human sexuality," the sexual violence epidemic barely registers in terms of law enforcement, which can be the sole recourse for many victims.[11] In the United States, only 230 of 1,000 sexual assault cases are even reported to the police, and of those reported, only 46 will lead to an arrest and 5 will result in a conviction. Indeed, prosecutions for rape and sexual assault are declining, down 40 percent between 2007 and 2017.[12]

The COVID-19 pandemic has only exacerbated the problem. Sexual assaults typically increase during states of emergency—by 45 percent during and after Hurricane Katrina, for example. The "pattern of gender differentiation at all levels of the disaster process, including physical and psychological risks, impact, and recovery, means that women typically bear the brunt of disaster effects," according to WHO. Minors are increasingly likely to experience abuse, including sexual abuse, and abusers are "more likely to murder their partners in the wake of personal crises."[13]

Patterns of increased demand for help from rape crisis centers and violence hotlines in 2020 and 2021 across Europe, Asia, and the United States indicate that the pandemic, especially during lockdown periods, followed the typical disaster pattern. Frustrations about lockdowns were often taken out on female domestic and health-care workers, older women, women with disabilities, and women isolated from technology.[14] All demands for help increased dramatically during those two years.[15] Lockdowns exacerbated domestic and relationship tensions. France reported a 30 percent increase in domestic violence cases. In Rio de Janeiro, cases of sexual violence were up 40–50 percent in 2020, and 90 percent of the causes were "related to the Covid-19 epidemic."[16]

As Dawn R. Gilpin observes in chapter 4, US gun sales, along with murders of female intimate partners, also increased during the pandemic. At the same time, the availability of sexual assault forensic exams (rape kits), child advocacy services, safe shelters, and other sources of refuge and protection for abused women decreased because of lockdown pressures and pandemic restrictions.[17] The effects from COVID-19 were so severe that some researchers called this uptick in sexual assault the "shadow pandemic," as multiple factors combined to simultaneously increase and reduce attention to an epidemic far older than COVID-19 and, in some ways, much more difficult to combat.

Another term for the increase in gender-based violence during COVID-19, according to the *Harvard Medical School Primary Care Review*, is *silent pandemic*. That term reflects both the direct and the indirect hardships the pandemic inflicted on women.[18] Because most countries around the world operate on gender discriminatory legal systems, women's rights during the pandemic crisis were rarely protected. Except in the 37 of 161 countries surveyed in 2018 that have laws granting men and women equal rights to own, use, and control land, the death of a male spouse or father from COVID-19 might mean that "women, girls and people in same-sex relationships lose access to the deceased's estate, as well as their share of the marital property or inheritance."[19]

What to Do?

The path forward for decreasing sexual violence remains unclear. Even the epidemic metaphor does not fully capture the problem. Unlike COVID-19, for example, sexual violence is not a new threat. Rather, it has plagued humanity since at least biblical times, making it more endemic than cyclical or novel. In addition, few treatments or interventions in the scourge of sexual violence have been consistently implemented let alone systematically evaluated. Nor have preventative measures—social "vaccines"—yet been identified. Moreover, wearing masks, full facial coverings, or any clothing type, no matter how conservative, does not guarantee a woman's safety from sexual assault, a point driven home by Jasmin Goodman and Wei Sun's discussion in chapter 16. Developed countries have been more successful at curtailing sexual violence than those in which women's and children's fundamental rights remain debatable, but developed countries have also been unable to eradicate it. As discussed in chapter 3, social structures even in the United States condone and even support the patriarchal power and male entitlements to women's bodies and lives that lie at the heart of the sexual violence epidemic. Indeed, that such structures endure does suggest a parallel to the dynamics of the COVID-19 pandemic, as the sexual violence epidemic is perpetuated and normalized at least in part by the same kinds of falsehoods, flawed assumptions, and denials that have fueled vaccine resistance and rejections of basic COVID-19 facts.

Despite these similarities, effective action against sexual violence is possible. Creative, anti-sexist public policy and actions by civil society organizations can make a difference in the short run, even if such acts do not completely transform societies or obliterate sexual violence. During the COVID-19 pandemic, for example, Spanish women were exempted from lockdown if they were experiencing domestic violence. They were also given a code—Mask-19—they could use to alert a pharmacist that they were victims of violence.[20] The UN Office for Disaster Risk Reduction also incorporated gender perspectives and gender-based violence awareness in its guidelines for emergency preparedness during the crisis. Those perspectives were included in WHO's 2019 health emergency and disaster risk management framework, which specified that services for women and girls must be prioritized at the beginning of any crisis, and women must be involved in decision-making processes all along.[21] Unfortunately, WHO's policies were totally absent from most countries' approaches to the pandemic.

Enforcement is essential to the effectiveness of such measures, however, and that is often where good intentions break down. South Africa is one of several nations (including Afghanistan) that have passed many women-friendly laws in recent decades, for example. Laws passed in South Africa since 1994 grant women greater access to employment and prioritize reducing violence against women and children. Yet, because of poor enforcement mechanisms and intransigent patriarchal attitudes, South Africa (like Afghanistan) remains among the most dangerous countries for women, with the highest levels of gender-based violence and femicide in the world, both of which have increased during the pandemic.[22]

Overall, policies that do not produce social change are ineffective in the long run. UN resolutions designed to address rape as a war crime have brought international attention to underlying causes for sexual violence during war—with implications for stressful times like those of the pandemic. Seven such resolutions were passed between 2008 and 2019, including Resolutions 1820, 1888, 1960, and 2467. All called for member states to recognize sexual violence and rape as punishable war crimes and to hold perpetrators of these crimes accountable. Resolution 1888 even called for establishing the Office of the Special Representative of the Secretary-General on Sexual Violence in Conflict. But because funding for such agendas is vulnerable, and they rarely include clear sanctions on governments or mandates for systemic cultural changes, these resolutions and others like them do little to counteract the "masculinity training" most men receive around the world. Without systemic changes, too many men will continue to believe that their lives are worth more than women's lives and that manliness means being strong and physically and emotionally dominating, especially over women.[23] Moreover, male soldiers may continue to be taught through "combatant socialization" to view rape as an acceptable weapon of war, an approach military leaders may use to recruit new members and to create solidarity within a fighting force.[24]

Even worse, too many men, including athletes such as Oscar Pistorius and political leaders such as Donald Trump, Jair Bolsonaro, and Boris Johnson, receive adulation and support for their "manly" violent and sexually transgressive—even unlawful—behavior. That's because "human subjects can be roused by what disgusts them . . . [and] licentiousness . . . can be a draw," as Rose explains. Voters seem increasingly enticed by role models and leaders who help them feel better about their own conscious or unconscious violent, biased, and lascivious tendencies. When asked how she could support

Trump despite his moral failings and her strong religious views, one voter explained in 2016, "'We are all sinners.'" After accusations of sexual assault appeared to enhance Supreme Court nominee Brett Kavanaugh's popularity with the Republican base in 2018, Senate Majority Leader Mitch McConnell observed that "only brute sex was rousing enough" to turn his party "on fire."[25] Acceptance of violent and abusive politicians encourages political leaders to bolster their power by denying the existence of their own and others' guilt for sexual offenses or even by denying that the offense even exists. Blaming victims offers a useful alternative to self-blame; that tactic is also a specialty of patriarchal social structures.

At the other extreme, characterizing women and girls as passive victims in need of male protection can do more to reinforce the power differentials that undergird patriarchal entitlement than to protect women. Policies based on that approach reinscribe the "gender essentialism" and feminine dependency that can promote the use of violence to keep women and girls under male control.[26] The playwright and activist Eve Ensler and others label the latter phenomenon "disaster patriarchy," as patriarchal forces take advantage of a crisis, such as the virus or a destructive hurricane, "to reclaim power—on the one hand, escalating the danger and violence to women, and on the other, stepping in as their supposed controller and protector."[27]

Such missteps and persistent biases can leave sexual violence survivors and their allies discouraged and overwhelmed. The underlying need to dismantle patriarchy, retrain males in the values of gender equity, increase societies' respect for women's and nonbinary people's autonomy and agency, strengthen support services for victims of assault, and allot additional resources to address today's twin pandemic, as many analysts suggest, can seem impossible to accomplish, especially in a world suffering from immense hardships and threats from environmental hazards, social and economic injustices, and a viral pandemic, all of which exacerbate sexual violence.[28] The same is true for implementing recommendations to grant girls and women equal access to educational and economic opportunities with boys and men, destroy supports for toxic masculinity (including patriarchal family systems), and abolish institutions that promote male dominance and female inferiority. Achieving such goals is likely to require generations of concerted effort against strong opposition. So, the question remains, what can be done now, under patriarchal, unjust, irrational regimes that are unlikely to disappear anytime soon?

Disrupting Systems: Allies and Agency

If possibilities for quickly and totally undoing the cultural dynamics that produce and promote sexual violence by men against persons perceived as women are remote, especially during stressful times like the present, then disrupting those dynamics one step at a time at community and individual levels may be the next best thing. Widescale social change can begin with incremental efforts that disrupt narratives and educate the public about alternative beliefs and courses of action.

Bring in the Men

One important transformation that can begin in families, educational institutions, and social service agencies is recognizing that sexual violence is not a women's (or victims') issue. Rather, it is a men's (or perpetrators') issue and will never be resolved until men/perpetrators commit to combating it. Even though most men are not perpetrators of sexual violence, "all men [even gay or trans men] have some relationship to the issue" by virtue of their cultural connection with the norms of masculinity that perpetuate the gender inequities driving sexual assault by men against women. That connection can vary, of course, along a spectrum. At one end, men can accept concepts such as the "toughness, dominance, and willingness to prove manhood by any means" implicit in many of those norms. At the other, men can completely reject that form of masculinity. But even at the rejecting end of the spectrum, men can experience "masculinity challenges" that can lead to gender-based violence (including against homosexual or transgender men) in a culture that associates any form of masculine weakness with failure and humiliation. Having experienced or witnessed violence in his own life can increase the chances that a man will react violently to those challenges.[29]

Working against masculinity norms, such as risk-taking, aggression, and violence, men in some regions—from Canada to Brazil, the United Kingdom, and South Africa—have become allies in the fight against sexual violence. Even before the 2017 revival of the #MeToo movement, Canadian organizations included the White Ribbon Campaign, which formed in response to the Montreal massacre of female engineering students in 1989. The campaign now has headquarters in eleven countries, including the United States and China. (Other pre-#MeToo activism includes *Un violador en tu camino*, discussed by Deborah Martin and Deborah Shaw in chapter 5.)

Numbers of ally groups and men participating in women's anti-violence groups have also grown in the United States since the 1980s, especially on college campuses. Men's Action to Stop Violence Against Women started in Atlanta, Georgia, in 1981. In addition to assisting with legal cases, Men's Action educates men and boys about the psychological and economic abuse that can be as harmful to victims as physical abuse.[30] In communities around the country in the 2010s, lots of men stuffed their feet into high heels (often red) for a Walk a Mile in Her Shoes event to show support for gender equity and to challenge concepts of masculinity that perpetuate sexual violence. One participant in 2015 stated that walking in the march meant standing up and making clear that sexual violence is everyone's problem.[31] Confirming the role of art in addressing sexual violence, visual images have been important recruitment tools for these movements.

Some groups have more recently built on Walk a Mile's kind of symbolic allyship by creating more inclusive community marches and immersive educational events to engage men in the issue of sexual violence. For example, Kendra Wyckoff, the executive director of Peace House in Park City, Utah, explains that after the COVID-19 shutdown, her organization chose to develop marches and educational programs connected with existing community events, using male community leaders, such as the police chief, to help recruit men in the fight to eliminate domestic and sexual violence. Wyckoff believes that awareness events, such as Walk a Mile, which her organization sponsored from 2013 to 2019, should be accompanied or replaced by more nuanced educational experiences in order to expand the male ally base.[32]

That change is consistent with general approaches to good allyship, which has been defined as challenging and motivating other men to join the fight, recognizing the structures that create both oppression and privilege for women and men, giving voice to marginalized communities, and welcoming criticism of allies' own actions and approaches. Not dominating groups or reinscribing male privilege and power are important caveats in good allyship, as is maintaining a balance in displaying masculine efforts to overcome privilege without diverting attention from women's experiences or efforts.[33] But involving men in the solution is "a critical ingredient in ending violence against women," according to the scholar Erin Casey. Research suggests that assuming men's interest in helping and recognizing the strengths men can lend to the cause is critical, as is approaching men as part of the solution rather than just the source of the problem.[34]

Demonstrating that gender equity is to men's advantage is a related approach recommended by Denis Mukwege, a gynecological expert in treating rape injuries and cowinner of the 2018 Nobel Peace Prize, along with the human rights activist Nadia Murad. Mukwege, a Congolese native, who has worked tirelessly to support women's rights in Congo and around the world, understands the concept of allyship. He speaks in order to amplify the voices of women who have been silenced, and he recognizes that his role is to stand beside women, not in front of them. He also knows that he can approach men about this issue when women in his country cannot. Starting in 2010, he used that privilege to work with tribal leaders of the Warega to couple the issue of women's rights with improved farming practices. He gradually convinced leaders and other Warega men that their wives' workloads were too heavy, questioned the gendered allocation of work, and then explored how cooperation between the sexes could improve their farming outputs and increase their income. As the program proved successful at achieving those goals, support for changes in the distribution of labor grew, discussions about the role and rights of women and the prevention of sexual violence ensued, and Mukwege was invited to replicate his program for other tribes in other regions. Mukwege believes strongly that male role models and peer-to-peer transmission of ideas for reform were crucial. "Overall," he explained, "we've found that men tend to be more receptive when the trainers are male too."[35]

The importance of men's direct involvement in violence prevention has led some US ally programs to consider men who are bystanders to the issue—neither victims nor perpetrators—complicit by their silence. Such programs seek to train men to look for "red flags" among their acquaintances—including excessive alcohol use and isolating their partners from other people—to intervene in nonconfrontational ways and to "undermine the sense of peer support for gender inequality."[36]

Such interventions in what scholars and therapists consider contemporary rape culture is critical to preventing and addressing sexual assault. Rape culture is sustained by beliefs and myths about rape and coerced sex. They include the idea that women are aroused by rape, that their dress or behavior indicates that they want rough sex, and that men rape because they cannot control their sexual urges.[37] Some men believe that sexual assault or rape is a justifiable punishment for a particular woman or for women in general whose success or independence seems a direct challenge to male authority or entitlement to certain activities or opportunities.

Prevention appears to be the most potent way to address sexual assault because experienced therapists say that reforming violent behavior is extremely difficult. Perpetrators are rarely driven to change their behavior because of guilty or remorseful feelings or because they fear for their children's welfare or find God. Men who commit sexual assault and otherwise abuse women are primarily interested in themselves and their own feelings, therapists have found. The only thing that works is compulsion—changing an abuser requires "placing him in a situation where he has no other choice." A man who abuses or assaults his wife or partner is not typically motivated to stop unless the partner leaves him "or a court demands change and threatens to jail him."[38] It is far better to focus on the vaccine of prevention and train new generations of men to understand that using force is neither their prerogative nor the best medicine for their toxic rage.

Women's Voices and Agency: Art Voices Speak

> How do you make this world, this life, in all its mystery and injustice, matter? Maybe this is the purpose of art . . . to see what's in front of us, to allow the truth in, with all its sorrow and brutality.
>
> —Eve Ensler, *Necessary Targets: A Story of Women and War*

Because preventive measures for the sexual violence epidemic remain weak, the roughly 90 percent of victims who are women (or perceived as women) have had to develop their own approaches to quelling this epidemic.[39] One important tack they have taken is speaking out and redefining themselves as survivors, thereby asserting their agency. But even the term *survivor* points to the limited control victims have over perpetrators, whether they are known to them (as in two-thirds of cases) or strangers. The term also suggests the uncertain and sometimes revictimizing forms of support victims receive from law enforcement, family, and friends. Becoming a survivor, therefore, primarily represents the control victims can have over their own responses to the threat or experience of sexual violence, as well as their identification with other survivors and their public engagement with the issue.

Art, Activism, and Sexual Violence exemplifies this type of survivor anti-violence strategy. The book's compendium of survivors' and allies' voices, expressed through the arts, demands responses in public spaces.[40] Through drama, poetry, dance, narratives, sculpture, paintings, drawings, quilts, needlework, T-shirts, and social media images, these artists' voices create a compelling form of agency directed at the injustice, degradation, disruption, and physical and emotional pain inflicted on people perceived as women by sexual predators in their homes or elsewhere. In most cases, they also assert victims' ability to transform the harm done to them and others like them into actions that redefine a harsh reality through creative works and emotional connections with viewers, readers, or audiences. And while ordinary narratives about and analyses of sexual violence can be compelling and effective, art voices such as those in this volume have the capacity to create a different and deeper impression on viewers, audiences, and readers and to shift public perceptions of this persistent form of violence.

Many of the pieces discussed and displayed in this volume illustrate the intensified impacts and dramatic effects of art. The works demonstrate art's ability to articulate, explore, complicate, and signify the impact of sexual violence. While educating and resonating with viewers emotionally, art can also change attitudes and behavior. Nik Zaleski and Elizabeth Johnson Levine's foreword, for example, describes an attendee at one of their productions, *With Each Other*, who confessed that he used to think that anyone drunk at a party "somehow deserved" sexual assault. But when he heard those words spoken onstage, he realized "how stupid it sounded," and he promised that he would "never think that again." Another young man, after seeing Ruta Butkus Marino's *Discomforters* quilt exhibition, described in chapter 12, commented: "I now have an open mind on the subject of sexual abuse." Art works.

Sometimes art's messages are indirect, relying on form as well as content. Stephanie Leigh Batiste's poem/play and the dance performances discussed by Sydney Burrows exemplify that effect. Eschewing a confrontational approach, Batiste's work in chapter 6 instead offers a poetic journey that balances the joys and pleasures of sexual desire and romance—"Smiling with you, / learning your ways, sharing mine"—with the disappointments of betrayal—"I am left / in love / with a figment of my imagination." Then comes seduction and abuse—". . . all shallow, he was just huntin' gold / . . . Yanking my chain and runnin' game"—and the hard lessons of love turned mean—". . . don't get burned / Learn to love the game and try not to let it change / Your golden giving ways."

Like Batiste's performers, the dancers and choreographers Burrows discusses in chapter 7 "must dig deep into . . . personal experiences and emotions to guide the . . . work." Dancers use and reclaim their bodies, which in some cases have been harassed and abused within the dance world. Exploring this relatively recent dance genre requires novel combinations of familiar and newly composed music, gestures, lighting, costumes, and sometimes spoken word to help audiences "pull out the pain when they need it," according to the choreographer Jinah Parker. At the same time, audiences understand from a dance's coordinated group performance that those who have experienced sexual violence or abuse are not alone. Indeed, both Batiste's play and the dances Burrows explores exemplify through their performative structures a collaborative approach to hurt and harm that can heal as well as energize and empower.

Some of the artworks in *Art, Activism, and Sexual Violence* utilize the ironic juxtaposition of homey symbolism with the horrors of destructive sexual violence within domestic settings to express their messages. Given that two-thirds of perpetrators are known to their victims, including family members and close friends, these works correctly identify home as potentially the most dangerous place a victim can be. Ruta Butkus Marino and Susanne Slavick deliberately re-create and then undermine the association of home with love, support, and comfort by disrupting cozy images—quilts and pillows—with startling visual messages that wrench viewers' attention away from those objects' conventional associations. Those images strip off pretenses about the comforts of home and confront viewers with the horrors of domestic violence and incest, often perpetrated in the name of (a controlling) love. Viewers' shock at those provocative images can change minds and motivate action against sexual violence.

The quilts in Marino's *Discomforters* series, discussed in chapter 12, draw viewers in with their colors and fabrics, like traditional-looking baby quilts that use a pink pattern with white polka dots or baby blue flowers on white fabric. But beneath the innocent and conventional appearances are subversive visual messages, such as the phallic shape of a boy's quilt. Marino's titles can also startle; one exhibition was titled *Home Is Where It Happens*. And the quilts include chilling quotations taken from Marino's site, Project Unbreakable. The texts detail the manipulations of sexual violence committed at home: "Daddy wants to play a special game"; "He said it was my duty as 'a good, Christian wife'—whether I liked it or not"; "This is what daddys and daughters do"; "I hate you for making me do this to you"; "He said he would give me twinkies." Such testimonials can be more effective than the grim statistics about domestic violence and incest by immersing viewers in the horrors of victimhood, even as the words also wrench their hearts.

Equally shocking are Slavick's red-stained pillow images representing the role of gun violence in family life. The charred scarlet depressions in the middle of the pillows proclaim that the violence can be deadly, as the resting places for weary heads or sites of sexual intimacy become targets of rage and retribution. As Slavick explains in chapter 13, this ultimate violence against domestic partners often accompanies assault that punishes victims for not cooperating with the sexual demands of a domestic partner. As further exemplified by Marino's quilts, love that leads to violence is always possessive, and often tyrannical. Recipients of such love fail to identify its pathology at their peril.

Both Luzene Hill and Clarity Haynes redefine and resist victimhood through their art. Hill's installation of meticulously knotted cords—each one "unique, specific, and countable"—discussed in chapter 8, enabled her to use her own body, traumatized by rape, as an art-making tool. She first scattered the cords around her as she lay on the gallery floor. She then stood up and transformed the "trace of violence" made by her body imprint through the "ritual action" of hanging the knotted cords one by one along the gallery wall. Surprisingly, the process of hanging the cords took ten days. Although she did not originally intend her work to be primarily about her own experience of rape, the process of hanging the cords had a personal impact on her sense of agency, even as it also empowered other victims of sexual assault who witnessed her performative installation.

Haynes fled before a sexual attack became a rape, but their narrow escape only reinforced a sense of vulnerability to the male rage that incites sexual assault. Right after the attack, the second in recent years, Haynes was terrified to go outside. But as they explain in chapter 9, Haynes was "determined not to let the assault interrupt [their] groove." So, they found an inner power. "The bullshit that accumulates, the misogyny that lands on me," Haynes writes," is not mine and never was." They laughed when they wanted to, and they painted. In response to the violence, Haynes began creating torso portraits of "monumental bodies, protectors. Gargantuan icons. Women who can't be knocked down." Haynes survived as a lesbian feminist artist telling the truth about women's lives, and obliquely about LGBTQ lives, by "finding language, in words and art, to tell the truth." That victims rather than perpetrators feel they must remake themselves in order to forestall violence is a sad commentary on that truth today.

Two chapters in *Art, Activism, and Sexual Violence* interrogate clothing as a symbol of both victimhood and resistance. Goodman and Sun address in chapter 16 the truism that certain types of clothing increase a woman's chance of becoming a target of sexual assault. Although there is some truth to the impact of clothing as a trigger to some perpetrators, it need not be seductive clothing.[41] Indeed, the idea that victims' provocative clothing incites sexual violence becomes ridiculous in the face of exhibitions of the clothes victims were actually wearing as well as of statistics: 15 percent of sexual assault victims in the United States are under twelve, meaning they might be attacked while wearing bunny pajamas or overalls. Even many teens, the largest targeted age-group, report having worn very modest clothing at the time of their assaults. One nineteen-year-old reported that she was wearing sweatpants and had a 102-degree fever when she was attacked the second time.[42]

Emily Bonistall Postel, Elaina Behounek, and Alesha Durfee describe a creative project in chapter 15 that engages indirectly with the myth that seductive clothing causes sexual assault and utilizes sex-neutral clothing as a mechanism for fighting back. In the Clothesline Project, which the authors have fielded in several communities, survivors and their allies design and display T-shirts that advertise to the world the emotional and the physical pain inflicted by sexual assault, as well as survivors' strategies for recovery. These shapeless shirts demonstrate that clothes, like bodies, can send a message of resistance and defiance in the face of sexual violence, thereby transforming victims into survivors.

The plethora of compelling social media images included in Leslie-Jean Thornton's chapter suggests how important visual expression is to sharing and protesting various acts of sexual violence. As Thornton explains in chapter 17, some images, like protesting hands and shocked eyes, become tropes in the popular understanding of the vicious harm sexual assault often inflicts on its victims and the depth of the trauma that can haunt survivors throughout their lives. From Thornton's discussion, it seems possible that social media is having an important impact on victims and survivors, as it allows them to replace the isolation of their abuse with a virtual community of understanding and acceptance.

Perhaps because of the deep cultural impact of nonstandard sexual identities and desires, sexual violence is practically endemic to the lives of transgender people. Overcoming the effects of that violence is not easy, but for this book's contributors, art offers healing empowerment. The trans artist Sean Shannon's coming-of-age story and accompanying poetry in chapter 10 exemplify trans vulnerability to sexual violence. As a transitioning boy, Shannon incited paternal rage, as his very existence affronted conventional patriarchal hierarchies of sexual identities and couplings. Young Shannon learns that his identity shift blurs both physical and psychic boundaries, "which non-trans people have the luxury of believing they can safely keep asunder."[43] That blurring makes some men, like Shannon's father, angry enough to abuse his gender-bending son "with his fists and his words but mostly his fists" as he tries to turn him into "the son he always wanted." That goal was apparently shared by a son of his father's friend who raped Shannon at age eleven. But the trauma did not stop when Shannon became a transgender woman. Perceived as "a man in makeup and women's clothing," a not-real woman, Shannon still feels after forty-six years "like I'm the only person who really believes me."

The possibility of suicide is a theme in Shannon's work, and her poem's final line—"maybe there's no use in counting the years any longer"—indicates that it remains an option. Yet Shannon's work also offers a way out of despair. Making art with language has repeatedly saved her life: "I write because I have to," she explains.

Psychic pain is similarly evident in the work of Chloe Dzubilo and Jennifer Patterson, yet their art also provides tools for resilience and recovery. Dzubilo's provocative line drawings and accompanying handwritten texts discussed in chapter 11 offer the healing possibilities of exposure—"outing" perpetrators of sexual violence and calling them by their names. *Bud-No-Wiser* exemplifies this technique, as the beer-soaked "funny uncle," whose looming presence drives girls to hide in closets, is revealed with his exposed erect penis as the sexual predator he really is. The doctor in "Behind closed doors" is likewise exposed as a titillated voyeur offering medical treatment more for what ails him than for what ails his transgender patient, lying prone on the examining table. In her exposure of a sexually predatory religious institution that has violated believers' trust as well as their bodies, Dzubilo asks how many priests it takes to ruin a community of children. The answer is just one.

The title and first lines of Patterson's poetic ruminations on sexuality and violence in chapter 14 offer a calming analogy between embroidery and resistance: "Each stitch new. Breaking to shape anew." Like the stitch her needle splits as she creates a new stitch, her queer body is split—"marked . . . traumatized. . . . a site of wreckage . . . a battleground." Reminiscent of Hill's work, Patterson's "ritual of transference" works to "translate skin into words into threads." After and sometimes during writing, Patterson maps "the words with embroidery thread." She discovers "the mind-body connection that's evident in sewing and writing." Embroidery and knitting can activate the parasympathetic nervous system, she explains, "which helps quiet the often highly activated 'fight or flight' response that many people with trauma histories and post-traumatic stress disorder (PTSD) have to manage daily." Although repetition can be the enemy of healing by becoming a compulsive disorder, Patterson finds comfort in repetition when her "hands are occupied, fingers entangled in thread." She writes from "inside the wound," both recognizing the harms she has suffered and critiquing herself, acknowledging her wounded selves and putting them in conversation with her "wise elder future selves." Through it all, she follows her mantra: "Stitch. Write. Repeat."

Encouragement

As hopeless as the scourge of sexual violence against women sometimes seems, these artists and their allies, who are mobilizing to redefine masculinity, clarify what constitutes violence, and work to stop it, offer some hope. Illuminating a subject that has long lain in the shadows is itself a healing act of resistance. Although the daily diet of news about battered and murdered women around the world can be excruciating, now and then a positive sign appears and suggests that resistance and defiance may have made a difference. In May 2022, for example, one of the largest sources of sexual violence against women, girls, and boys in the United States—the Southern Baptist Church—finally decided to publicize the names of offending ministers and church officials for the first time in its history. The list of seven hundred names had been kept secret for ten years. It is not clear what will happen next. But at least a light has been shone.

Notes

1. World Health Organization, "Violence against Women," fact sheet, March 9, 2021, www.who.int/news-room/fact-sheets/detail/violence-against-women. The categories "men" and "women" in these statistics are not fully explained, but the presumption is that both the men and the women are presumed to be cisgendered, although that presumption is rarely put to the test in their victimization.

2. Åsa Regnér, "Op-Ed: Trafficking in Women and Girls Is Moving Online Due to COVID-19," UN Women, December 8, 2020, www.unwomen.org/en/news/stories/2020/12/op-ed-trafficking-in-women-and-girls-is-moving-online-due-to-covid-19.

3. World Bank, "Gender-Based Violence (Violence against Women and Girls)," last modified September 25, 2019, accessed June 2, 2023, www.worldbank.org/en/topic/socialsustainability/brief/violence-against-women-and-girls. According to the South African government, a woman was killed every hour there in 2020. Nobuhle Judy Dlamini, "Gender-Based Violence, Twin Pandemic to COVID-19," *Critical Sociology* 47, no. 4–5 (2021): 588.

4. Dlamini, "Gender-Based Violence," 583–84. The 2015 cost of each rape in the United States was $151,423. Each year, rape costs the United States more than any other crime ($127 billion). National Sexual Violence Resource Center, "Statistics about Sexual Violence," 2015, www.nsvrc.org/sites/default/files/publications_nsvrc_factsheet_media-packet_statistics-about-sexual-violence_0.pdf.

5. The latest statistics about sexual violence for lesbians and bisexual women

are from 2015. National Sexual Violence Resource Center, "Statistics about Sexual Violence."

6. National Sexual Violence Resource Center, "Sexual Violence and Transgender/Non-binary Communities," 2019, www.nsvrc.org/sites/default/files/publica tions/2019-02/Transgender_infographic_508_0.pdf.

7. Tuck Woodstock, "Who Is Committing Violence against Trans Women," *Portland (OR) Monthly*, October 2020, www.pdxmonthly.com/news-and-city -life/2020/10/who-is-committing-violence-against-trans-women.

8. Woodstock, "Violence against Trans Women."

9. Williams Institute, University of California, Los Angeles, School of Law, "Transgender People over Four Times More Likely than Cisgender People to Be Victims of Violent Crime," press release, March 23, 2021, https://williamsinstitute .law.ucla.edu/press/ncvs-trans-press-release.

10. Jacqueline Rose, *On Violence and on Violence against Women* (New York: Farrar, Straus and Giroux, 2021), 142.

11. Rose, *On Violence*, 142. Inadequate as law enforcement can be in handling sexual assaults, the response of police is the only measure available for determining that offenses have been taken seriously. It would be far better for victims to have recourse to other mechanisms through which the harms inflicted by sexual violence and the behaviors and attitudes that perpetuate such violence can be addressed.

12. Denis Mukwege, *The Power of Women: A Doctor's Journey of Hope and Healing* (New York: Flatiron Books, 2021), 174–75.

13. Taylor Walker, "A Second, Silent Pandemic: Sexual Violence in the Time of COVID-19," *Harvard Medical School Primary Care Review*, May 1, 2020, https:// info.primarycare.hms.harvard.edu/review/sexual-violence-and-covid.

14. Dlamini, "Gender-Based Violence," 585–86.

15. Walker, "A Second, Silent Pandemic."

16. For a review of global statistics about the rise of sexual violence during the pandemic, see Emma Graham-Harrison, Angela Giuffrida, Helena Smith, and Liz Ford, "Lockdowns around the World Bring Rise in Domestic Violence," *Guardian*, March 28, 2020, www.theguardian.com/society/2020/mar/28/lockdowns -world-rise-domestic-violence.

17. Walker, "A Second, Silent Pandemic."

18. Walker, "A Second, Silent Pandemic."

19. Dlamini, "Gender-Based Violence," 587.

20. Dlamini, "Gender-Based Violence," 589.

21. Neetu John, Sara E Casey, Giselle Carino, and Terry McGovern, "Lessons Never Learned: Crisis and Gender-Based Violence," *Developing World Bioethics* 20, no. 2 (2020): 67–68.

22. Dlamini, "Gender-Based Violence," 588. Other countries usually included

in the list of the world's most dangerous countries for women are (in descending order) India, Afghanistan, Syria, Somalia, Saudi Arabia, Pakistan, Congo, Yemen, and Nigeria. The United States is also among the top ten because of the prevalence of sexual violence. Note that all the countries on the list are in Asia, Africa, and the Middle East except one. Spencer Feingold, "10 Most Dangerous Countries for Women," *Stacker*, November 19, 2018, https://stacker.com/world/10-most-dangerous-countries-women.

23. Mukwege, *The Power of Women*, 249–51, 228–29.

24. Bridget Margueritte Carter, "Rape as a Weapon of War: A Critique of Wartime Rape Practice and Its Neglect by the International Community and the Global Patriarchy" (PhD diss., Webster Vienna Private University, 2021), 83.

25. Rose, *On Violence*, 14, 17, 156.

26. Carter, "Rape as a Weapon of War," 83.

27. V (formerly Eve Ensler), "Disaster Patriarchy: How the Pandemic Has Unleashed a War on Women," *Guardian*, June 1, 2021, www.theguardian.com/lifeandstyle/2021/jun/01/disaster-patriarchy-how-the-pandemic-has-unleashed-a-war-on-women.

28. See Dlamini, "Gender-Based Violence," 588.

29. Tal Peretz and Chris M. Vidmar, "Men, Masculinities, and Gender-Based Violence: The Broadening Scope of Recent Research," *Sociology Compass* 15, no. 3 (2021): e12861, https://doi.org/10.1111/soc4.12861.

30. Jeff Hearn, Kopano Ratele, Tamara Shefer, and Anisur Rahman Khan, "Men, Masculinities, Peace, and Violence: A Multi-level Overview on Justice and Conflict," in *Routledge Handbook of Feminist Peace Research*, ed. Tarja Väyrynen, Swati Parashar, Élize Féron, and Catia Cecelia Confortini (London: Routledge, 2021), 316. See also White Ribbon, "About White Ribbon Campaign," 2019, https://whiteribbonworld.com; and Men Stopping Violence, "About Us," accessed May 31, 2023, https://menstoppingviolence.org/about-us.

31. Walk a Mile in Her Shoes, "The International Men's March to Stop Rape, Sexual Assault & Gender Violence," accessed May 31, 2023, http://walkamileinhershoes.com/index.html#.YpEN2ZPML00.

32. Kendra Wyckoff, phone interview with the author, June 17, 2022.

33. Peretz and Vidmar, "Men, Masculinities, and Gender-Based Violence." In previous work, these authors describe a pedestal effect for men who become active in anti-violence work. They explain that men, who often make the same claims that women activists have long made, frequently receive more respect and praise than the women do, rise to the top of organizations' public work, and get paid higher speaking fees. In short, male leaders in the field can manipulate their own hegemonic masculinity to access this sexist "reward structure." See, for example, Michael A. Messner, Max A. Greenberg, and Tal Peretz, *Some Men: Feminist Allies and the Movement to End Violence against Women* (New York: Oxford University Press, 2015), 139.

34. Erin Casey, "Strategies for Engaging Men as Anti-violence Allies: Implications for Ally Movements," *Advances in Social Work* 11, no. 2 (2010): 276, https://libkey.io/libraries/158/articles/372622300/full-text-file.

35. Mukwege, *The Power of Women*, 249–51, 228–29.

36. Peretz and Vidmar, "Men, Masculinities, and Gender-Based Violence."

37. Lundy Bancroft, *Why Does He Do That? Inside the Minds of Angry and Controlling Men* (New York: Berkley, 2003), 189.

38. Bancroft, *Why Does He Do That?*, 360.

39. This and other statistics about sexual assault victims and perpetrators are from the Rape, Abuse and Incest National Network (RAINN), the nation's largest anti–sexual violence organization. See New Orleans Sexual Assault Response Team, "Sexual Assault Statistics," statistics compiled by RAINN, accessed May 31, 2023, www.nolasart.org/statistics.html. The site offers a statistical breakdown of assault victims by age and race and assesses the effects of assault. The statistics are mostly troubling, including the fact that only about 36 percent of victims receive medical care and that girls aged sixteen to nineteen are four times more likely than the general population to be victims of sexual assault.

40. Our search for art directed at sexual violence revealed no male artists whose work actually addresses the issue.

41. Recent research has indicated that individuals may interpret particular types of clothing as a trigger for objectifying the wearers, making them appear lacking in personhood or agency and increasing their vulnerabililty to violence. Bhuvanesh Awasthi, "From Attire to Assault: Clothing, Objectification, and De-humanization—a Possible Prelude to Sexual Violence?," *Frontiers in Psychology* 8 (March 2017): 338. www.ncbi.nlm.nih.gov/pmc/articles/PMC5344900. As these responses are culturally constructed as well as individualized, it seems equally likely that form-fitting clothing as well as shapeless burquas could trigger objectification of their wearers under certain circumstances.

42. New Orleans Sexual Assault Response Team, "Sexual Assault Statistics."

43. Rose, *On Violence*, 93.

19

Who's Missing?
The Negative Space of Sexual Violence

Dawn R. Gilpin

"Negative space" refers to the empty space around an image that helps define it: a shape exists only insofar as it can distinguish itself from what surrounds it, the not-shape. What is the thing and what is not the thing must both be identifiable in order to make sense of what one is seeing. The process of creating, of telling stories, even of conveying information, always entails making choices about what to include and what to leave out. Sometimes, what is left out constitutes its own story, or series of stories.

In planning and assembling this volume, we have tried to represent a range of perspectives, contexts, and situations. No single book can be thoroughly comprehensive, however, so there are inevitably some gaps, some negative space. Not all of that space is the result of deliberate choices on our part, as there were contributors we wanted to include but were unable to reach or who were not available at the time. This chapter is intended to acknowledge those missing voices; to point to some artists, writers, and thinkers not included here who have something important to contribute to the subject matter; and to stimulate others to work in new directions. This book is meant to represent the beginning of a conversation, not the final word.

Categorically Missing

Although we have sought to be as intersectional as possible with this volume and are proud of the slate of artists and scholars represented here, there are a number of voices regrettably absent from the conversation—not for lack of effort, but because a book like this one requires a specific type of art or writing that can be difficult to locate, especially for communities that are not our own. As two white women in academia, we have been keenly aware of the limitations of our own personal and professional networks and done our best to reach beyond, but there is still a great deal of room for more inclusiveness.

To start, this book heavily emphasizes women, who represent the most frequent victims of sexual violence (90 percent in the United States, according to the Rape, Abuse and Incest National Network [RAINN]).[1] Yet significant numbers of men are also subjected to sexual assault, and their perspective is worth examining. Indeed, male college students between the ages of eighteen and twenty-four are more than five times as likely to be sexually assaulted as their nonstudent peers.[2]

When it comes to the communities most impacted by sexual violence, according to RAINN, Indigenous Americans are twice as likely to experience sexual violence as any other race. Prison inmates are also disproportionately vulnerable, and 60 percent of sexual violence in US prisons is perpetrated by prison staff.[3] People with disabilities are more than three times as likely to be sexually assaulted as nondisabled individuals, while children with intellectual disabilities are nearly five times as likely as their peers to become victims of sexual violence.[4] A 2018 NPR investigation found that, according to unpublished US Justice Department statistics, "people with intellectual disabilities are sexually assaulted at rates at least seven times the rate for people without disabilities."[5] There are also relatively few counselors and mental health providers who specialize in working with these populations, amplifying the challenges of being a survivor.

Almost 20 percent of Black women are rape survivors, while 41 percent report having experienced sexual coercion or other forms of sexual assault. Reporting rates are known to be especially low among Black women, and they are less likely to be believed than women of other races. Especially worrisome given the structural racism within US society, a staggering 86 percent of Black girls in the juvenile justice system and Black women in prison, collectively, experience sexual violence.[6]

Intimate partner violence is particularly rampant in the LGBTQIA+ community: the 2010 National Intimate Partner and Sexual Violence Survey (NISVS) conducted by the Centers for Disease Control found that 44 percent of lesbian women and 61 percent of bisexual women reported having been raped, stalked, or physically attacked by an intimate partner during their lifetime, compared to 35 percent of heterosexual women.[7] The most vulnerable are transgender individuals, 47 percent of whom have been sexually assaulted at some point in their lives; that rate rose to 53 percent among

Black, 58 percent among Middle Eastern, 59 percent among multiracial, and 65 percent among Indigenous American transgender survey respondents.[8]

According to a 2022 report by the National Asian Pacific American Women's Forum, general discrimination against Asian American women is on the rise. Since the pandemic began, East Asian women in particular report dramatically increased levels of harassment and feeling less safe in their everyday lives, while Native Hawaiian and Pacific Islander women are the most vulnerable to sexual harassment, reportedly by 52 percent.[9]

We wish we had been able to include a broader spectrum of gender and sexual identities and intersections here, but one constant of positive space is that it is finite, while negative space is infinite. We hope that others will step into this realm with us and help to highlight an even more diverse range of artists, scholars, and activists working in and around the subject of sexual violence. Some places to start for inspiration:

- In 2015, the Australian activist Belinda Mason curated a multimedia art installation, *Silent Tears*, to explore the stories of twelve women who had either experienced sexual violence while disabled or become disabled as a result of sexual violence.[10]
- A Long Walk Home is a Chicago-based organization that centers Black women and girls. Founded in 2003, the nonprofit combats sexual violence through training in art, activism, and leadership. Cofounder Salamishah Tillet was awarded the 2022 Pulitzer Prize for Criticism for her writings on race and popular culture.[11]
- The 2017 volume *Religion, Disability, and Interpersonal Violence* contains a number of chapters of potential interest, but we would like to highlight "Ableist Shame and Disruptive Bodies: Survivorship at the Intersection of Queer, Trans, and Disabled Existence" by Lydia X. Z. Brown. She touches on some themes addressed in this volume, such as the nature of personal boundaries and self-determination. Brown writes, "As sexuality is intricately tied to notions of gender identity (themselves dependent on the able-normative body), disabled people exist more often as objects in othering narratives than as subjects, let alone narrators, of their own."[12]

Global Reach

While chapter 5 focuses dramatically on international performance activism and there are other discussions of the issues related to sexual violence worldwide throughout *Art, Activism, and Sexual Violence*, including in chapter

18, the book primarily concentrates on sexual violence committed and art produced in and about the United States. Accurate data are, as always, difficult to find, largely due to underreporting (especially in the case of sexual violence against men and boys), but a 2020 study sought to analyze global trends based on available figures. The researchers found that between 1993 and 2017, sexual violence against women was indeed more prevalent than against men (2,816.1 versus 1,193.9 per 100,000) in both wealthier and lower-income countries.[13]

For a more international perspective, there are a number of outstanding creators/artists and activists worth investigating. Here are just a few:

- Regina José Galindo is a Guatemalan artist who puts her body center stage in powerful performances.[14] Most relevant to this volume is her show *Perra*, in which she carved the word *perra* ("bitch" or "whore") into her leg with a knife to protest sexual violence against women in her country.[15]
- Panmela Castro, a native of Rio de Janeiro, Brazil, has used street art to highlight the problem of sexual violence within the favelas and spread information about the phenomenon more effectively than traditional channels.[16]
- South African artists and activists Jenny Nijenhuis and Nondumiso Msimanga, both survivors of sexual assault, launched an "artivism" initiative in 2016 called Dirty Laundry: they solicited donations of underpants and strung thirty-six hundred pairs—indicative of the number of assaults estimated to occur in South Africa each day—throughout the city of Johannesburg as a provocative installation to raise awareness.[17]

A Variegated Palette of Genres

One of the unusual features of this book is that it includes a wide range of styles and genres of art, from paintings, textiles, and poetry to dance and other performing arts. However, there remain countless types of art that are unrepresented here, in some instances because of the physical constraints of a book. Their absence is not meant to imply there are no sculptors, glassmakers, tattoo artists, jewelry makers, musicians, potters, and additional artists doing meaningful work related to the subject, nor do we intend by our selections here to set boundaries on what can or should be considered "art." Some examples of other forms of art missing from our volume include work by the following:

- Cousins Ellie Clougherty and Kristen Malinowski, who are close friends, graduates of the University of Virginia with degrees in neuroscience, and sexual assault survivors, cofounded the company Kamaria, which makes jewelry that, aesthetically, "celebrates the beauty of imperfection" and materially helps college student survivors of "power inequality trauma," such as sexual assault, with assistance for rent, counseling, and tuition.[18]
- The musical artist Trapper Schoepp, a member of RAINN's National Leadership Council, is committed to including men in the conversation about combating sexual violence. In a 2020 profile, he stated: "It's one thing to show solidarity behind the scenes, but we need to be more vocal as men. The time for accountability has to be now, or else nothing will change. This is not a political issue, it's an issue any decent human should care about."[19]
- The cartoon artist Diane Noomin, in *Drawing Power: Women's Stories of Sexual Violence, Harassment, and Survival*, brings together cartoons by sixty-three artists that address sexual violence, rape, stalking, and assault. Edited by Noomin, with a foreword by Roxane Gay, this book is a smorgasbord of content related to this issue produced by survivors.[20]

The Endemically Invisible

There is a thrumming drumbeat throughout the literature on sexual violence in any context, population, or time period: "underreported," "limited data," "full extent of the issue unknown." A great deal of sexual violence takes place in the shadows of obscurity. The reasons for this incomplete portrait are many. In some cases, it is the result of institutions focused solely on a limited range of visible, measurable outcomes, leaving behind the vast numbers of people, especially women, subjected to ongoing psychological and emotional control, intimidation, and terror that may never stray beyond the strictures of the law while nonetheless constituting abuse. In many such cases, even friends and family are unaware or do not acknowledge that the patterns of behavior they observe constitute forms of sexual violence, especially if certain forms of coercion are condoned by local communities, justified by religious beliefs, or encoded as a form of gendered virtue and traditional values.

In other cases, the missing data are the casualty of patchwork, decentralized systems of information collection, leaving up to local agencies or the media the decision of how to frame a particular incident. Others decide not to report because there are no readily and safely accessible services or for fear of retaliation by the perpetrator of the violence. And in many—too many—instances, those who have experienced sexual assault or abuse do not report because they have legitimate reasons to feel that they will not be believed or that they may even suffer worse consequences at the hands of those who are supposed to protect them.

Artists, including some contributors to this volume, may find themselves "reporting" their experience only through their art itself or only coming to recognize over time and through the process of creation that they have been violated. Art is a bold assertion of self, a refusal to be muzzled, a conversation that draws others in and helps find shared points of connection through which to drive social change. It means making something out of nothing, breaking up the negative space of silence.

Notes

1. RAINN, "Scope of the Problem: Statistics," accessed June 12, 2022, https://rainn.org/statistics/scope-problem.

2. RAINN, "Victims of Sexual Violence: Statistics," accessed June 12, 2022, https://rainn.org/statistics/victims-sexual-violence.

3. RAINN, "Victims of Sexual Violence."

4. Center for American Progress, "Sexual Violence and the Disability Community," February 12, 2021, www.americanprogress.org/article/sexual-violence-disability-community.

5. Joseph Shapiro, "From the Frontlines of a Sexual Assault Epidemic: 2 Therapists Share Stories," NPR, January 18, 2018, www.npr.org/2018/01/18/577065301/from-the-frontlines-of-a-sexual-assault-epidemic-two-therapists-share-stories.

6. National Black Women's Justice Institute, "Black Women, Sexual Assault, and Criminalization," April 11, 2021, www.nbwji.org/post/black-women-sexual-assault-criminalization.

7. Centers for Disease Control, "NISVS: An Overview of 2010 Findings on Victimization by Sexual Orientation," 2010, www.cdc.gov/violenceprevention/pdf/cdc_nisvs_victimization_final-a.pdf. The abbreviation LGBTQIA+ incorporates many forms of sexual identity and orientation—lesbian, gay, bisexual, transgender, queer (or questioning), intersex, asexual, and "+" to signify gender and sexual identities for which there are yet no descriptive terms.

8. Sandy E. James, Jody L. Herman, Susan Rankin, Mara Keisling, Lisa Mottet, and Ma'ayan Anafi, *The Report of the 2015 U.S. Transgender Survey* (Washington, DC: National Center for Transgender Equality, 2016).

9. National Asian Pacific American Women's Forum, "The State of Safety for Asian American, Native Hawaiian, and Pacific Islander Women," March 2022, www.napawf.org/our-work/march-2022/state-of-safety.

10. Silent Tears, accessed May 31, 2022, https://silenttears.com.au; see also

Belinda Mason, "Silent Tears: Disability and Violence through the Eyes of Female Victims," *Guardian*, August 24, 2015, www.theguardian.com/artand design/gallery/2015/aug/24/silent-tears-disability-and-violence-through-the -eyes-of-female-victims.

11. A Long Walk Home, "Our Mission," accessed May 15, 2022, www.along walkhome.org/about-us.

12. Lydia X. Z. Brown, "Ableist Shame and Disruptive Bodies: Survivorship at the Intersection of Queer, Trans, and Disabled Existence," in *Religion, Disability, and Interpersonal Violence*, ed. Andy J. Johnson, J. Ruth Nelson, and Emily M. Lund (New York: Springer, 2017), 163.

13. Nasrin Borumandnia, Naghmeh Khadembashi, Mohammad Tabatabaei, and Hamid Alavi Majd, "The Prevalence Rate of Sexual Violence Worldwide: A Trend Analysis," *BMC Public Health* 20 (2020): 1835.

14. Regina José Galindo, accessed June 20, 2022, www.reginajosegalindo.com.

15. Regina José Galindo, "Perra," accessed June 20, 2022, www.reginajose galindo.com/en/perra-2.

16. Panmela Castro, "Rede NAMI," accessed June 3, 2023, https://redenami .com.

17. SA's Dirty Laundry, "About," accessed June 20, 2022, www.sasdirtylaundry .co.za/about.php.

18. Jess Feldman, "These NoVA-Born Cousins Are Designing Jewelry for a Great Cause," *NorthernVirgina*, September 2, 2020, https://northernvirginiamag .com/style/shopping/2020/09/02/these-nova-born-cousins-are-designing -jewelry-for-a-great-cause; Kamaria, accessed June 15, 2022, https://kamaria.com.

19. RAINN, "Musician and RAINN Supporter on How Men Can Help End Sexual Violence," May 12, 2020, www.rainn.org/news/musician-and-rainn -supporter-how-men-can-help-end-sexual-violence.

20. Diane Noomin, ed., *Drawing Power: Women's Stories of Sexual Violence, Harassment, and Survival* (New York: Abrams ComicArts, 2019). See also Nat Wassell, review of *Drawing Power: Women's Stories of Sexual Violence, Harassment, and Survival*, edited by Diane Noomin, *Cultured Vultures*, September 17, 2019, https://culturedvultures.com/drawing-power-review.

Contributors

STEPHANIE LEIGH BATISTE is associate professor of English at the University of California, Santa Barbara, and director of the Hemispheric South/s Research Initiative. Her research and teaching areas include African American literature and culture, race and racism, Black performance studies, American studies, cultural studies, and US history. Her award-winning book *Darkening Mirrors: Imperial Representation in Depression-Era African American Performance* focuses on the relationship between power and identity in Black theater, film, and dance. She is coeditor of the New York University book series Performance and American Culture. Also a creative writer and performer, she has written three plays—*Stacks of Obits*, *Young Love Found and Lost: Six Poems in a Circle*, and *Blue Gold and Butterflies*—and done collaborative adaptations and original work with students. She has performed her solo show *Stacks of Obits*, about street murder in Los Angeles, nationally and internationally.

ELAINA BEHOUNEK is assistant professor in sociology and criminal justice at Middle Georgia State University. She studies intimate partner violence, sexual assault, fear of crime, and educational inequality. Her work has included explorations into emotional labor and burnout by domestic violence and sexual assault advocates. Among her publications is the article "The Safety of Women and Girls in Educational Settings: A Global Overview and Suggestions for Policy Change." She is a member of the American Society of Criminology and the American Sociological Association.

SYDNEY BURROWS is a dancer, writer, and digital strategist and a master's student in English at the University of Rochester in New York. She also serves as assistant director for digital strategy and engagement at the University of Rochester Office of Advancement and is assistant editor of *DIY Dancer*, an online and print international dance magazine. She is a company member of PUSH Physical Theatre. Her publications include the article "#MeToo: Sexual Assault and the Arts" and pieces about dance as cultural celebration and a means of connection during COVID-19 isolation.

T DE LONG (formerly Tara De Long) is a New York City–based rap artist whose work has been performed and exhibited in museums, galleries, and festivals around the world. De Long has released both solo and collaborative albums and appeared in and produced art films, performance projects, and videos. De Long was a member of the original lo-fi hip-hop group Bedroom Productions, formed in the mid-1990s. De Long has produced and curated music and performance art programs, including the Warm Up series at MoMA PS1. In 2007, De Long transitioned to T De Long. A partner of and artistic collaborator with Chloe Dzubilo, De Long serves as executor of Dzubilo's estate in collaboration with Participant Inc.

ALESHA DURFEE is professor and chair of the Department of Women's and Gender Studies at St. Louis University. Her service, research, and teaching focus on intersectionality, gender-based violence, and domestic violence. She coordinated the Clothesline Project for several years while at Arizona State University and has been a volunteer domestic violence advocate. Her work has been published in the journals *Violence against Women*, *Gender and Society*, *Feminist Criminology*, and *Feminist Teacher*. She is the recipient of a National Institute of Justice Researcher-Practitioner partnership grant, a National Science Foundation grant (with Jill Messing), and a writing fellowship from the Women's International Study Center.

DAWN R. GILPIN is assistant dean for research and associate honors professor at Arizona State University's Walter Cronkite School of Journalism and Mass Communication. Her work explores cultural dynamics within and around mediated social systems, from organizations to communities to subcultures, and narrative flows of power through media. In recent years, her research has focused on gun culture in the United States, alongside emergent cultures and issues of mis- and disinformation within global information environments. In work coauthored with Leslie-Jean Thornton, she has used visual imagery and memes as entry points into these subject areas.

JASMIN GOODMAN is a postdoctoral research fellow in the Department of Communication, Culture and Media Studies at Howard University. A critical race, gender, and media scholar, her work focuses primarily on social media, digital streaming, and Black popular culture. She has recently expanded her research to include social justice and activism. She is also founder and principal of the J. Michelle Group, a strategic intelligence and engagement firm that specializes in using research and strategy to help brands, companies, and government agencies develop culturally responsible and engaging strategies for diverse populations.

CLARITY HAYNES is a queer feminist artist, writer, and educator living in New York City. They are best known for their Breast Portrait Project, a multidisciplinary, socially engaged work that is grounded in the practice of painting from observation and features unconventional painted portraits of torsos, focusing on queer, trans, cis female, and nonbinary bodies. In 2020–21, they created Birth Altar, a life-size celebration of the bravery and resilience conveyed by images of childbirth. They teach drawing at Brooklyn College and painting at Trestle Gallery and are a member of the Corpus VI and tART collectives.

LUZENE HILL is a multimedia artist, best known for socially engaged conceptual installations and performances. Her work reflects interdisciplinary scholarship in visual art, women's studies, and precontact culture of the Americas. Recent work, employing Indigenous matrilineal motifs, asserts female agency and challenges male dictated hierarchies. An enrolled member of the Eastern Band of Cherokee Indians, Hill lives and works in Atlanta, Georgia. Her work has been exhibited throughout the United States, as well as in Canada, Russia, Japan, and the United Kingdom. Recent residencies include a 2020 Social Engagement Artist Residency and a 2020 Invited Artist Residency, Anderson Ranch Arts Center. Hill's work is featured in the PBS documentary *Native Art NOW!*

JENNIFER KARASH-EASTMAN is director of St. Bonaventure University's Sexual Assault Campus Prevention Program in Allegany, New York. The program is funded through the US Department of Justice, Office on Violence Against Women. Her research addresses various issues within the fields of women's studies, gender theory, and social justice activism, including migrant writings, particularly within the Spanish-speaking world. In addition to journal articles, including "Women in the Future of the Theology of Liberation," she authored an entry about the Caribbean for the volume *Gender and Identity around the World.* She also works as a trainer and educator, developing and marketing educational materials as a digital learning specialist and consultant.

SALLY L. KITCH is University and Regents' Professor of Women and Gender Studies at Arizona State University (ASU). She is also founding director of ASU's Institute for Humanities Research and the Humanities Lab and was named a Distinguished Sustainability Scientist in ASU's Global Futures Laboratory in 2017. Kitch specializes in cultural, racial, and feminist theory; US women's history; gender ideologies and the environment; and feminist epistemology. She is the author of numerous journal articles and book chapters, as well as seven books, three of which have won national prizes. Her recent publications include *The Specter of Sex: Gendered Foundations of Racial Formation in the United States*; *Contested Terrain: Reflections with Afghan Women Leaders*; "Protection and Abuse: The Conundrum of Global Gender Inequality"; and "Eco-Sin: A View from the Pandemic."

ELIZABETH JOHNSON LEVINE is a choreographer, dancer, and educator with a focus on socially engaged dance practices. Her work connects communities through choreography by promoting civic dialogue and participatory experiences. She has special interest in working with youth and elders, developing embodied structures for learning, and promoting leadership development and health through the arts. In addition to her dance training in the United States, she has studied at the London Contemporary Dance School and taught and performed internationally. Currently associate artistic director of Dance Exchange, she was creative codirector (with Nik Zaleski) of CounterAct from 2016 to 2019 at Arizona State University, a campus-wide arts-based initiative for sexual violence prevention.

RUTA BUTKUS MARINO is a textile artist living in Beachwood, Ohio. Her recent body of work uses the medium of quilts to tell the story of sexual assault. A former librarian and senior curator at the Regina A. Quick Center for the Arts at St. Bonaventure University in New York State, she is currently the administrative assistant for the Department of Psychology and the Department of Exercise Science and Sports Studies at John Carroll University in Cleveland, Ohio. She served as the coordinator of *The Artist as Quiltmaker* biennial exhibition at the Firelands Association for the Visual Arts in Oberlin, Ohio, from 2010 to 2020. Marino completed a quilt about human trafficking in 2020.

DEBORAH MARTIN is professor of Latin American film and culture at University College London. She is the author of the books *The Child in Contemporary Latin American Cinema*, *The Cinema of Lucrecia Martel* and *Painting, Literature and Film in Colombian Feminine Culture 1940–2005: Of Border*

Guards, Nomads and Women, as well as numerous articles and book chapters on Latin American cinema. With Deborah Shaw, she is coeditor of *Latin American Women Filmmakers: Production, Politics, Poetics*. Martin is currently working on feminist and environmentalist activism in Latin America and its relationship with film and visual culture.

NICOLA OLSEN is an independent scholar, educator, and theater artist. She specializes in theater for youth and the cultural/social significance of art. Olsen is a working director and dramaturg and served as dramaturg on a mainstage production of *Machos* during the COVID-19 pandemic. She has a background in high school teaching and administration of fine arts departments in secondary education.

JENNIFER PATTERSON is a grief worker who uses plants, breath, and words to explore survivorhood, body(ies), and healing. A queer and trans affirming and centering, trauma-experienced herbalist and breathwork facilitator, Patterson offers sliding-scale care through her private practice Corpus Ritual. She is the author of *The Power of Breathwork: Simple Practices to Promote Wellbeing* and editor of the anthology *Queering Sexual Violence: Radical Voices from within the Anti-violence Movement*. Her work has been published in *VIDA: Women in Literary Arts*, *580 Split*, *OCHO: A Journal of Queer Arts*, and *Feminist Wire*. She has an master's degree from Goddard College.

EMILY BONISTALL POSTEL is the state director of Marsy's Law for Kentucky, the bipartisan effort that successfully secured constitutional rights for crime victims in Kentucky. She leads a broad coalition of state legislators, victim advocates, community organizations, survivors, staff, students, and volunteers. As a subject matter expert in victimology, she is an educator and activist whose work is committed to the welfare of crime victims and focuses on the ways research and practice intersect to effect social change.

SEAN SHANNON is a writer, English instructor at the University of Wisconsin–Platteville, and artist-of-many-trades. Her first novel, *The Prostitutes of Lake Wiishkoban*, was short-listed for the Dundee International Book Prize and was a quarterfinalist for the Amazon Breakthrough Novel Award. She is also the author of the *50 Critical Thinking Exercises for Humanities Classes* books. She has written about her experiences as a transgender rape survivor in the anthology *Queering Sexual Violence*. Currently, she is working on a history of how politics has influenced American education over the past fifty years.

DEBORAH SHAW is professor of film and screen studies at the University of Portsmouth, England, and research lead for the School of Film, Media and Communication. Her research interests include transnational film theory, Latin American cinema, film and migration, and screen studies and gender and sexuality, and she has published widely in these areas. She is the founding coeditor of the journal *Transnational Cinemas* (now *Transnational Screens*). Her books include *Contemporary Latin American Cinema: Ten Key Films* and *The Three Amigos: The Transnational Filmmaking of Guillermo del Toro, Alejandro González Iñárritu, and Alfonso Cuarón*. Her coedited books include *The Transnational Fantasies of Guillermo del Toro*, *Latin American Women Filmmakers: Production, Politics, Poetics*, and *Sense8: Transcending Television*.

SUSANNE SLAVICK is an artist, curator, and university professor emerita at Carnegie Mellon University. Her curatorial projects include *When the Bough Breaks* in 2019; *Marx@200* in 2018; and the traveling exhibits *Unloaded*, 2015–19, which explored the impact of guns in US culture, and *Out of Rubble*, 2011–15, which featured international artists responding to the aftermath of war. Slavick has exhibited her own work across six continents, most recently at the Godwin-Ternbach Museum in New York City. Her work has been recognized by the National Endowment for the Arts and the Pennsylvania Council on the Arts. In 2019, she received the College Art Association Distinguished Teaching of Art Award. Selected essays and articles have appeared in *Journal of Visual Culture*; *Technology and Culture*; *Formations of Identity: Society, Politics, and Landscape*; *Cairo: Images of Transition*; *Hyperallergic*; *Cultural Heritage and Arts Review*; *Cultural Politics*; *Frontiers: A Journal of Women Studies*; and *Guernica: A Magazine of Art and Politics*.

WEI SUN is associate professor and director of graduate studies in the Department of Communication, Culture and Media Studies at Howard University. She is a Fulbright Specialist in communications/journalism. Her research interests include intercultural communication, new media studies, and health communication. Her publications have appeared in *Qualitative Research Reports in Communication*, the *Journal of Faculty Development*, and the *Howard Journal of Communications* and in several books. She was recently guest editor for a special issue on COVID-19 for the *Howard Journal of Communications*.

STEVEN TEPPER is the dean of the Herberger Institute for Design and the Arts at Arizona State University. Tepper, a sociologist, is a leading writer and speaker on higher education and US cultural policy, and his work has fostered national discussions around topics of cultural engagement, creative work and careers, art and democracy, and the transformative possibilities of a twenty-first-century creative campus. He is the author of *Not Here, Not Now, Not That! Protest over Art and Culture in America* and coeditor and contributing author to *Engaging Art: The Next Great Transformation of America's Cultural Life*. He has published widely on the topic of education and careers in publications such as the *Chronicle of Higher Education*, *Inside Higher Education*, the *Huffington Post*, *Fast Company*, and the *Wall Street Journal*.

LESLIE-JEAN THORNTON is associate professor at Arizona State University's Walter Cronkite School of Journalism and Mass Communication. Formerly a journalist, she retains an avid interest in how information is shared online. As an academic, she explores what those messages mean in the broader context of history, culture, society, and changing technology. As a practicing artist, Thornton has most recently focused on how the news is shaped and shared visually. She intends for her work with #MeToo imagery to give voice to the voiceless and make visible that which is hard to see. She has published about Twitter and gender issues in *Sex Roles* and about visual communication in *Visual Communication Quarterly* and in several book chapters.

NIK ZALESKI is a facilitator, narrative artist, and intimate somatics coach rooted primarily in the reproductive justice movement. She has founded several companies and projects at the intersection of health and the arts, including For Youth Inquiry Participatory Theater Company, Swarm Artist Residency, and Ag47 Artist Mentorship Collective. She is an ensemble member of Sojourn Theatre, Erasing the Distance, and For Youth Inquiry. Zaleski codirected CounterAct at Arizona State University from 2016 to 2019. She currently consults on organizational development, arts-based organizing, and storytelling for various organizations through her cultural strategy company, Murmur.

Index

Page numbers in *italics* refer to illustrations